Umberto Mariani

Umberto Mariani

edited by David Rosenberg

SKIRA

Cover
Senza titolo, 2013
Vinyl and sand on lead sheet
80.5 x 60.5 cm (31¾ x 23¾ in.)

Art Director
Marcello Francone

Design
Luigi Fiore

Editorial Coordination
Vincenza Russo

Copy Editor
Doriana Comerlati

Layout
Fayçal Zaouali

Translations
Robert Burns, Christopher Huw Evans,
Lidia Filippone for Language Consulting
Congressi, Milano

Photo Credits
Courtesy of Opera Gallery

First published in Italy in 2016 by
Skira Editore S.p.A.
Palazzo Casati Stampa
via Torino 61
20123 Milano
Italy
www.skira.net

Printed and bound in Italy. First edition

ISBN: 978-88-572-3067-2

Distributed in USA, Canada, Central & South
America by Rizzoli International Publications,
Inc., 300 Park Avenue South, New York,
NY 10010, USA.
Distributed elsewhere in the world by Thames
and Hudson Ltd., 181A High Holborn,
London WC1V 7QX, United Kingdom.

Contents

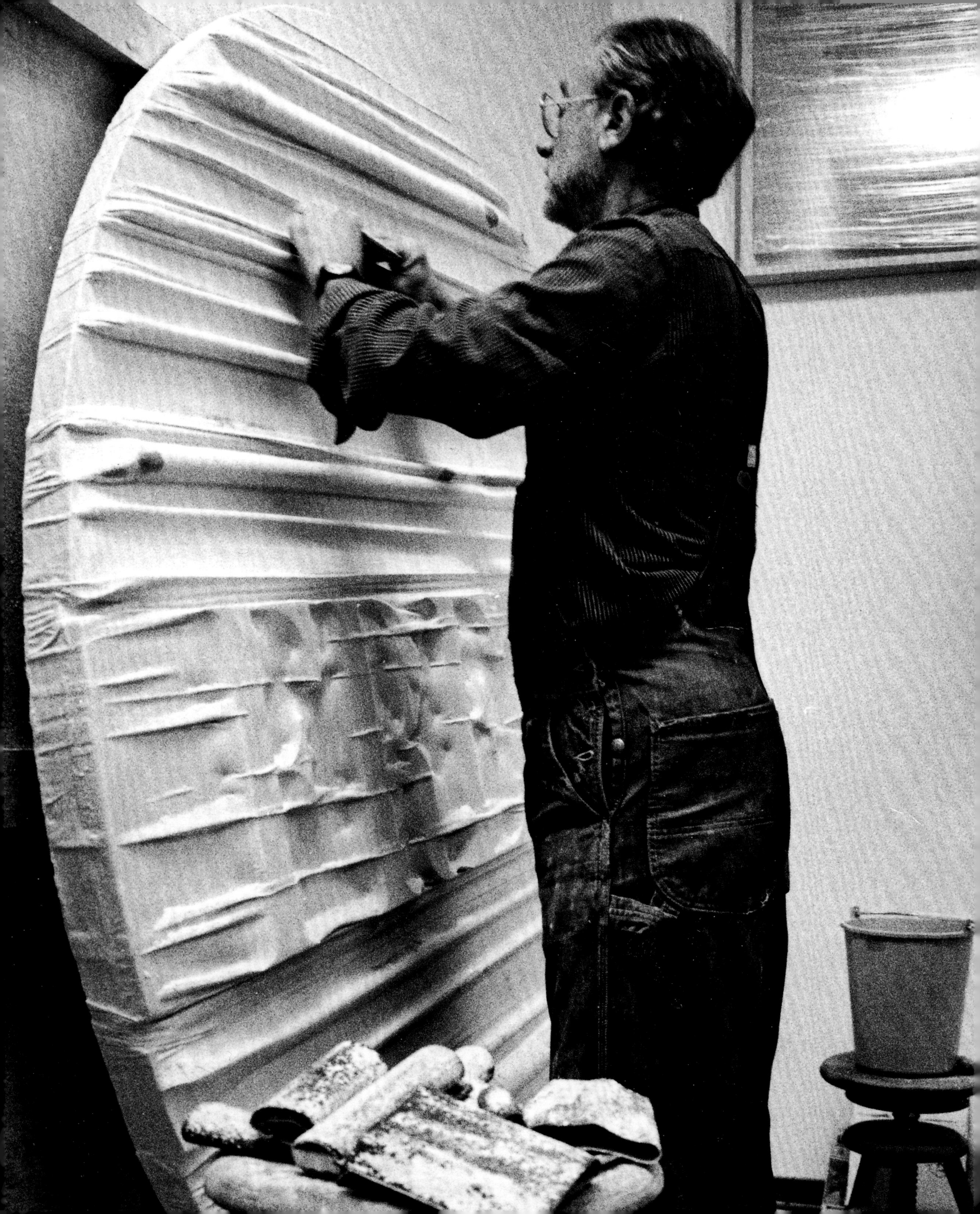

La Grande Bellezza, or Life in the Folds On Umberto Mariani

David Rosenberg

Umberto Mariani in his studio while working on one of the eight sculptures for Frette, 1999

In mathematics, we judge a proof by its coherence and elegance. If we apply the same criteria to Mariani's work, then we can be sure we are dealing with a linchpin of the modern and contemporary art scene. Behind the evident and mesmerizing beauty of his works, not only lies a lifetime of work and reflection, but also, in the background, the whole history of modern and contemporary art in Italy and Europe since the 1960s. And beyond, a reflection and a series of practices falling within the broader arena of the history of Western art and of Arab Muslim and Eastern cultures come through.

Although Umberto Mariani was born in Milan, and has lived and worked there for many years, he does not consider himself a pure Milanese, since his family comes from Reggio Emilia. Umberto came into the world in November 1936, two years after his elder brother. His parents had met some years earlier. Like many young people at that time, they encountered one another on the main street of a small town, where groups of young men and women used to stroll in the evening and observe each other from a distance. One day, they both found themselves at the back of a tram. And started talking. They liked each other, met up often and in the wake of it decided to get married. At the time Umberto's father was working as an accountant. During the war, the family left Milan to escape the bombing. Children did not go to school, their mother gave them lessons.

In 1944, on their return to Milan, the young Umberto could not go back to school. For years he had been suffering from various health problems and was often bedridden. It was at that time that he began to paint and draw, making watercolours of the landscape from postcards. But he had no idea of being or wanting to become an artist. To him, painting was simply a way of relieving the boredom of too long days spent cloistered in his bedroom. Finally, he recovered and was able to go back to school. It did not take his art teacher long to notice the skills of this budding painter, who had taught himself the basics of drawing. Umberto regularly won the drawing competitions that the teacher organized. It was him who advised his parents to enrol him in the Brera Art School. When he finished his secondary schooling, his father allowed him to choose between the Academy of Fine Arts and the Polytechnic, where he would be able to study in order to become an architect. Umberto chose the second option and filled in the registration form, but he changed his mind on his way to the university. He threw the form in a rubbish bin, at last admitting to himself that what he wanted most was to become a painter. He eventually enrolled in the Brera

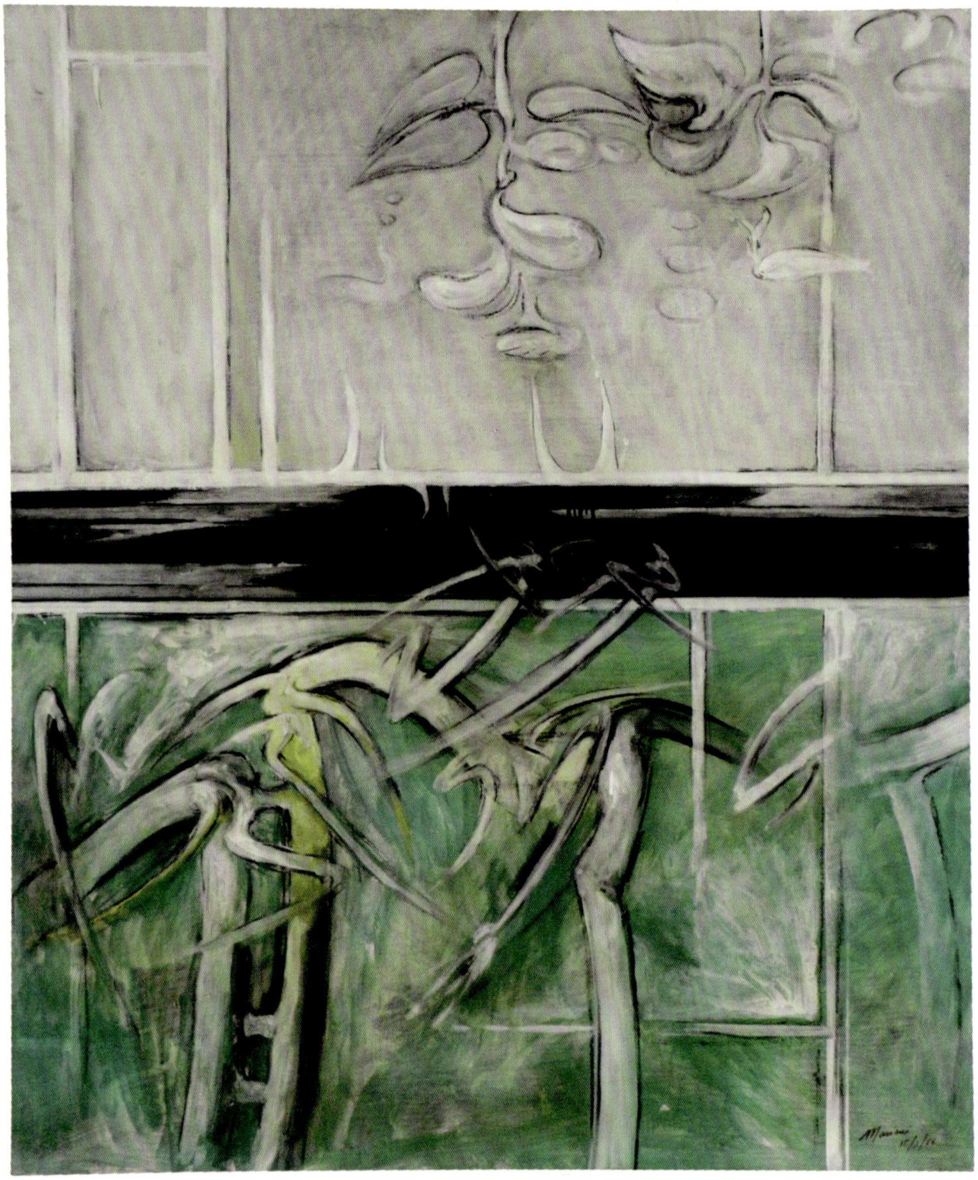

Umberto Mariani
Serra n. 1, 1966
Morgan's paint on canvas
140 x 120 cm (55⅛ x 47¼ in.)

Academy. It was customary at the time to choose a speciality: painting, sculpture or decoration. He went for decoration and found himself studying under Achille Funi. Funi was a well-known artist who had earned his reputation during the Fascist period. A friend of Costanzo Ciano, the viceroy of Libya, he had been responsible for numerous decorative projects and frescoes in Italy and Libya. Although close to the Cubo-Futurists before the First World War, Funi was best known as one of the advocates of the 'return to order' and Italian neoclassicism. During the years of his training, Umberto painted many frescoes with his teacher, sometimes surreptitiously introducing his self-portrait, as in a scene depicting a group of monks received by Cardinal Borromeo. Mariani was twenty-two, and had certainly learned the techniques, but he was seeking a pictorial style more in tune with his concerns at the time.

During the post-war years, there was much debate of socialist realism in the Leftist circles in Italy; it was a subject that came up occasionally when the artist was talking to his father, a former member of the Italian Communist Party since the early 1930s. Renato Guttuso was one of the emblematic representatives of this committed kind of painting, as were Edouard Pignon and Pablo Picasso in France. And then there were the abstract painters, like Emilio Vedova, Piero Dorazio and Afro... But he did not feel attracted to either of these styles. Instead, it was the work of Francisco Goya, which he discovered at an exhibition devoted to the *Caprichos* and *Disasters of War*, that stirred his imagination and influenced his work at the time. Paradoxically, he found Goya's works more stimulating and inspiring than many of his contemporaries. It raised, in his view, 'very profound human and social issues'.

In 1958, when he finished his studies, Umberto won an award from the academy and was offered a stay in Brussels to visit the World's Fair. There, he saw for the first time a series of pictures by Constant Permeke, a naturalistic Belgian painter with expressionistic accents. They hit him like a bolt from the blue and provided him with a new source of inspiration. He would continue to paint canvases in the same spirit until around 1962 and 1963. In the meantime, he was called for military service. Once released from the army, he went back to work in Funi's studio. He participated in some major decorative projects, including that of St Peter's Basilica in the Vatican and the large frescoes in the dome and apse of the shrine of Sant'Antonio in Rimini.

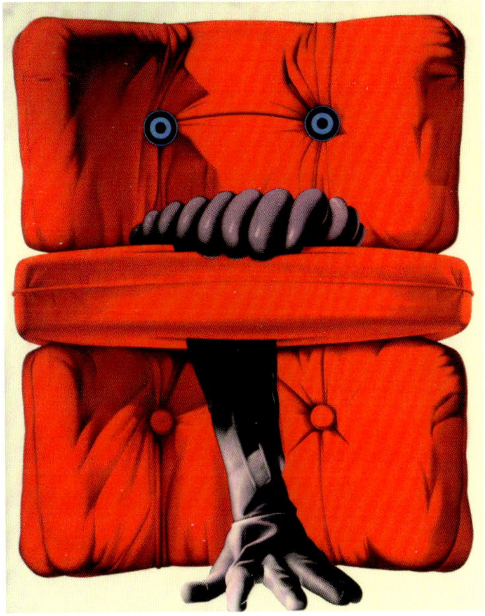

Umberto Mariani
La vergine incognita, 1969
Acrylic on canvas
92 x 76 cm (35⅞ x 29⅞ in.)

In 1963, Umberto met Ritva Raitsalo, a young Finnish designer. He fell in love with her and a few months later drove off from Milan to join her in Helsinki. Together, they decided to travel around the country, in search of the architecture of Alvar Aalto. Their wanderings took them to Rovaniemi, a town a few miles away from the Arctic Circle where the famous architect had designed a large number of buildings.
On this journey Umberto painted seaside landscapes, alternating gouache and pastel compositions on paper with ones in acrylic on canvas. The couple got married in 1965. On his return to Italy, Umberto moved into a studio on Via Andrea del Sarto in Milan. It had a garden in an inner courtyard that was to become the dominant subject of his paintings. A great upheaval took place in his work in 1965. On a trip to Turin, he discovered the work of the English artist Graham Sutherland and that gave him an aesthetic shock of a kind he had rarely felt before. 'Plants looked like birds, birds turned into flowers…' It was, he said, 'the feeling of ambiguity': a strange universe, at once dreamlike and familiar, that was to inspire him for a whole year, until the painter was gradually able to detach himself from his master.
The artist was changing, just like the city where he lived and worked. The former industrial centre of Milan was in the process of becoming an international capital of fashion and design. This was also the heyday of the magazine *Domus*, of Arne Jacobsen, Verner Panton, Eero Saarinen, Gerrit T. Rietveld, Ettore Sottsass, Gae Aulenti and Joe Colombo… One of the great artistic and intellectual challenges of the time lay, according to the artist, 'in the confrontation between nature and artifice'. This precisely is evident in his paintings of the period. From a strictly formal point of view, the paintings of 1967–74 were perfectly in tune with the times. The joint influence of various currents can clearly be discerned: British and American Pop Art (let us remember that in 1964 Umberto was in Venice and had visited the famous Biennale at which Robert Rauschenberg was awarded the Grand Prize), psychedelia and the work of Konrad Klapheck, Allen Jones and Domenico Gnoli. Mariani was also interested in the Narrative Figuration movement, promoted by the French critic Gérald Gassiot-Talabot, whose main exponents he met on a visit to Paris in 1967. But there was also and above all a less obvious link with the representatives of German New Objectivity. Mariani was a frequent visitor of the Galleria del Levante, which at the time showed Christian Schad, Otto Dix, George Grosz, Max Beckmann and Franz Radziwill; artists whose meticulously finished pictures and almost tactile handling of paint made a strong impression on Mariani, by his own admission.
Satin or rubber gloves, leather boots, fragments of the female body, strange plant forms, iconic objects of design from the time… There were all the ingredients of a fetishist eroticism related to the sensuality of the materials, the smooth opulence of the design forms often combined with two parts of the female anatomy that seem to delight the painter in particular: the leg and forearm. Mariani thus composed a remarkable portrait gallery by assembling what could be described as 'anthropomorphic' puppets. A stack of objects could end in evoking a head with a caricatured smile or a grotesque body, as in some of Enrico Baj's paintings. A tufted cushion served to draw the outlines of the head of the *Presidente dell'Associazione delle Cliniche Neuropsichiatriche* (*Chairman of the Association of Neuropsychiatric Clinics*) while the handset of a telephone made a pair of blue eyes for the *Conservatore della Biblioteca Nazionale* (*Curator of the National Library*) and a twisted electric wire evoked the lips of

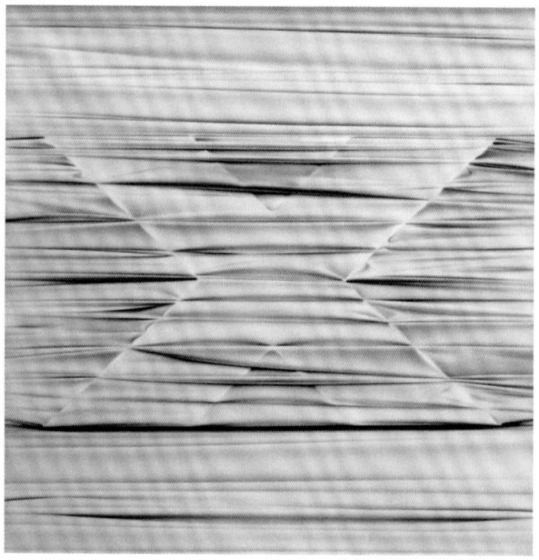

Umberto Mariani
Alfabeto afono: X, 1976
Acrylic on canvas
100 x 100 cm (39⅜ x 39⅜ in.)

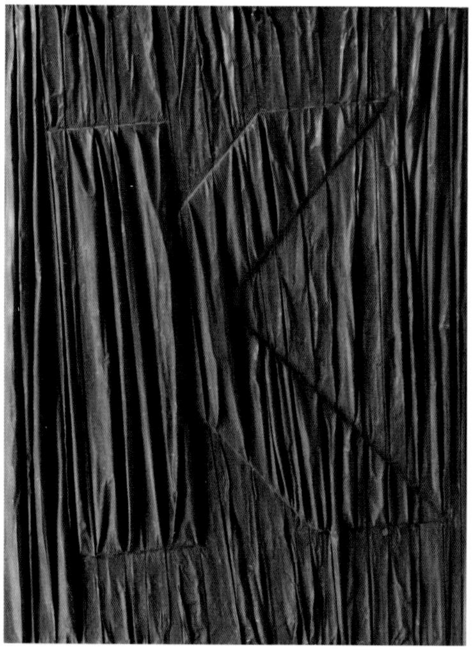

Umberto Mariani
La forma celata: K, 2010
Folded lead sheet
80 x 60 cm (31½ x 23⅝ in.)

La vergine incognita (*The Unknown Virgin*). Composed in the manner of a web or a grid with alternating vertical and horizontal lines, Umberto's 'plant' paintings already had the frontal character that we know, but this time accentuated by a diffuse, almost clinical white light, of the kind you might find in an operating theatre or a photographer's studio. Hence a sort of *cadavre exquis*, a puzzle in which the different elements are piled up or overlap with one another. This is at once mechanical and organic, natural and artificial, monumental and copulatory. It is exhilarating today to rediscover these brightly coloured works, which seem to make up a testamentary inventory, an imaginary museum of the objects and fantasies of the time.

This period in the artist's life was also marked by an intense exchange of ideas and many discussions with his Milanese colleagues Paolo Baratella, Fernando De Filippi and Giangiacomo Spadari, painters with whom Mariani believes in retrospect to have had 'more ideological than purely artistic affinities'. In 1968, the four artists were invited with Vittorio Gobbi to Paris to take part in the Salon de la Jeune Peinture, where they created an 'installation-environment' around the emblematic figure of a police officer. Just like Paris, Milan became a focus of political protest. Artists, including Mariani, demonstrated against the way cultural institutions were managed; a protest that would culminate in the symbolic occupation of the Milan Triennale and the Venice Biennale. It was also an important moment from the point of view of the recognition of Mariani's work. The French critic Edouard Jaguer, who had been introduced to his work by Enrico Baj, organized the artist's first solo exhibition in Belgium at the Galerie Arcanes and published his works in his magazine *Phases*. The artist also exhibited in Finland, at the Nykytaiteen Museo in Tampere, and his works featured prominently in the 6th International Exhibition in Knokke-Heist. Mariani then devoted himself to a series of works emblematic of the post-1968 ideology that were inspired by Honoré Daumier, an artist whose satirical spirit and innate sense of irreverent political caricature had already influenced Mariani's earlier pictures.

It was during this period of intense creative and political activity that Mariani's artistic journey began to take a more coherent and structured turn. His technique evolved through the use of the airbrush, which resulted in the realization of a series of pictures entitled *La citazione differente* (*The Different Quote*) which included, among others, a tribute to Piero Manzoni. It was here that the motif of drapery made its first real appearance in his work. In this regard, Mariani happily admits that the use he made of the theme or motifs at the time was directly influenced by Manzoni's famous series of *Achromes*. Manzoni is an artist for whom he feels a true admiration.

In 1974 Mariani painted the first pictures in the *Alfabeto afono* (*Aphonic Alphabet*) series. It began with a commission from a famous restaurant in Milan, the Saint Andrews, for which he produced a picture figuring the letter 'S' and 'A'. According to Mariani, this work reflected the intellectual concerns of the time related to the theme of communication or to the inability to communicate; a current of thought of which Jacques Lacan, in the artist's view, was one of the most important representatives. At the time Mariani asked himself: 'How to give a plastic form to such a literary and abstract concept?' It was this, he says, that made him think of camouflaging the alphabet, which is 'the source and foundation of our verbal communication', or covering it with a veil. To the dual aspect, at once visual and aural, of the letter corresponds the dual aspect of the drape, which is both veil and gag.

Umberto Mariani
Teorema: tela + oggetto, 1979
Acrylic and mixed media on canvas
120 x 195 cm (47¼ x 76¾ in.)

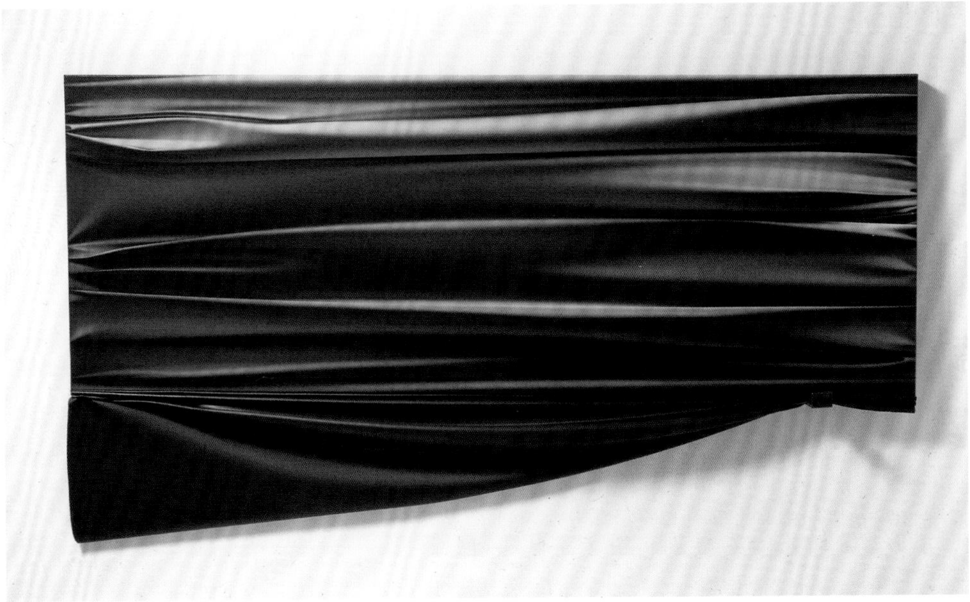

Visually, this work is distinguished by the extreme sobriety of the compositions, which from now on are reduced to the inclusion of a stylized form (this or that letter reduced to a geometrical object) within the frame of the canvas. We still find Mariani's taste for the effect of materials and textures, but assuming this time a form of solemnity and monumentality. There is also something more radical, the quest for a not only visual but also physical presence of the picture, seen as an object or material structure in the exhibition space.
It was out of this line of research and these considerations that the *Teorema* (*Theorem*) series were born, a series to which the artist devoted himself from 1977 to 1980. During this period Mariani worked on the form of the elongated rectangle, a shape directly inspired by the distinctive architecture of the rooms of the Ferrara museum where he had exhibited. The artist's approach was growing a little more radical. At this point, his works were a long way from the arabesques of Pop and Psychedelic Art, as if the pendulum had reached the end of its swing and was now heading off again in the opposite direction. From this moment on he worked between a direct presentation and representation of the materials themselves. Felt, oil or acrylic on canvas: Mariani produced black or white monochrome compositions with surfaces that were at times almost smooth, at others draped. 'By chance', he said, 'I moved from the representation of the object to the pictorial object itself and its materiality. I used plastic film, fabric... I combined illusion with reality, visual with the material.'
Paradoxically, this very specific series did not lead the artist down the road of a stripping down of his work and a progressive accentuation of its minimal and abstract character. In fact, Mariani's work split into two separate branches: the first, entitled *Relitti di scena* (*Stage Wrecks*) led to the famous *Forma celata* (*Hidden Form*) – a series of pictures on which the artist has been working from 1991 until the present day – while the second took the form of a kind of travel diary entitled *Autobiografico* (*Autobiographical*).
Just as the *Alfabeto afono* must be seen in the wider context of the intellectual concerns of the post-1968 era linked to the growing importance of social sciences (psychoanalysis and linguistics in particular) and questions related to language and communication, the *Relitti di scena* works cannot be separated from the specific artistic context in Italy in the early 1980s. In Europe as in the United States, this was

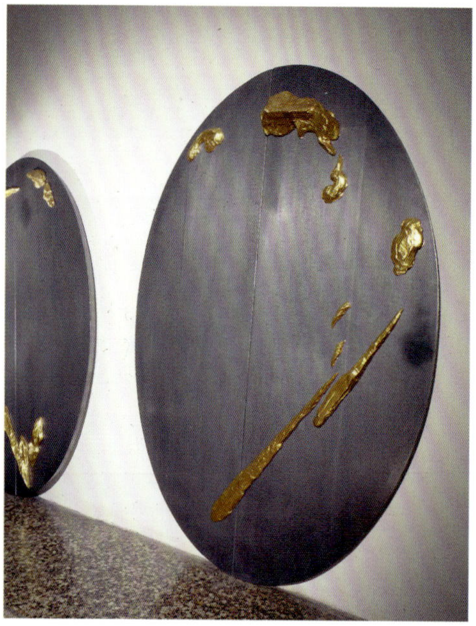

Exhibition *Specchi: Michelangelo Pistoletto – Umberto Mariani*, Galleria La Polena, Genoa, 1991

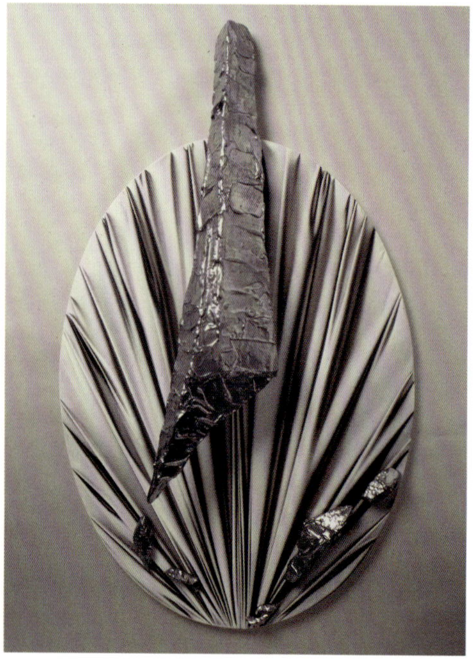

Umberto Mariani
Specchio n. 67, 1988
Acrylic and lead sheet on carved wood
230 x 130 x 60 cm
(90½ x 51¼ x 23⅝ in.)

the time of the return of figuration – or at least of a strong interest in figurative painting practices – that resulted among other things in the emergence of Figuration Libre in France, Neoexpressionismus in Germany and the Transavanguardia in Italy. Achille Bonito Oliva, who coined the name of this last movement, insisted on the 'theatrical' character of the pictorial work; the artists connected with it called a 'return to traditional forms of painting', extolling the subjective nature of art, the use of myth and imagination and the mixing of genres and quotations.

Although not a member of this movement, Mariani was particularly receptive to these ideas, as was already apparent from some works from 1979 – such as *Il luogo dell'illusione* (*The Place of Illusion*) or *Teorema: tela + oggetto* (*Theorem: Canvas + Object*) – and was already committed to what he called 'the way of theatricality'. Play of light, drape or curtain, combination of objects and images…

At the time some highlighted the 'Pirandellian' nature of his work, straddling real life and theatre. Mariani looked with renewed interest at the paintings of Giorgio de Chirico and René Magritte, which he regarded as *mises-en-scène* in the full sense of the term: he was particularly interested in the way they used the effects of perspective, the divisions of space and the arrangement of objects and accessories, which he transposed into three dimensions by using structures in relief. He worked meticulously, each year producing a dozen works in a baroque spirit that combined a number of recurrent elements: the pen, the set square, the curtain, sometimes a letter in relief… Each work was conceived as a true installation that fit into the surrounding architecture and was then illuminated with oblique light, emphasizing shadows and crevices and accentuating the dramatized character of the work. The fragmented nature of the compositions of the 1960s and 1970s can be found again here, but this time in a concrete and tangible way, as if the frame of the image and the painting had shattered and pieces of it were scattered all over the picture rail. Little by little, following the internal logic of the unfolding of his work, the movement of the pendulum again led Mariani to progressively restrict the number of elements in his compositions. With the two series *Ferri* (*Irons*) and *Specchi* (*Mirrors*), elements that had previously been multiplied and projected outside the frame were limited in number and gradually brought back inside it. The artist mainly worked with oval frames in which he painted drapes with an airbrush.

To this were added pieces of Cor-ten steel, carved and gilded wooden shapes or sheets of lead. In these works there is a sort of constant toing and froing between positive and negative: at times the shape of an object appears in relief (a letter, for example), at others there is just the outline of its empty silhouette. Sometimes a question mark is shown with a number or another punctuation mark. The work retains its theatrical and metaphysical aspect, but in a more frugal and sober manner. These are, according to the artist, strange mirrors not reflecting our image, but that of our questions.

In 1990, while working on a new tribute to de Chirico depicting a beach, Mariani used a sheet of lead shaped in such a way as to suggest the fluttering of a flag in the wind. And without him being truly aware of it at the time, these small pieces of drapery were going to act as a trigger. In fact, it had all been there right in front of his eyes for a long time. The drape was not to be content with discreetly haunting the whole history of art, fascinating it since the time of ancient Greece and Rome and right up until the Renaissance and the 18th century. Whether painted or sculpted, drapery is everywhere and holds a pre-eminent place

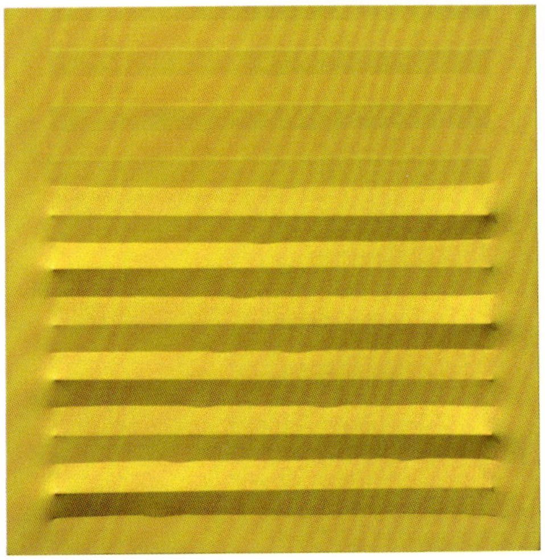

Agostino Bonalumi
Giallo, 1978
Acrylic on canvas
70 x 70 cm (27½ x 27½ in.)

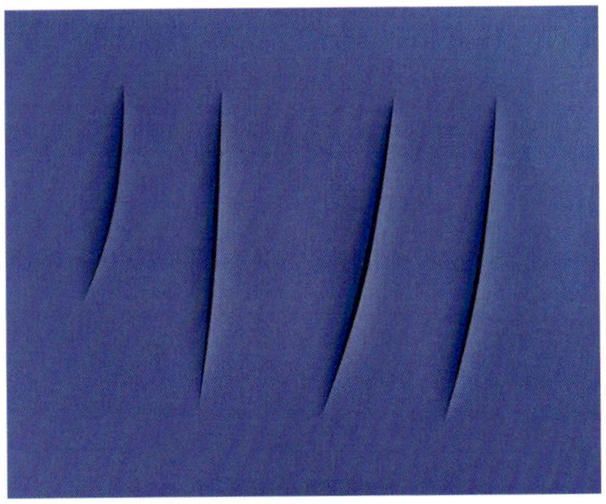

Lucio Fontana
Concetto spaziale. Attese, 1960
Water paint on canvas
65 x 81.5 cm (25½ x 32⅛ in.)

in the representation of the human being. And the more attention he paid it the more he discovered the subtlety, ingenuity and elegance with which every artist has treated this subject, which is anything but incidental. Much has been said about what drapery at once conceals and reveals, about the symbolism of the colours chosen for it and many other things. And ever since his debut as a painter, Mariani himself had first delighted in satin drapes, in the deep, soft cushions of the design of the 1960s, and then in those veils that had covered his alphabet and finally in the great theatre curtains deployed in his baroque compositions. There may be no single answer able to explain this fascination with folds. Above and beyond conjectures about the origin of or reason for such a passion, what matters is merely to see what the artist has done with it, what form he has given it.

After all, this 'practical question' – whether the 'practice' be painting or sculpture – has always been there for Mariani: How to bring the surface of the canvas to life, what presence, what relief to give to it? It is a question that relates to an entire segment of the history of post-war Italian art, to an area of artistic research that had first been opened up and explored by Lucio Fontana with Spatialism and his famous *buchi* ('holes') and *tagli* ('slashes') and then further investigated by artists like Paolo Scheggi, Enrico Castellani and Agostino Bonalumi, or by Dadamaino and his *Volumes*. Mariani's strength lies in having found his own way among his peers, in having been able to understand and appreciate them while knowing how to distinguish himself, in order to offer something unique and singular, in the end something that is his. Indeed, in my opinion, quite apart from the undeniable plastic qualities of his works, the sumptuousness of his palette and the precision and majesty of his compositions, he has a visual language that belongs to him alone. This is what makes him both unique and irreplaceable and has contributed to the influence Italian art exercises today.

Mariani has always been attentive to things, to the world around him, as well as to the materials he uses. When he started working with sheets of lead he felt, he says, what he handled was a dense and heavy fabric, a 'mute' material with which he could pass from the illusion of relief to relief itself.

This is where the pieces of the puzzle came together and he was able to get his research into drapery to gel and 'give substance to his desire to go beyond representation, to succeed in animating the surface of the picture, in giving it a life and a presence that is not only physical but also spiritual'.

Among the artists previously mentioned, the elasticity of the fabric was used to create an effect of relief and reaching out towards the viewer, a phenomenon expressed by the Italian word *estroflessione* or eversion. For Mariani, the process is reversed: the fold sinks into the fabric and no longer alludes to the idea of relief or projection but to depth (*introflessione* or introflexion).

So if we want to draw parallels between his work and that of some of his colleagues, it might be more accurate and relevant to point to the creations of Mariano Fortuny and Roberto Capucci, two great Italian fashion designers who worked in their own way with and in folds.

We should not be misled by this comparison: there is no room for chance or accident, in contrast to what may happen with a piece of fabric. In Mariani, the drapery has been staged, it is the product of a rigorous act of construction. Although the work of preparatory drawing is very intuitive in his own words, each composition is actually carefully worked out before being meticulously executed. The amplitude of undulatory movements, the depth of hollows, the height of ridges, and the arrangement of folds, all this is

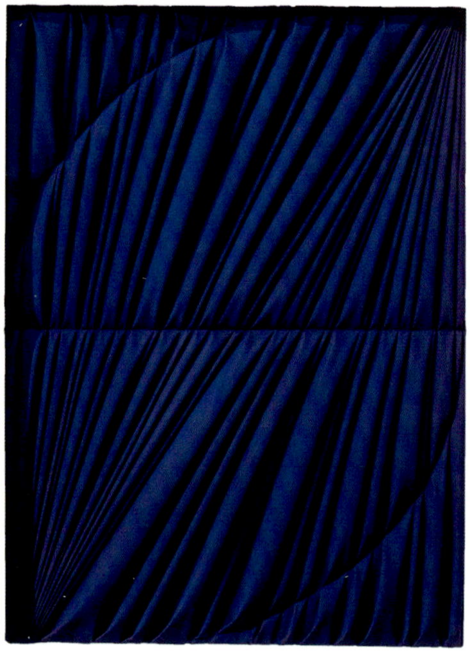

Taghelmoust: il velo, 2013
Vinyl and sand on lead sheet
80 x 60 cm (31½ x 23⅝ in.)

subject to a reflection on the space which, according to the artist, fits into the tradition of the Renaissance where perspective made it possible to organize the gaze and the world in accordance with an intangible geometrical order. 'This is the great Italian tradition which I aspire to be a part of', says Mariani. And he adds: 'When I'm working, I always think of the great masters of the past.'

Sometimes the composition of the drapery, the monochrome colour and the presence of the work are self-sufficient, while at others Mariani reintroduces a 'hidden form' (*forma celata*), returning to the idea of a curtain covering a physical object whose presence we sense without being able to see it directly. In this respect, Gérard-Georges Lemaire has aptly said: 'Umberto Mariani has managed to turn his approach into a strange and fascinating version of the persistence of painting as an expression of its time and of a conceptual vision of that painting. In other words, his creations are "pictures" in the classical sense, but with a subject that has been reduced to a purely referential expression of an object which offers us a view of the mind. Once it has accomplished this reversal of perspective, the "picture" resurfaces in a new guise and can be experienced by the viewer both as an object of contemplation and as an object of meditation. This is where the strength and beauty of his aesthetic journey reside.' Sometimes the artist has received a sort of confirmation of his intuitions in a completely unexpected manner, such as when he met Tuareg tribespeople on one of his trips to Mali and then Niger. 'It was an artistic shock: the impression', he says, 'of coming face to face with one's own works as if they had come to life.' Out of this would come a series of works entitled *Taghelmoust: il velo* (*Taghelmoust: the Veil*), named after the traditional Tuareg headdress, in which the artist created a set of sculptures and paintings of an indigo colour. 'The penultimate colour in the spectrum, a mixture of blue and purple that mesmerizes me', declares Mariani. As does each of the hues and shades he uses in a monochromatic way: bright red, gold, silver, sunshine yellow, mauve, dark green, dark grey or shocking pink…

As was mentioned above, when Mariani began the series *Relitti di scena*, which allowed him to revisit not only Italian Metaphysical painting but also some aspects of Surrealism, the artist started to keep an 'autobiographical journal' of a very special kind, which would eventually take the form of a travel diary. It is part of his fascinating work, slightly on the fringes, as if it were clandestine. But it allows us to understand

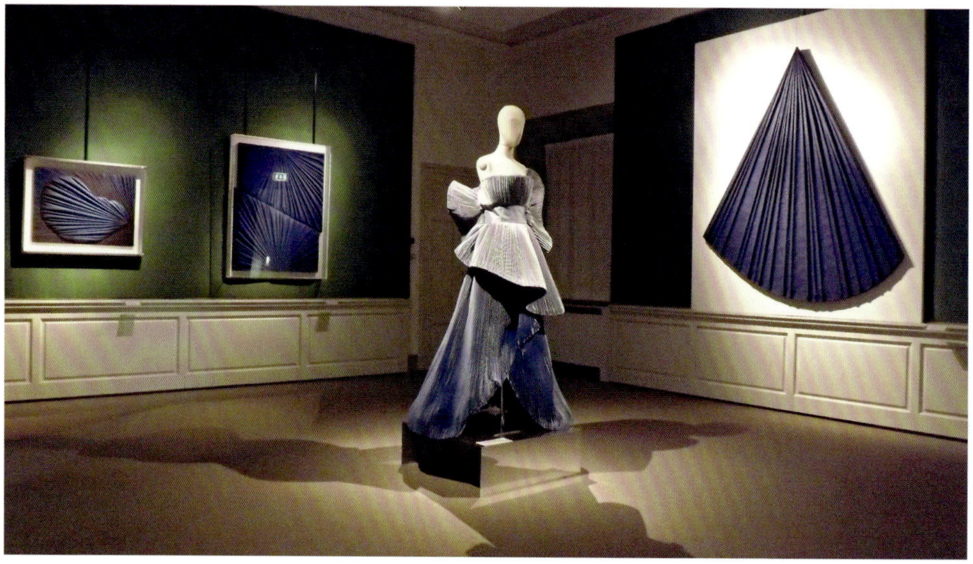

View of the exhibition *Mariani* chez *Capucci*, Villa Bardini, Florence, 2016

Autobiografico: Cuzco, 2006
Summer 1984: the ancient capital of the Inca Empire
Acrylic on wood
40 x 65 cm (15¾ x 25½ in.)

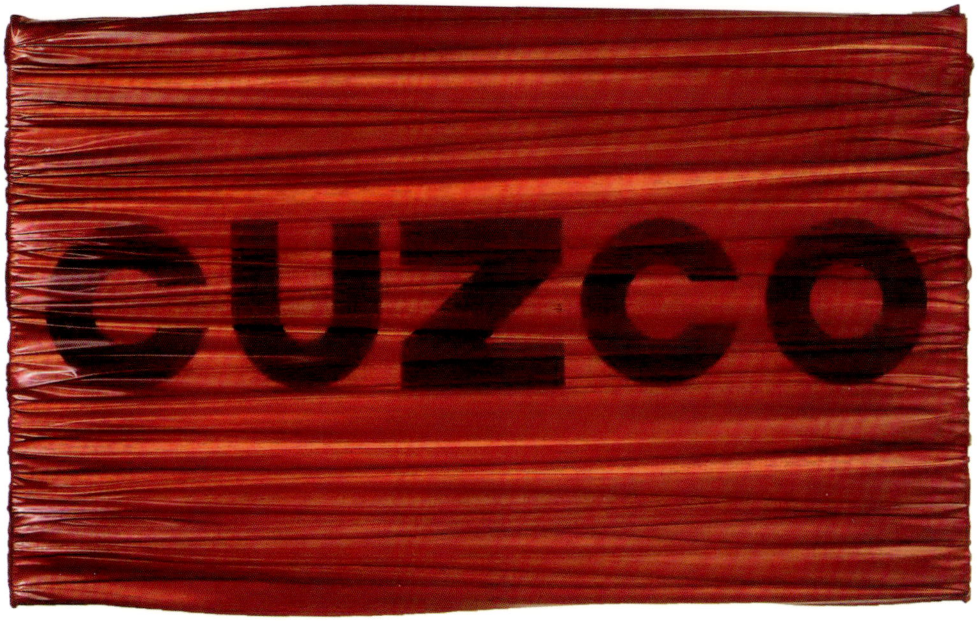

in retrospect where the artist was trying to go and what he was preparing to do. In Mariani, the starting point is always reflective; it is a point of return to himself and to the aesthetic, emotional or intellectual experiences that are at the root of the practice on which he is about to embark. The work enables him to resolve issues or to integrate experiences by giving them a perceptible form that makes sense in his eyes. It is hermeneutics applied to his own experiences. In an emblematic and radical way, the very first work of the *Autobiografico* series represents the artist's date of birth. Then there are, according to circumstances and events, pictures bearing the date of an important meeting or event related to his career as an artist, to his family or some of his friends' life. There are also forms of annotation, such as terse reports on his state of mind (*OK* or else *Crisis*). Each picture is like a bookmark of memory.

From a formal point of view, this calls to mind On Kawara's *Date Paintings* and Christo's wrappings, as well as the folds of Manzoni's *Achromes*. The horizontal formats are elongated, as if they were traffic signs. On plain monochrome backgrounds, the artist has painted simple dates or place names in block capitals: Titicaca, Lakagikar, Ulaanbaatar, Xinjiang, Rajasthan, Ténéré… And so we discover another aspect of the artist's life, that of a passionate traveller who has been all over the world, showing a preference for inaccessible or remote areas, for high mountain plateaus or polar seas. Surprisingly, this passion for travel arrived rather late in Mariani's life, and it was only around the age of fifty that he began to roam the planet, tramping across plains and mountains, creases and folds in the landscape that he calls 'the wrinkles of the world', just as he measures the pleats and folds of drapery with his hand and eye while working in his studio, in order to dig up or carry away all the deep *bellezza* from each day that passes.

Paris, February 2016

WORKS

On Beauty

Umberto Mariani

Beauty will save the world
F. M. Dostoevsky

It may come as a surprise to find that a writer like Dostoevsky, who largely dealt with demonic themes in his books and whose characters are nearly all damned, defeated and despairing, chose to place all his hopes in *beauty.*
But beauty does not manifest itself solely through serene and gratifying forms and contents.
The history of art and literature has shown to us that beauty is also to be found in Greek tragedy and in *terribilia*, in 'terrifying things'.
Grünewald's *Crucifixion* in Colmar is the most horrific image we can conceive.
His picture of Christ on the cross, his body riddled with putrid sores, takes us to the verge of despair and disgust. Yet in my view it can certainly be called noble and sublime art.
It is also clear that Goya's *Black Paintings* of the Quinta del Sordo in the Prado are not intended to lighten our spirits. They bear a dramatic and troubling message. The extraordinary quality of the painting that went into their creation does not want to annul the sense of tragedy that pervades them in any way, and nevertheless we cannot help but describe them as beautiful, indeed as stunningly so.
'I believe that today, more than ever, the artist has a para-religious mission to fulfil: to keep the flame of an inner vision lit.'
What I am quoting here are not the words of a 19th-century 'Nazarene', but a statement made by Marcel Duchamp in 1960. Shortly afterwards the world of art would be invaded by images barely worthy of a supermarket: tins of shoe polish, cans of soup, Polaroid photos, an endless series of celebrations of consumption, fetishist exaltations of everyday banality. The categories of the beautiful, the sublime, the spiritual, obliterated or treated with arrogant contempt. The historical avant-gardes, as Duchamp's aphorism makes plain, aspired to the regeneration of humanity, to the bestowal of a modern, up-to-date, contemporary dignity on it. It suffices to read the writings of Boccioni, Malevich and Kandinsky.
Kandinsky, Chagall and Klimt made explicit references to Byzantine and Russian icons, perhaps the highest peaks ever reached in

Senza titolo, 2015
Vinyl and sand on lead sheet
120 x 90 cm (47¼ x 35½ in.)

La forma celata, 2014
Vinyl and sand on lead sheet
80 x 60 cm (31½ x 23⅝ in.)

the history of art, expressions of an inner thought and feeling.
In my work I make constant reference to elements and subjects that have always been part of art history, to things like *drapery* and other archetypal forms, such as the ellipse, the egg and the cross.
There is nothing naturalistic or even realistic about my drapery, my folds. If anything they make use of symbolic forms and meanings. Their development follows a geometric logic and has recourse to linear rhythms and spaces. They are remote from the volumes of Masaccio, from the architecture of Piero and from the emphatic turbulence of the Baroque. Instead they are with no doubt closely related to the symbolic (today we would say abstract, mental, conceptual) and, in some way, labyrinthine iconography of the Byzantine world.
Gerhard Richter, Umberto Eco and Renzo Piano have for some time been reasserting the profound value of the 'idea of beauty'.
At the end of the 18th century Goethe wrote in his *Maxims and Reflections*: 'Perfection is already there when what is necessary is already being accomplished; beauty is there when what is necessary is accomplished but hidden.'
Oscar Wilde tells us: 'Beauty is a form of Genius – is higher, indeed, than Genius, as it needs no explanation. It is one of the great facts of the world, like sunlight, or springtime, or the reflection in the dark waters of that silver shell we call the moon.'
I am proud to make these words mine and intend to use them as a brief introduction to my work of the last thirty years, which has been focused on just this 'hidden form'.
With equal pride I consider myself as part of that recent, momentous phenomenon known as 'Made in Italy', an economic and, at the same time, cultural development that unites beauty and excellence.

Milan, November 2014

Senza titolo, 2015
Vinyl and sand on lead sheet
120.5 x 80.5 cm (47½ x 31¾ in.)

Senza titolo 2, 2016
Vinyl and sand on lead sheet
120 x 90 cm (47¼ x 35½ in.)

Senza titolo 3, 2016
Vinyl and sand on lead sheet
120 x 90 cm (47¼ x 35½ in.)

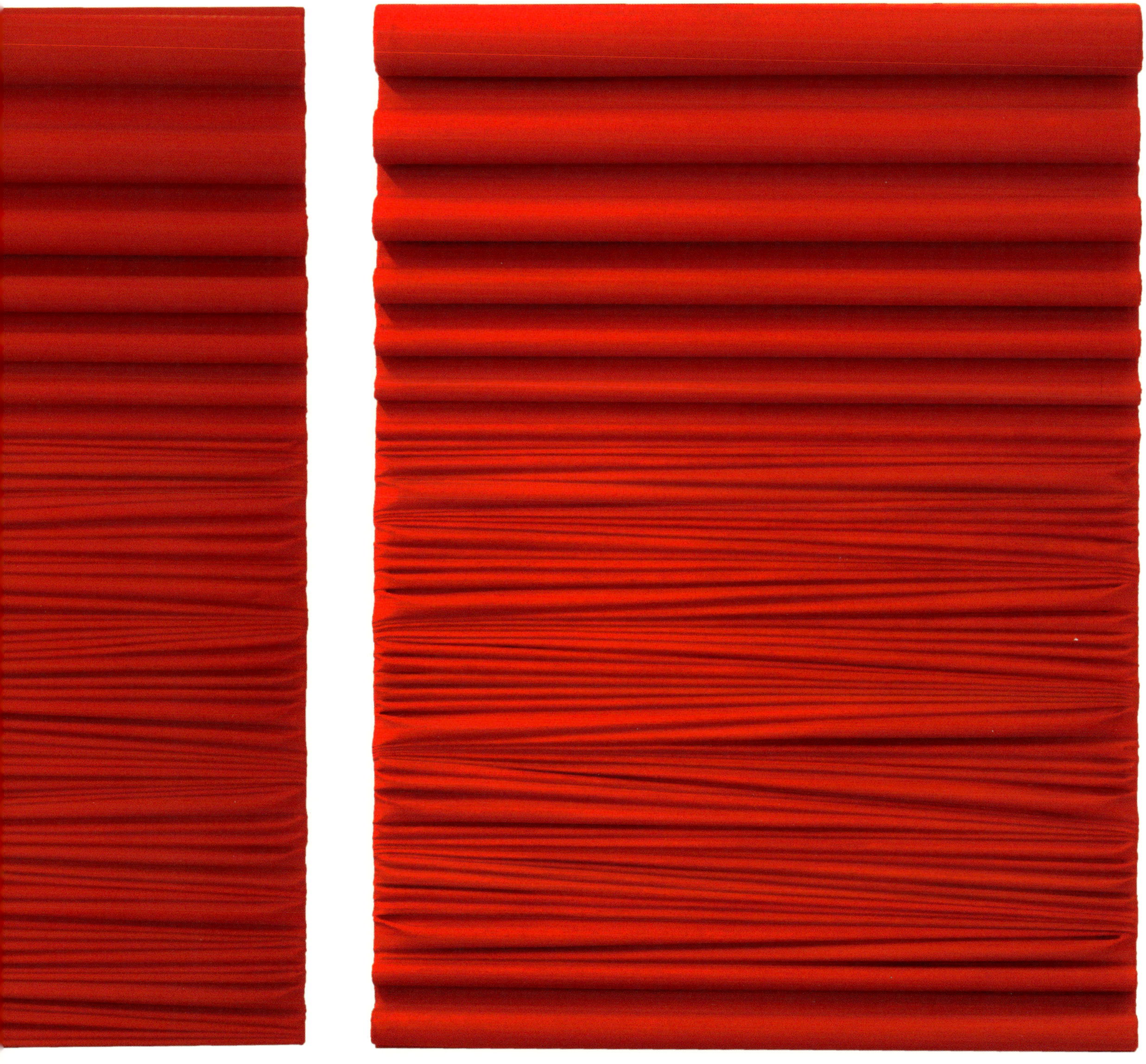

La forma celata, 2012
Vinyl and sand on lead sheet
28 x 20 cm (11 x 7⅞ in.)

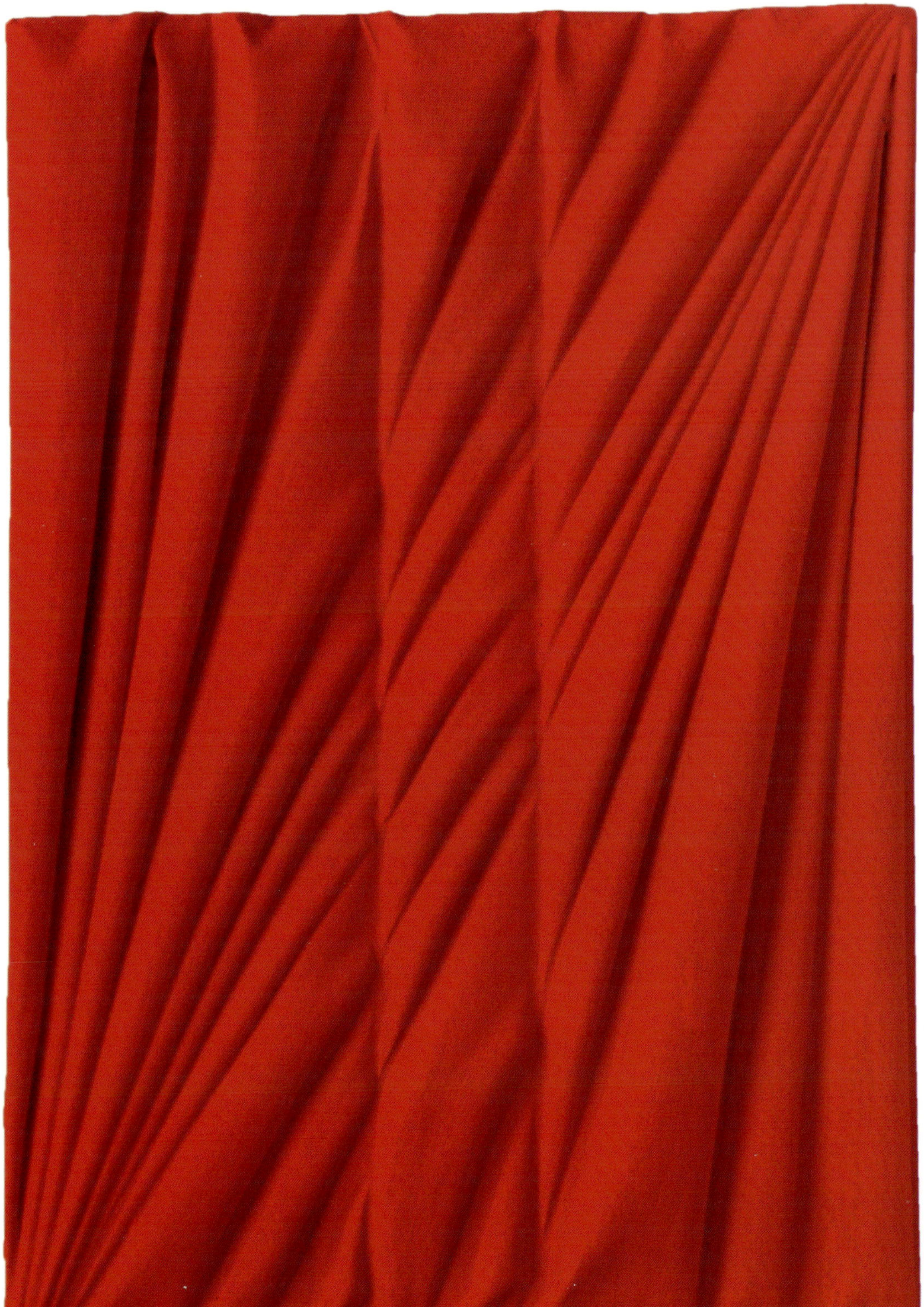

La forma celata, 2012
Vinyl and sand on lead sheet
28 x 20 cm (11 x 7⅞ in.)

Senza titolo, 2014
Vinyl and sand on lead sheet
80 x 60 cm (31½ x 23⅝ in.)

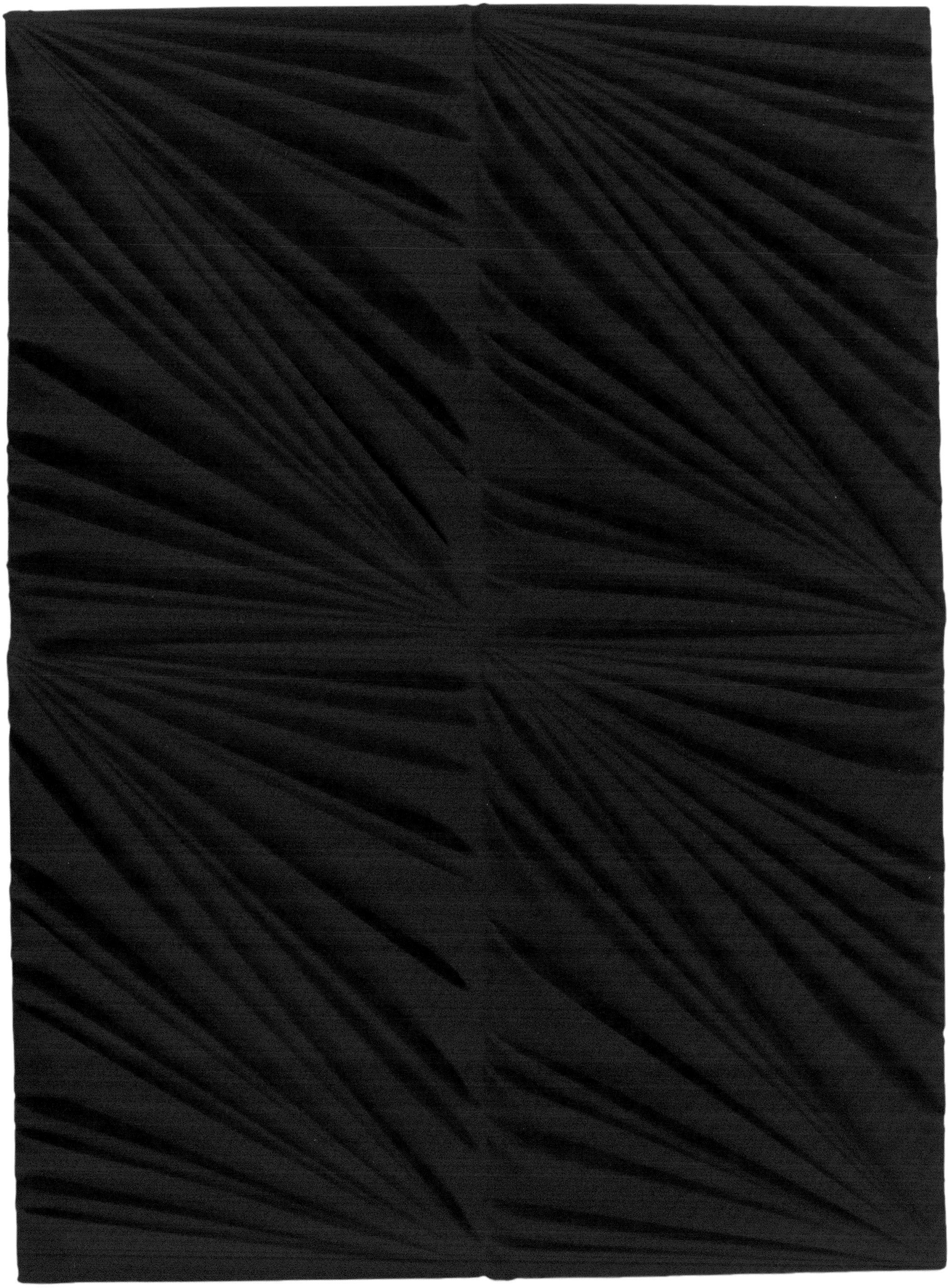

La forma celata 4, 2009
Vinyl and sand on lead sheet
28 x 20 cm (11 x 7⅞ in.)

La forma celata, 2015
Vinyl and sand on lead sheet
80 x 60 cm (31½ x 23⅝ in.)

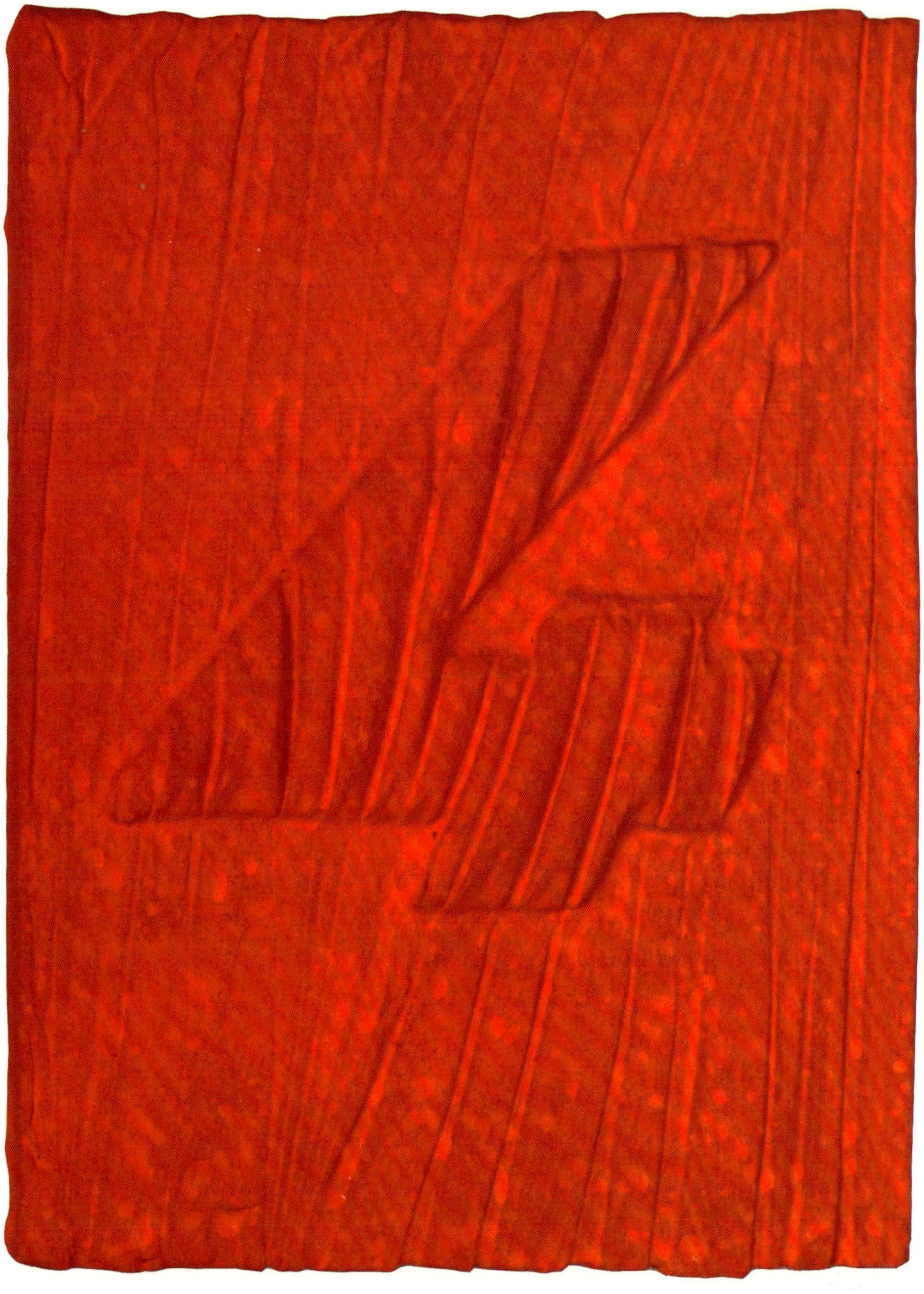

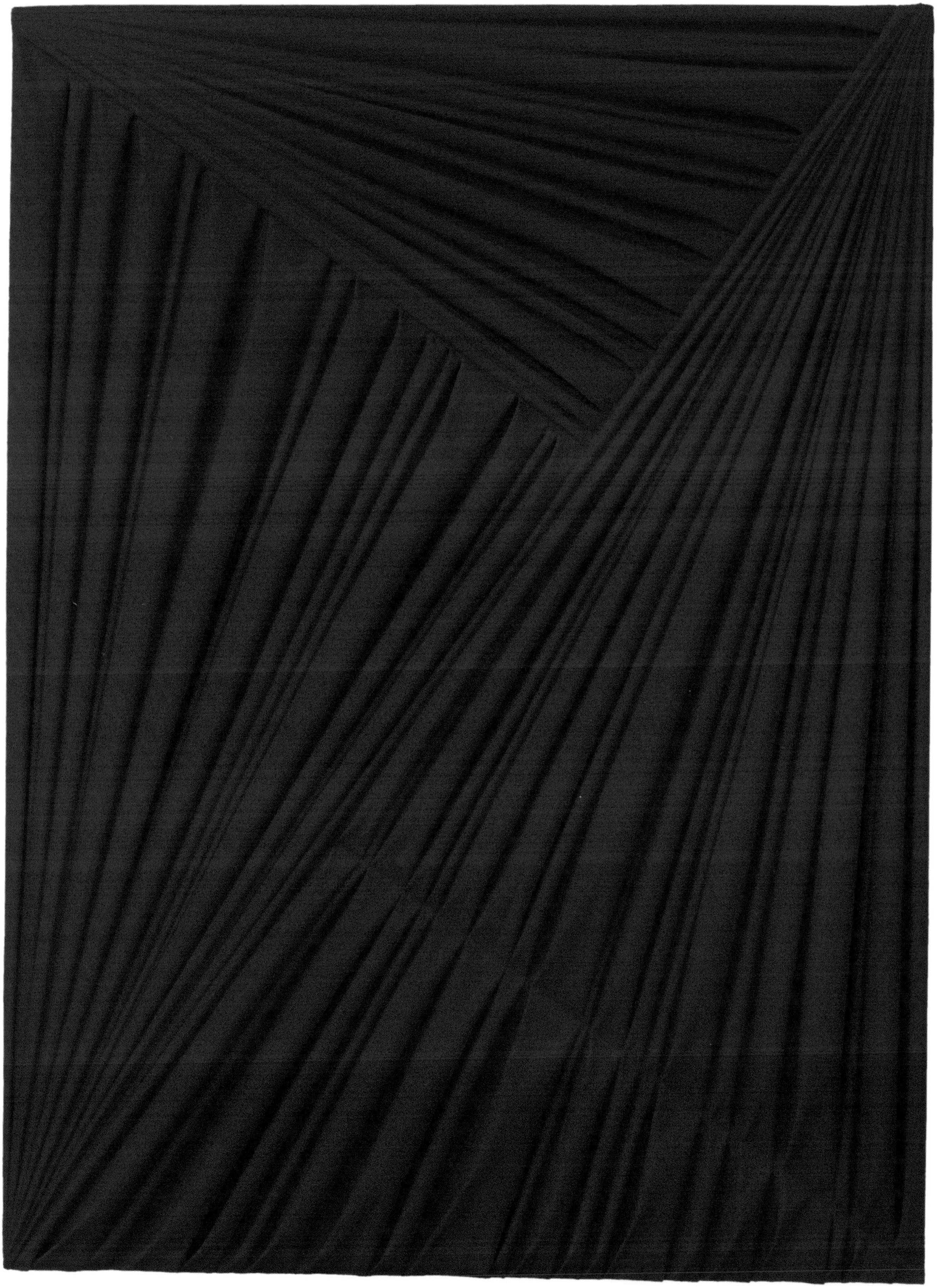

La forma celata, 2015
Vinyl and sand on lead sheet
120 x 90.5 cm (47¼ x 35⅝ in.)

La forma celata, 2013
Vinyl and sand on lead sheet
120.5 x 80 cm (47½ x 31½ in.)

La forma celata, 2015
Vinyl and sand on lead sheet
120 x 90.5 cm (47¼ x 35⅝ in.)

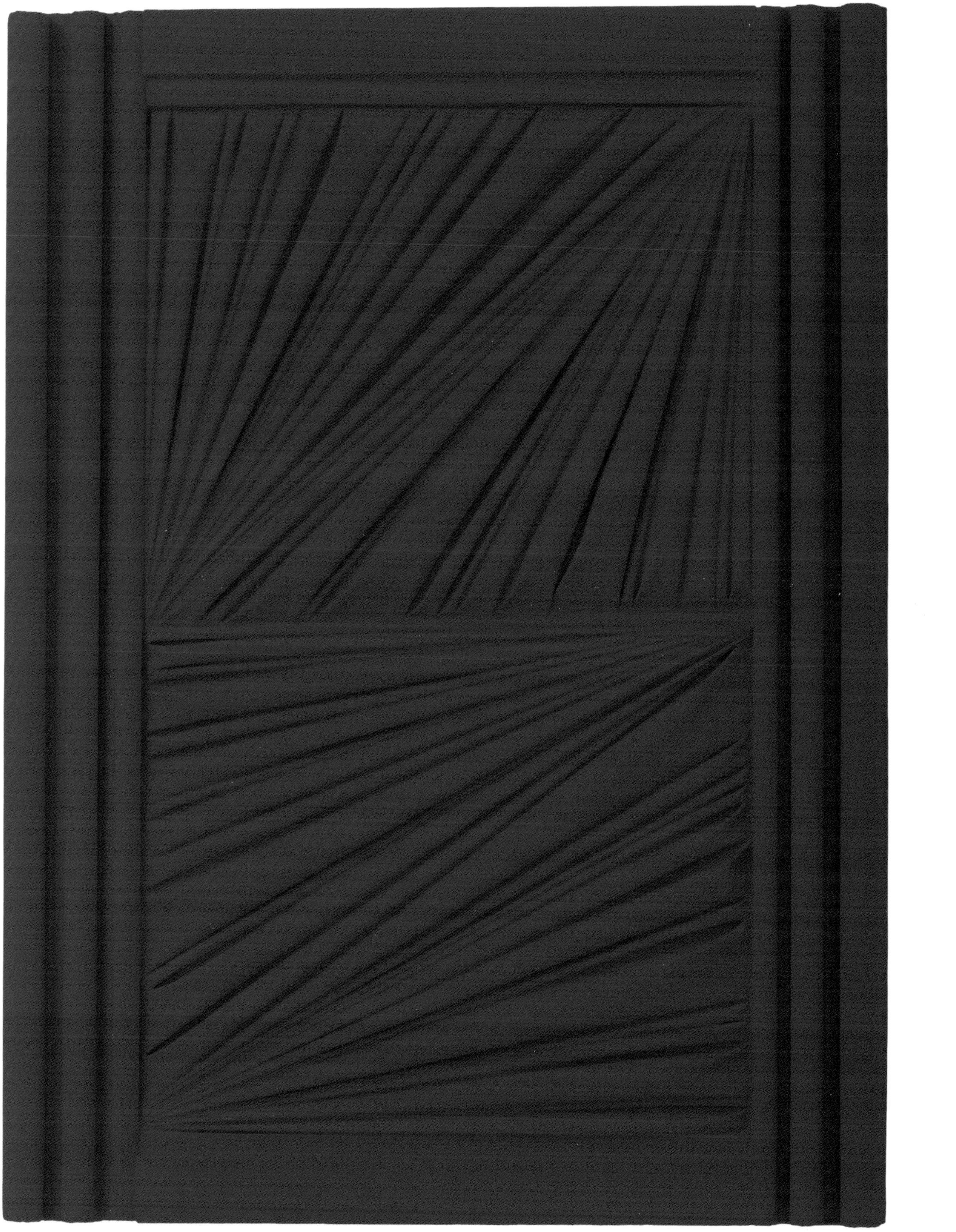

La forma celata, 2015
Vinyl and sand on lead sheet
80 x 60 cm (31½ x 23⅝ in.)

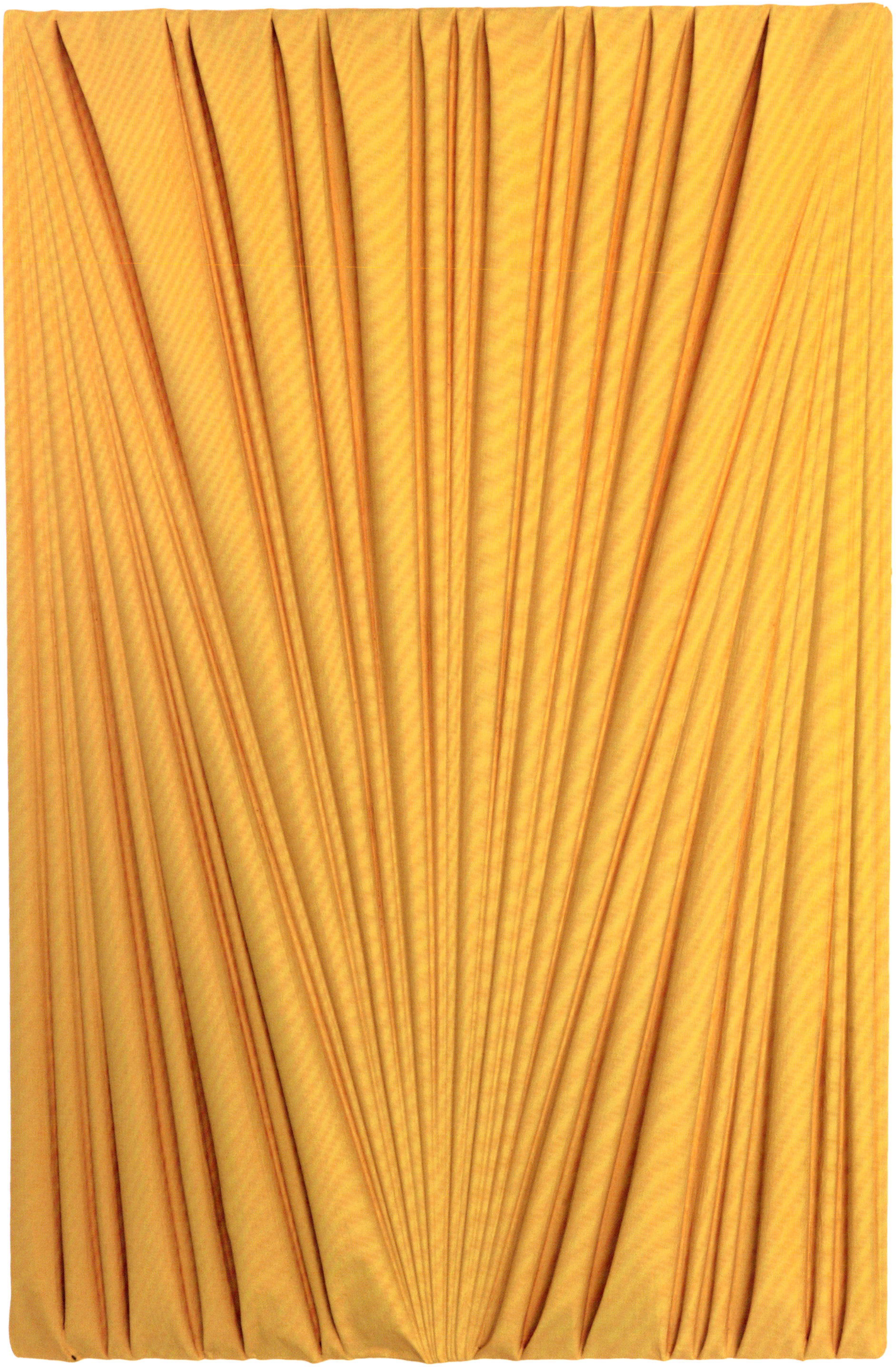

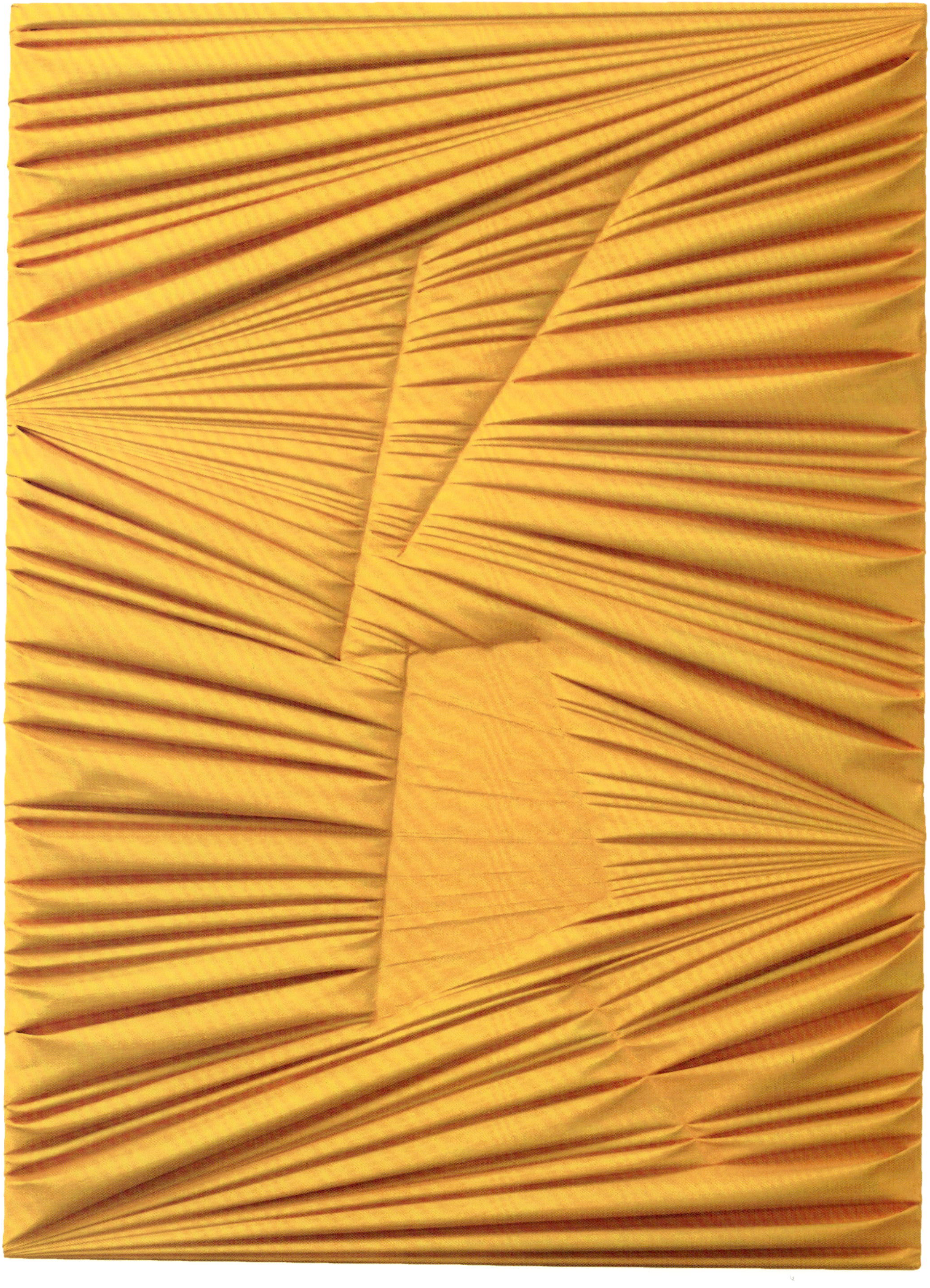

La forma celata, 2015
Vinyl and sand on lead sheet
120.5 x 90.5 cm (47½ x 35⅝ in.)

La forma celata, 2014
Vinyl and sand on lead sheet
42 x 33 cm (16½ x 13 in.)

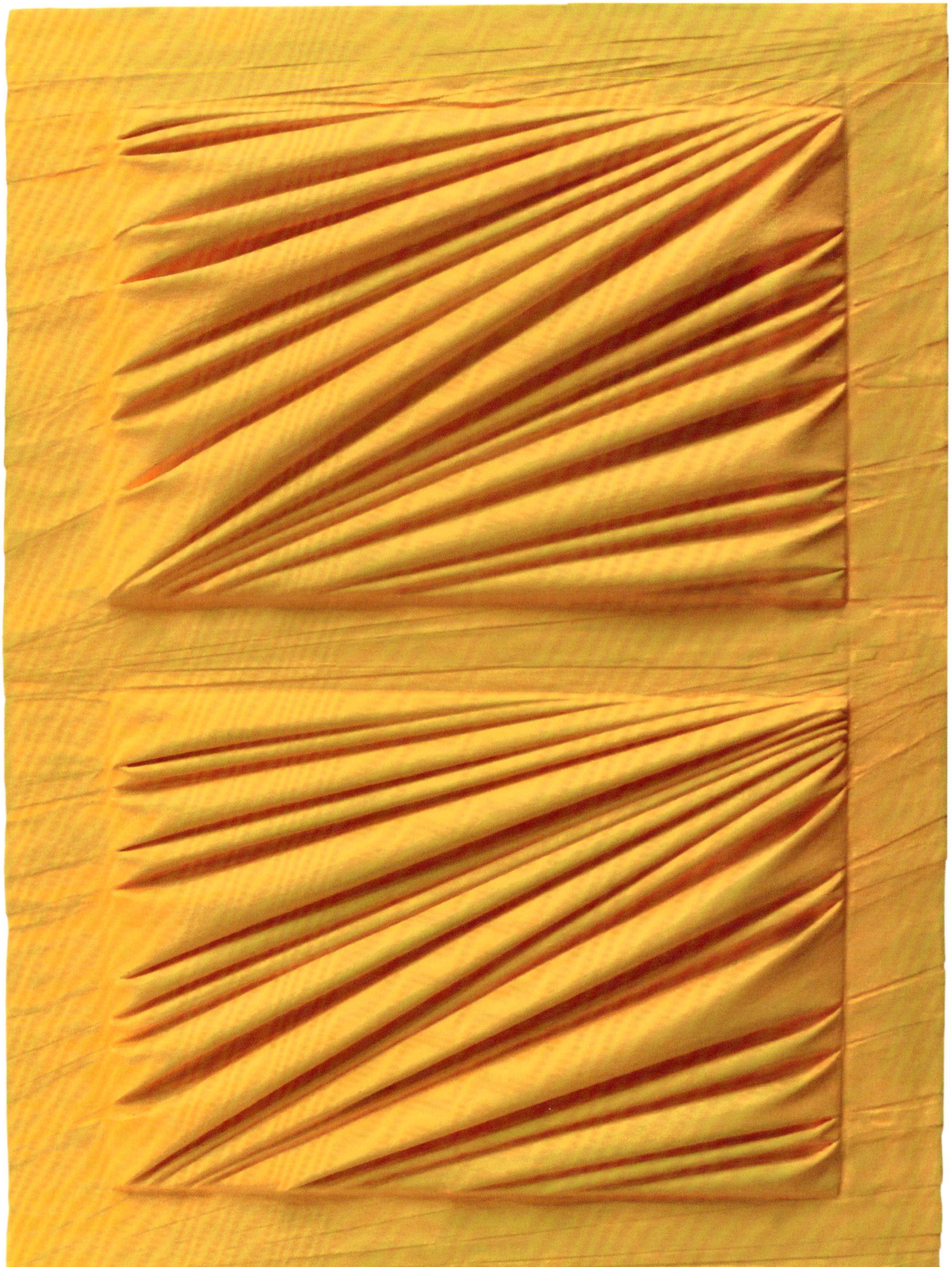

Senza titolo, 2015
Vinyl and sand on lead sheet
120 x 90 cm (47¼ x 35½ in.)

Pages 40–41
Senza titolo, 2013
Gold leaf on lead sheet
121 x 90.5 cm (47⅝ x 35⅝ in.)

La forma celata, 2013
Gold leaf on lead sheet
120 x 90 cm (47¼ x 35½ in.)

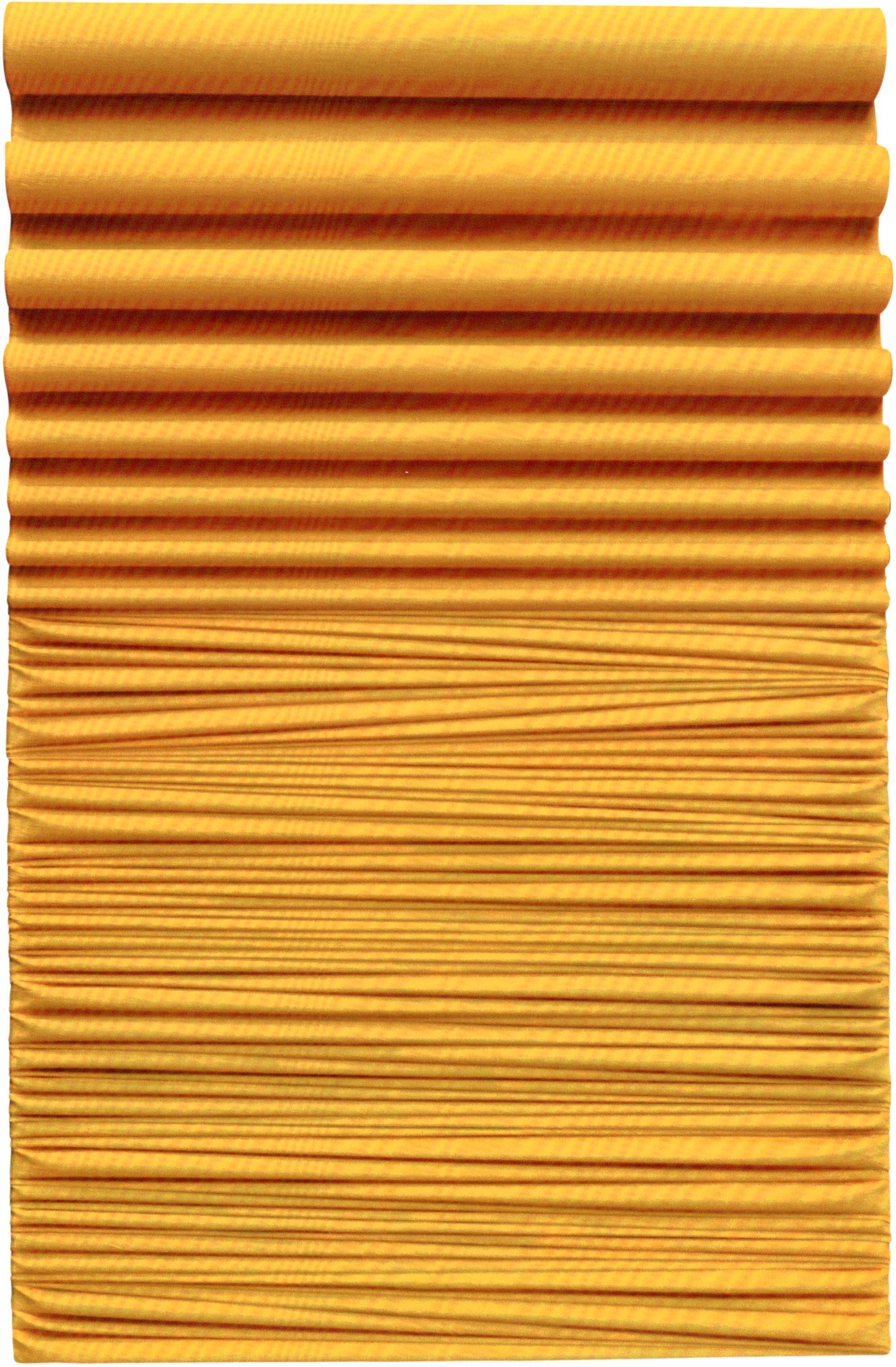

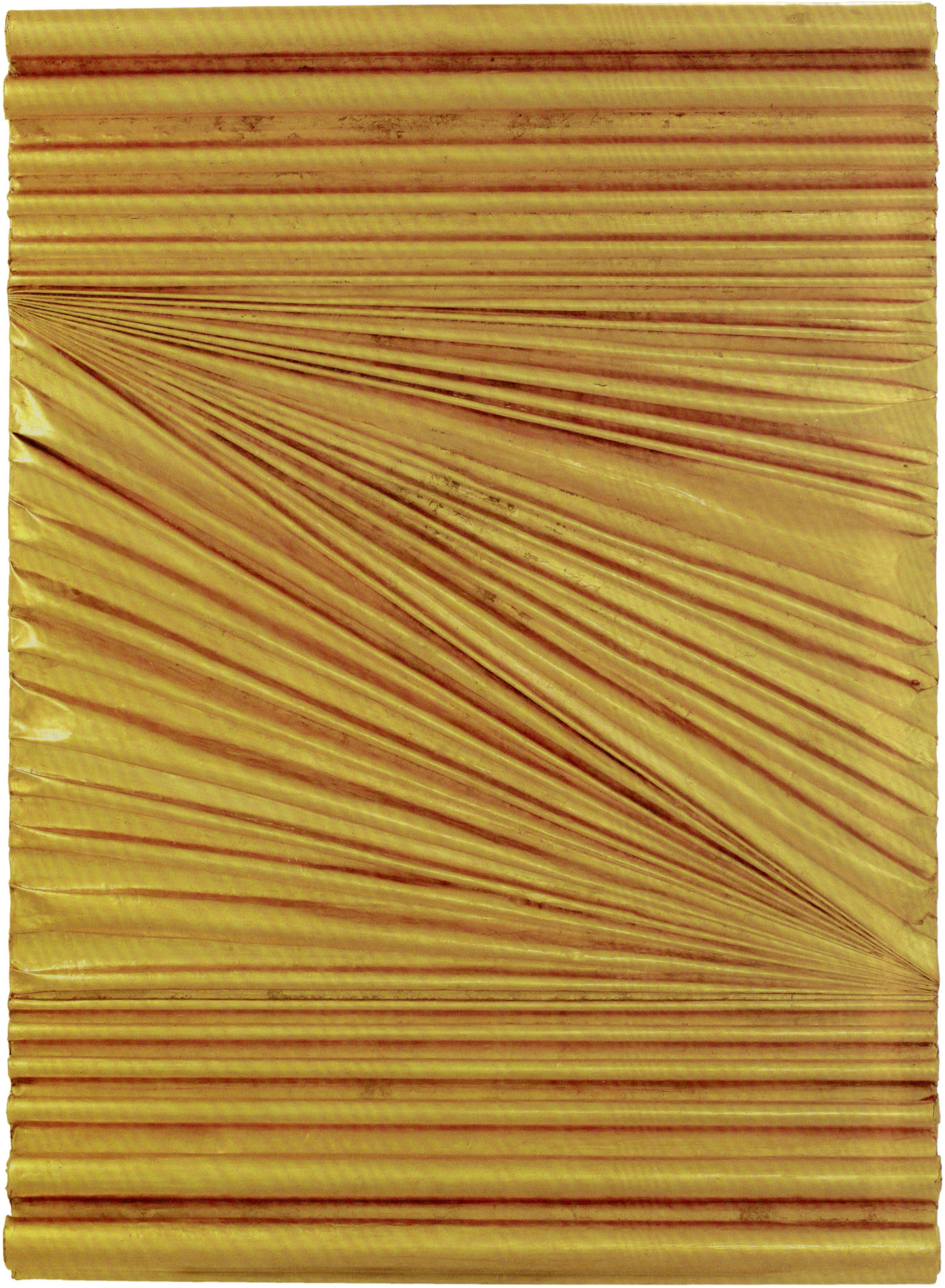

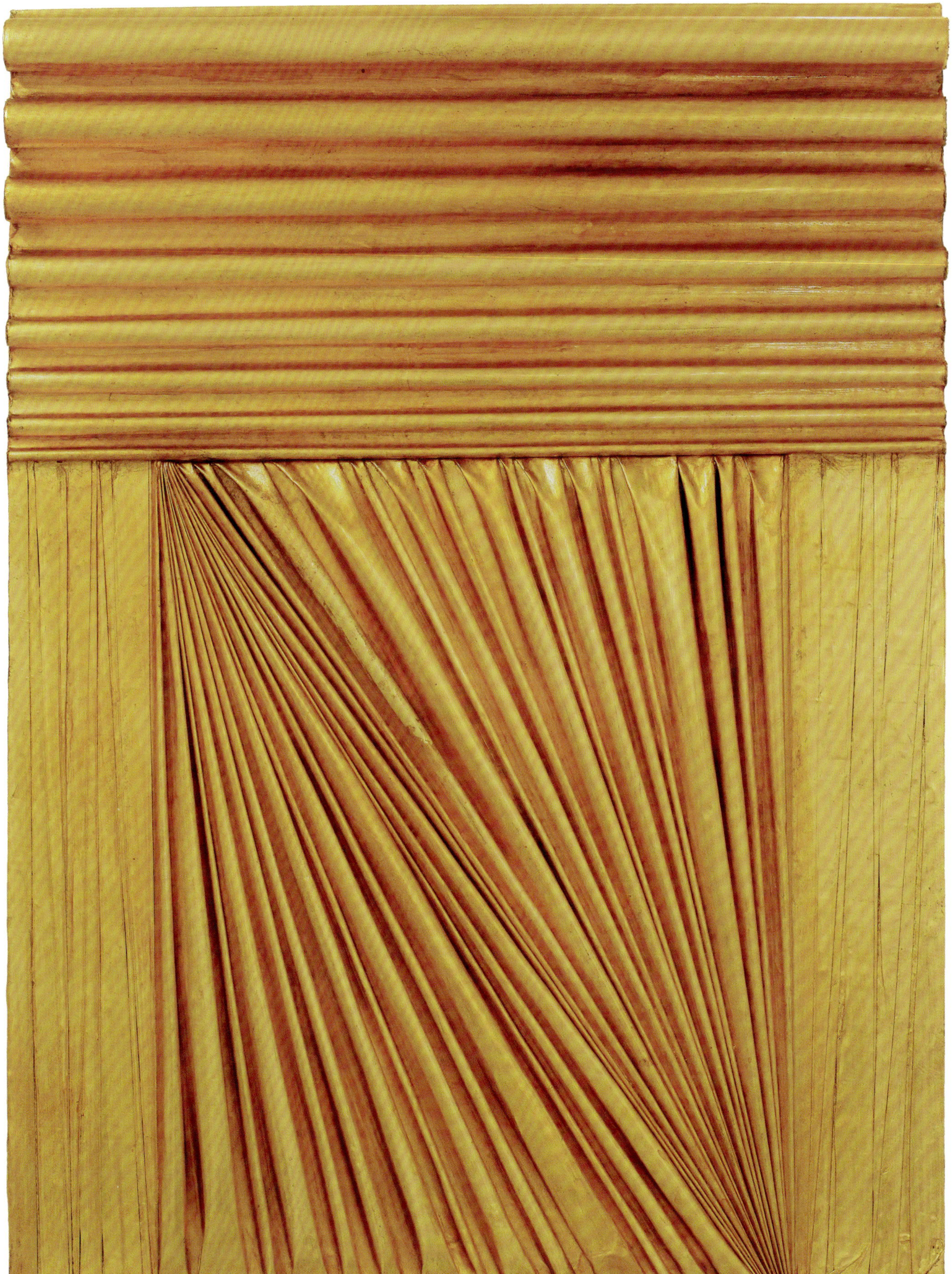

La forma celata, 2013
Gold leaf on lead sheet
120.5 x 90 cm (47½ x 35½ in.)

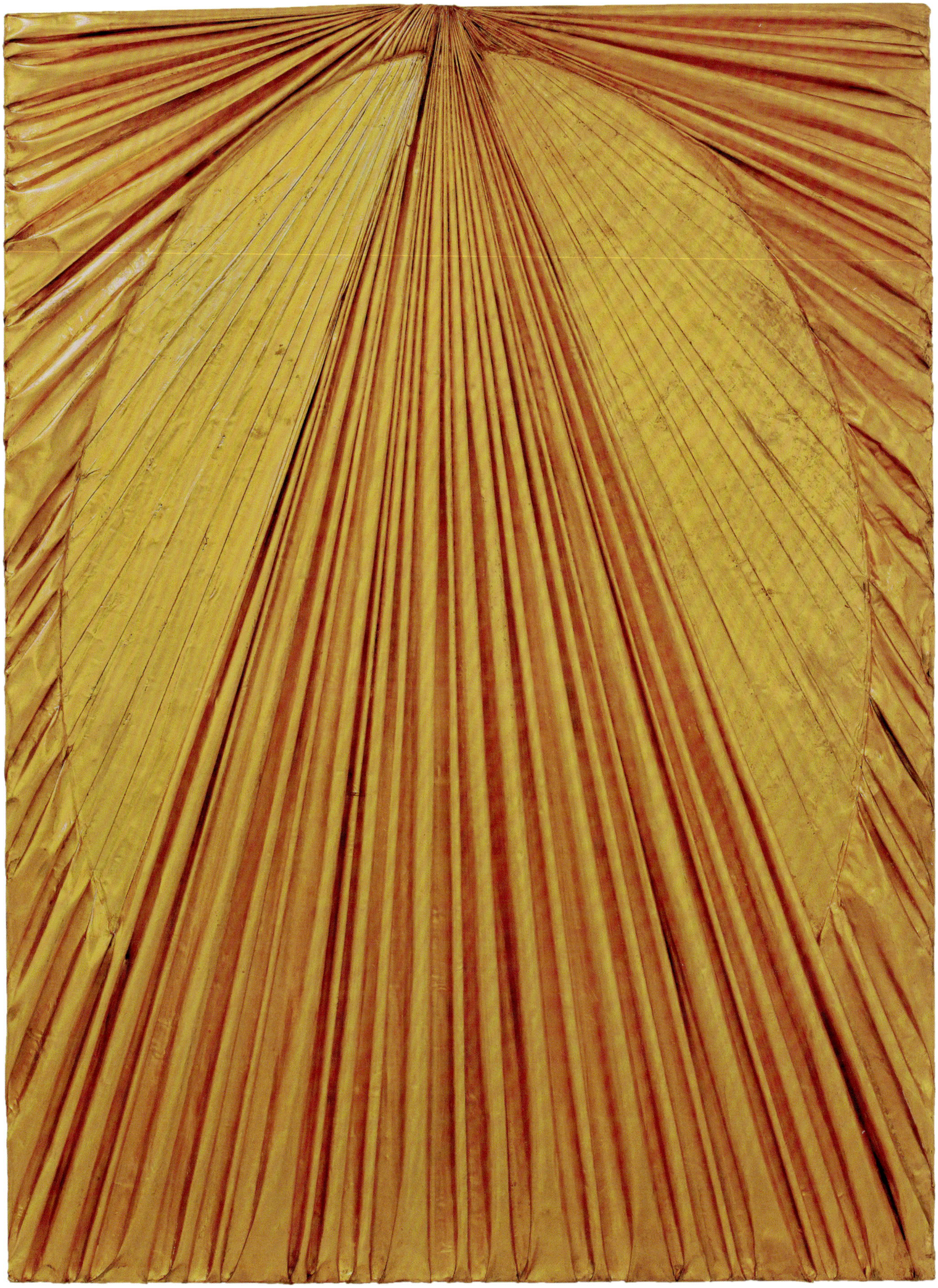

Senza titolo, 2005
Vinyl and sand on lead sheet
50 x 38 cm (19¾ x 15 in.)

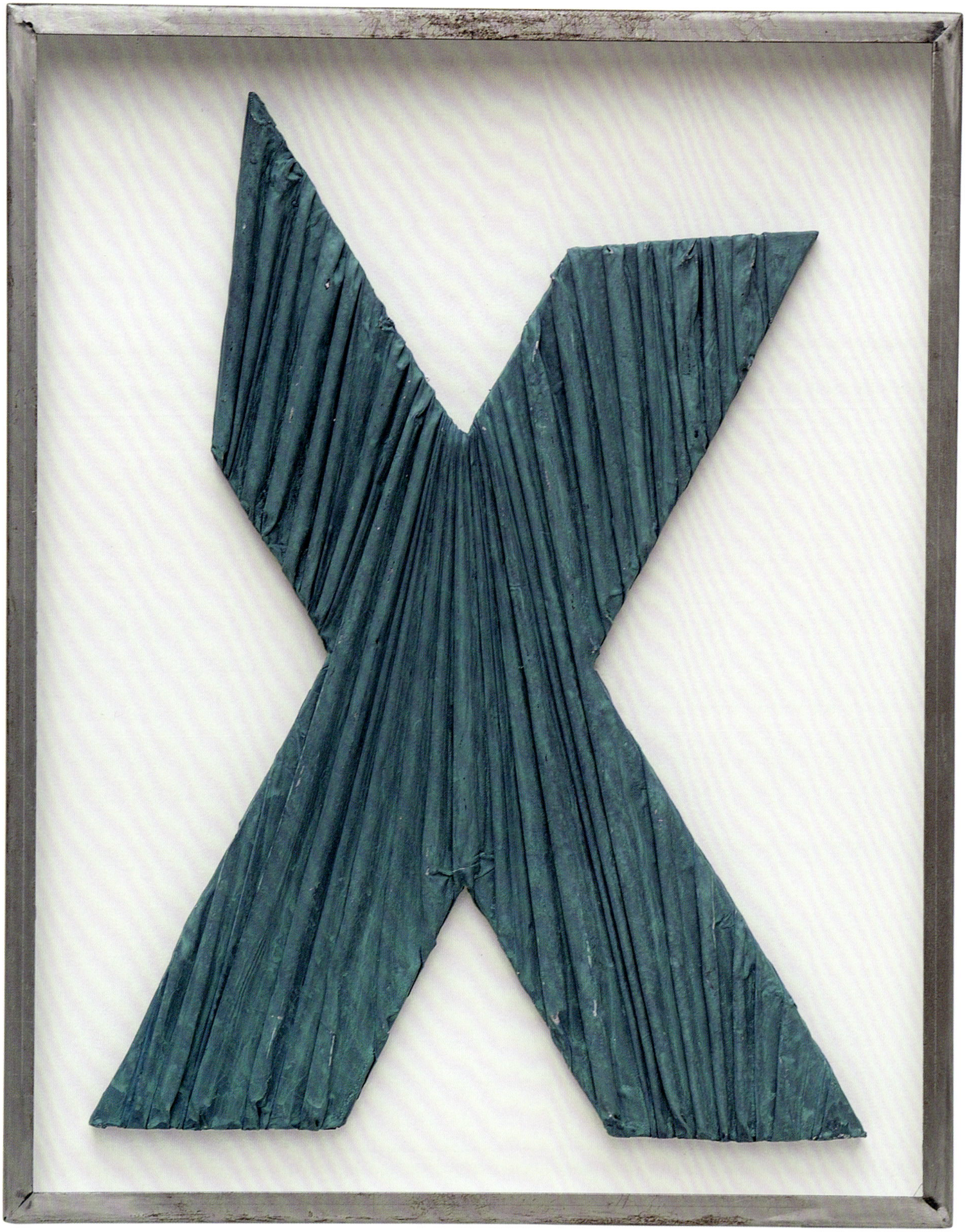

Senza titolo, 2006
Vinyl and sand on lead sheet
80 x 60 cm (31½ x 23⅝ in.)

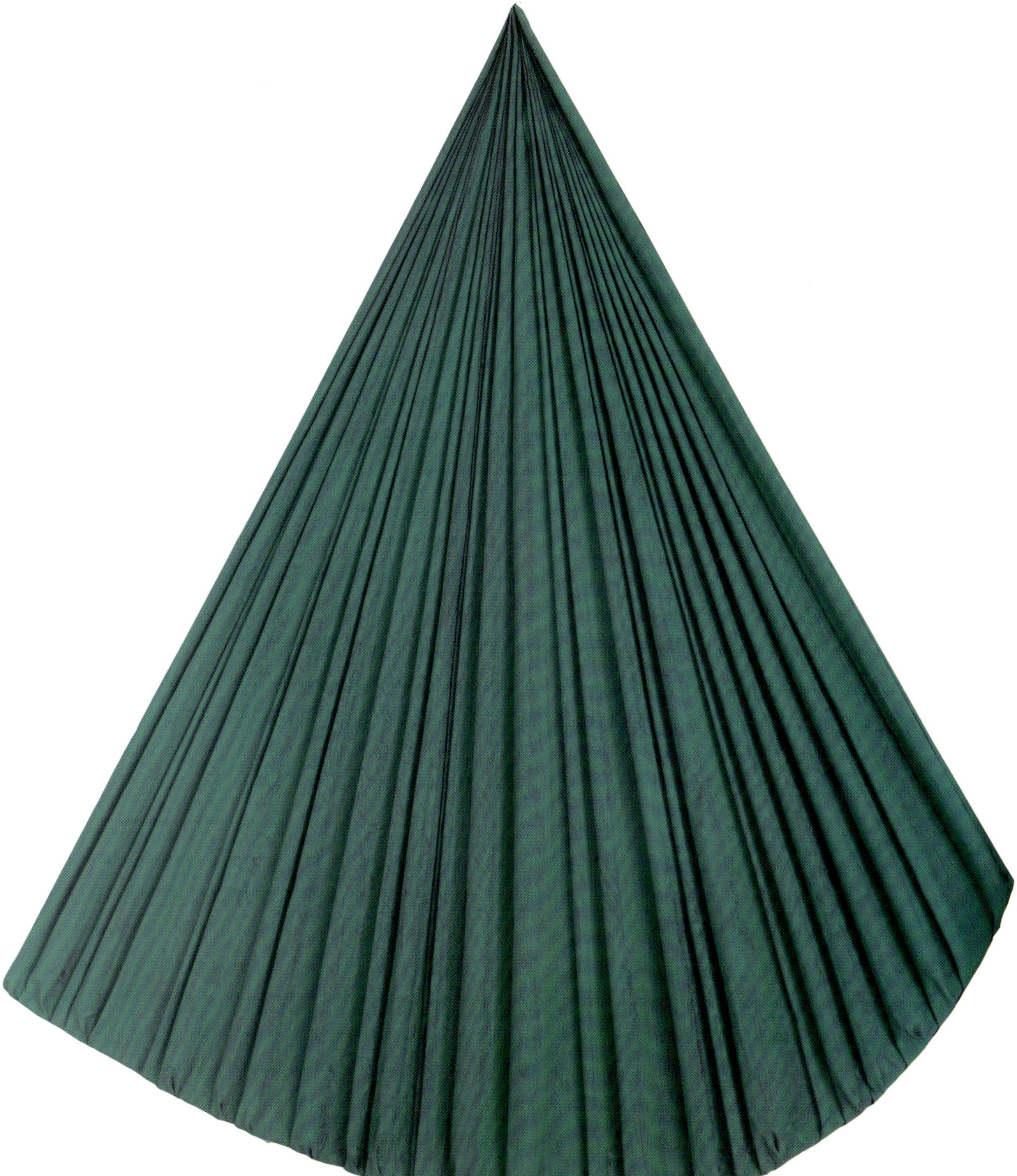

La forma celata, 2009
Vinyl and sand on lead sheet
42 x 33 cm (16½ x 13 in.)

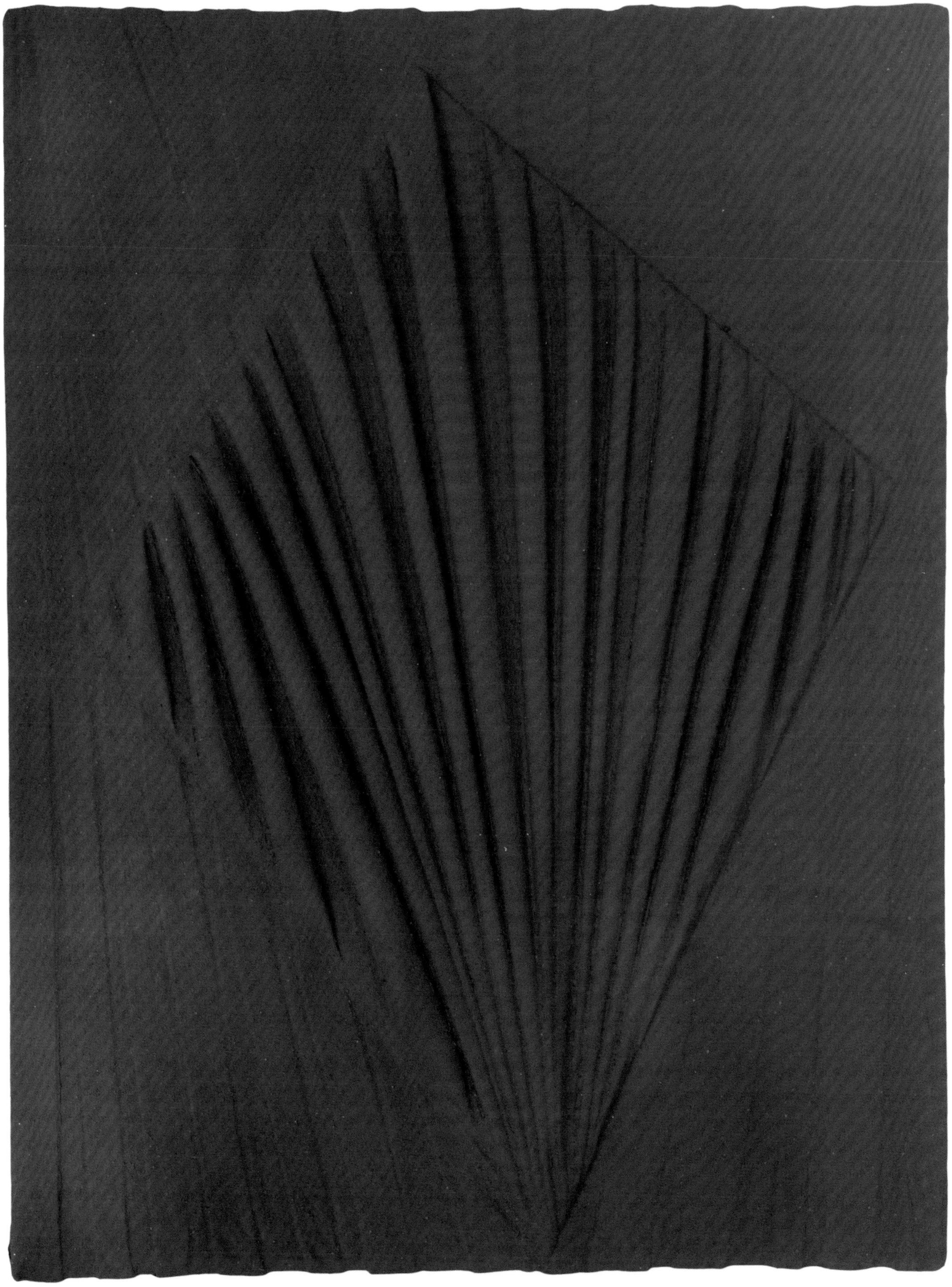

Umberto Mariani: Infinite Inflection

Bruno Corà

Preliminary remarks

If time – and in our case that occupied by the observation of the finished work – has some essential value, then it will be worthwhile saying that a great deal has passed since I first beheld the work of Umberto Mariani. It's been about half a century – it was in 1966, the beginning of my apprenticeship – since I became acquainted not only with Mariani's works but also with those of Bepi Romagnoni, Gianfranco Baruchello, Valerio Adami, Gianfranco Pardi and others. It was my dear friend Giangiacomo Spadari who pointed them out to me and also arranged for me to meet some of them.

But many more years would have to pass before I had the opportunity to measure myself hermeneutically – although I had been following it – with Mariani's painting. This happened in 1975 at the exhibition of the cycle of paintings *Alfabeto afono* (*Aphonic Alphabet*). I did not hesitate on that occasion – Mariani having invited me – to formulate a brief critical essay. Certain affirmations and points made at the time still seem to hold their ground as I prepare to turn my thoughts again to the artist's most recent works. Looking back at the text, I cite statements made regarding the 'ambiguous' quality of his painting. I wrote at the time: 'Mariani further and more closely combined the terms of his global definition of certain ambiguities of the real: ambiguity in the artistic idiom, ambiguity in language and its codes, objective ambiguity of one of his images as the equivalent of the ambiguity of the messages emitted by reality.'[1]

In pointing out that the comprehension of the meaning of the icono-letters of *Alfabeto afono*, unlike his previous painting cycles – the *Serre* (*Greenhouses*, 1966), the *Contestazione mondana: Flower Power* (*Worldly Protest: Flower Power*, 1967) and the other themes and formulations in which objects and anthropomorphic plant forms, in spite of the sketchiness of association, made absolutely decipherable the emblematic messages strongly infused with the 1960s consumer aesthetic – could only be achieved 'through two orders of interpretation: the first still regarding the forms of the image, the second about what they might mean as the first (or isolated) letters of an unknown word and, what's more, as letters deprived of their phonetic capacity'.[2] Furthermore, I commented on how Mariani, starting at the end of the 1960s, had already evidenced unsettling forms under the sheaths, imitation-skin membranes and manner of alluring 'agitated drapings'. Lastly, precisely regarding the draping I pointed out that this figurative theme – which Mariani did not later fail to emphasize, in that it belonged to all

La forma celata, 2015
Vinyl and sand on lead sheet
120 x 90 cm (47¼ x 35½ in.)

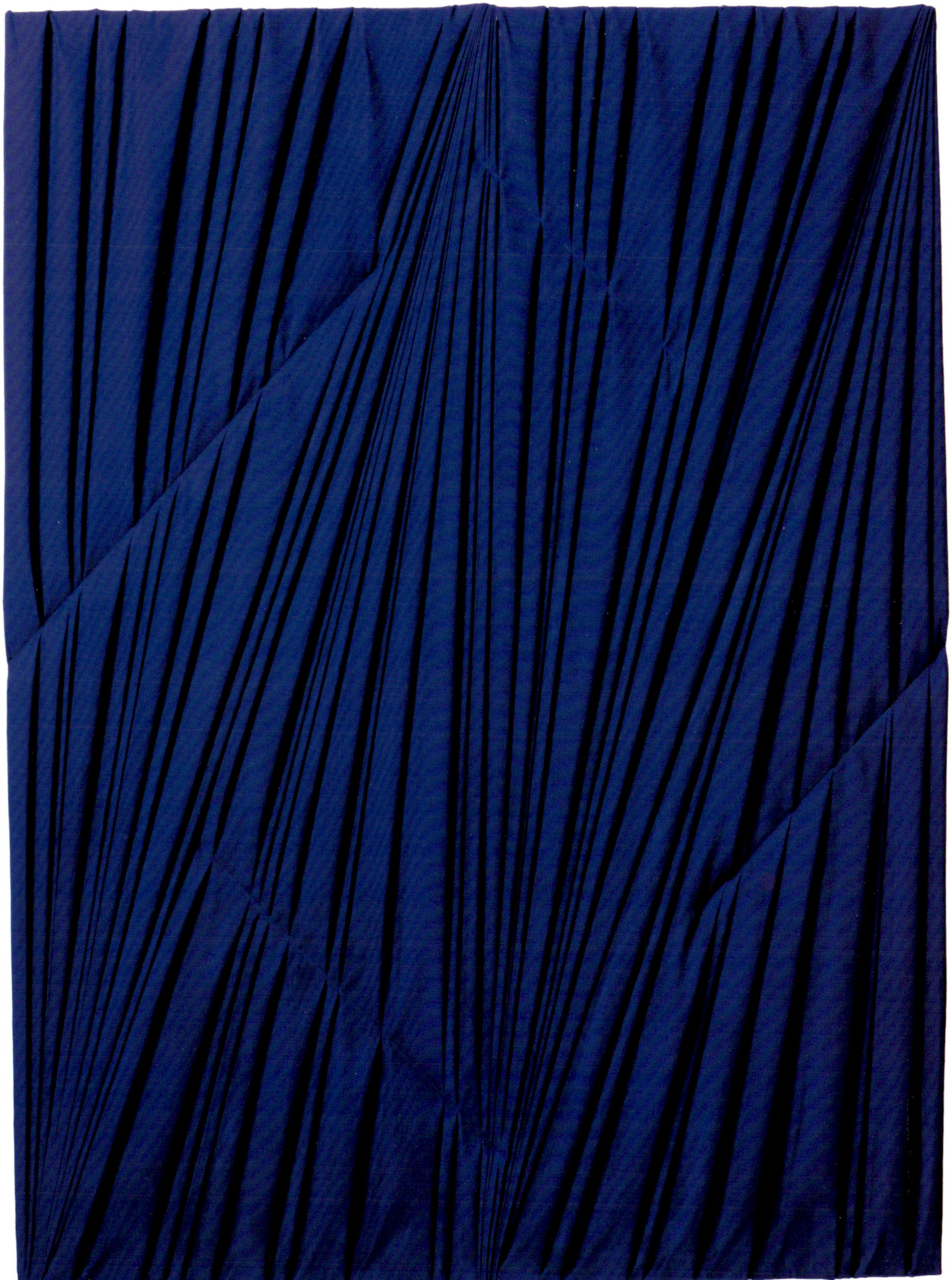

civilizations and all epochs, swathing, cooling, hiding – also became charged with a 'dramatic' aspect in evoking the shroud. I found it comforting to read a few years later that Guido Ballo[3] had with interest returned to the observations I had made regarding ambiguity in Mariani's images, *Alfabeto afono* and other things, focusing on certain aspects of that inalterable property that Mariani never lost.

When I saw photos of the most recent and contemporary cycle of works by the artist, at the acme of their congenital illusory qualities, I was prompted to take a trip to his studio in Milan, giving me the indubitable advantage of being once again able to witness the effective role of his hand-mind in the creation of the works. Although expertise, skill and mastery may seem to be obsolete, bygone virtues, having made room for other attributes of the generative impulse in art, when they are bountifully manifested it is certainly not in vain. Hence, standing before the many works still in progress and others already completed, all the pictorial and sculptural qualities whose objective power I had perceived in the photos revealed themselves with even more impact. A visit to the studio of a painter like Mariani is still one of the most fruitful moments for an observer interested in understanding both the idiom and the elaborative processes that give origin to the form and to the overall image of the work.

From the ambiguous to the real, from surface to relief

In the works labelled 'leads', which took form starting in 1991 using lead sheet, Mariani achieved a variegated paradigm that equals or perhaps outdoes that expressed earlier in *Alfabeto afono*. Indeed, in the elaboration conceived by Mariani, they have taken on differing pictorial-sculptural aspects and morphologies. They are nearly inexhaustible variations of a model imagery which, far from existing as a reference object, nevertheless exists in the mind of the artist, who thus affirms his freedom to act on and modify a pure idea, which, as such, is neither obligating nor rigid yet still demanding equally ideal outcomes.

The first 'leads', taking the form of surfaces in relief, bear the title *La forma celata* (*The Hidden Form*, 1991). They evidence many modalities that might seem to derive from his painting in the *Alfabeto afono* years (1974–76), based on folds and 'concealed forms', i.e. beneath the mimetic representation of a fabric that hides, in the case in question, box-like letters of the alphabet. Actually they include other elaborative processes developed subsequent to those works, and thus the inflections of the cycle *Teorema* (*Theorem*, starting in 1977), the cycle *Il luogo dell'illusione* (*The Place of Illusion*, 1979–80), the *Relitti di scena* (*Stage Wrecks*, 1980–94), *Zodiaco* (*Zodiac*, 1981–83), *Specchi* (*Mirrors*, 1985–93), and lastly the cycle titled *Autobiografico* (*Autobiographical*, since 1977).

The stations on this quite meaningful path had led Mariani, step by step, over the course of more than a decade, to introduce other materials into the work. Thus, alongside canvas with acrylic paints, he added oil on canvas and various other materials: from jersey and silk chiffon to wrought iron, carved wood, gold leaf, plaster, methacrylate, Kristall and lastly lead sheet. This path, certainly not followed instinctively but actually quite arduous, evidenced Mariani's need to free himself of the metaphorical exercise of 'representation' to achieve an increasing degree of verisimilitude, going from ambiguity to the realistic illusoriness. While initially the folds in the fabric were pure pictorial representation, he would later replace them with the folds of real fabric.

Up to this point, he has moved from 'represented' painting to 'presenting' painting. But later, with folded lead sheet on panel, Mariani's interests essentially turned to the phenomenological yield of that material. It not only is the real protagonist of the image of the work with its surface structured in folds, but also displays such ductility that it can 'conceal' or 'present', below or above its surface, geometric forms of every sort, or alphabetic letters through varying depths of imprints. In this morphological 'meditation', an essential role is played by the folds in the lead sheet, light, shadow, the surface and depth of the folds, and the imprint of the hidden forms of objects, which for the most part are not there.

This phase of the 'leads' thus takes a new linguistic common denominator composed of the *fold* which is no longer simulated and illusory but real and phenomenal with unlimited prospects for morphological development.

The fold, the unlimited form

As we observe the earliest 'leads', titled *La forma celata*, the famous 'wet folds' are called to mind because, by compressing and causing the fabric to adhere to the body, the water reveals, through the folds, 'more than nudity' (Gilles Deleuze). There is just a short jump from the 'wet folds' to those in Giuseppe Sanmartino's *Veiled Christ*. Few other works speak to us so clearly of the power of revealing-hiding, the compressing and adhering of folds to the body and thus to the form.

As 'folded matter', the lead sheet systematically elaborated by Mariani since 1991 ideally seems to constitute, because of the morphology of the *fold* which totally informs the works, the ideal object of Deleuze's thinking on the modern Neo-Baroque essence and its 'soul' precisely via the metaphor of the 'fold'. He begins by stating: 'The Baroque [...] endlessly produces folds. It does not invent things: there are all kinds of folds coming from the East, Greek, Roman, Romanesque, Gothic, Classical folds... Yet the Baroque trait twists and turns its folds, pushing them to infinity, fold over fold, one upon the other. The Baroque fold unfurls all the way to infinity.'[4]

After having introduced its formal aspect, Deleuze suggests the need for a cryptographic action if we want to achieve the understanding of the multiplicity and complexity of its distinctive trait; to succeed in seeing and reading 'the coils of matter, and the folds in the soul'.[5]

Before we venture along this hermeneutic path briefly mentioning a few works, we do well to recall – without any presumption of merit for Mariani (something he never claimed himself) as regards his work being in harmony with the most advanced concepts in contemporary physics – that contemporary physics arrived at the notion of curved space and curved matter because of the forces actively compressing it. Mariani's work would thus naturally mesh with the *Zeitgeist* of this period. So seeking to 'see' in the folds of the lead sheet with its 'hidden forms' means shifting the gaze rhythmically from zones in full light to zones in half or full shadow and then observing zones of light and zones of shadow again, without pause if, as it seems, the frameless work alludes to the infinite extensibility of that folded elaboration of the lead sheet. Moreover, in works like *Senza titolo* (*Untitled*, 2013, gold leaf on lead sheet, 120 x 93 cm, 47¼ x 36⅝ in.), the folds of the gilded sheet radiate from the centre toward the four sides, with a diagonal cut in the support bearing a non-apparent slip plane in the act of shifting. Such works evoke a spatiality that overflows their perimeter into external space.

Senza titolo (*Untitled*, 2014, sculpted lead sheet, 80 x 60 cm, 31½ x 23⅝ in.), whose radii of silvery folds extend from the centre toward the four sides, proceed with the same expansiveness beyond the edges of the work. The continuity of one fold in another is the generative principle in Mariani's lead sheet works. For that matter, this continuity

following page
Senza titolo, 2015
Vinyl and sand on lead sheet
120 x 90.5 cm (47¼ x 35⅝ in.)

is the very attribute and quality of space. Let us not forget that Boccioni underscored its presence in the sculpture *Unique Forms of Continuity in Space* (1913) and that Castellani, in his theoretical text 'Continuità e nuovo' published in *Azimuth* in 1959, made his own sort of reference to continuity, creating a work which now shares many qualities with Mariani's. In Castellani's structured surfaces, light and shadow, projections and recesses, alternate and, albeit differently, constitute an experience that cannot be ignored, certainly more than in Manzoni's *Achromes*, especially after 1974 when Mariani began to use lead sheet in his works.

Furthermore, given Deleuze's above thoughts on the Baroque and Leibniz, the continuum of folds in Mariani's lead sheet 'hidden forms' prompts us to contemplate an observation by the great German philosopher: 'The division of the continuous ought not be considered as that of sand into grains, but as that of a sheet of paper or of a tunic into folds [...] without the body ever dissolving'.[6]

At this point the question springs to mind: Is Mariani's work 'baroque'? I personally feel that his 'folds' consciously elude baroque turbulence and iconographically adhere to the conceptual and mental labyrinthine model.

The various works I saw in Mariani's studio, now exhibited, show a richness of variations that summon forth the act of modulating which consists in an unequal and continually varying process of shaping. Reading the folds of the soul of these works should consist of decrypting those variations as sensibilities expressed in forms. An undertaking that is as arduous as opinionable can more properly be replaced with the identification of the attitudes, modes and intentions that seem to emerge from the formative process of the works. In this sense, alongside the act of folding the lead sheet, it is possible to identify that of obtaining a linear trace of interruption in the folds from it. Hence in the work *La forma celata* (2012, white glue and sand on lead sheet, 80.5 x 60.5 cm, 31¾ x 23¾ in.) in which the use of the 'imprint' morphology is evident, as well as the introduction of opposing vectors in clusters of folds in *La forma celata* (2010, white glue and sand on lead sheet, 121.5 x 90.5 cm, 47⅞ x 35⅝ in.) and in contiguous horizontal, vertical and diagonal lines in *Senza titolo* (*Untitled*, 2013, white glue and sand on lead sheet, 79.5 x 60.5 cm, 31¼ x 23¾ in.).

Quite a few works exhibit the hidden oval forms of possible mirrors or other objects or symbols (cross, arrow, star) that are not observable because the very form, often geometrical, is presented without revealing its identity. This exercise, it must be said, has much in common with how we might think of Giorgio Morandi's still lifes, Claude Monet's *Water Lilies* or the many versions of Paul Cézanne's *Sainte-Victoire*. In all these cases, one finds oneself confronted with the artist's desire to meditate on the inexhaustible quality of the formative process and on the conception of space and the factors that determine it, precisely starting from that ceaseless modularity of folds and, in the final analysis, of the chromatic variations used.

Lastly, all the hidden forms evoke a phantasmatic apparition and with it the antinomic qualities of absence-presence that induce the observer to activate his imagination in the attempt to resolve an enigma.[7]

Mariani, like other masters preceding him, has entered the phase where the generative thought behind his work, while continuing to unfold its questions, stages the dramaturgy of language itself in the act of taking form.

[1] Bruno Corà, 'Alfabeto afono di Umberto Mariani', in exhibition catalogue, Sala Comunale, Alessandria, December 1976.
[2] Ibid.
[3] Guido Ballo, 'Umberto Mariani o dell'Ambiguità Fantastica', in *Umberto Mariani. Opere 1975-1984*, exhibition catalogue, Marie-Louise Jeanneret Art Moderne, Geneva, October 1984, pp. 2–3.
[4] Gilles Deleuze, *The Fold: Leibniz and the Baroque*, trans. T. Conley (Minneapolis: University of Minneapolis Press, 1993), p. 3.
[5] Ibid.
[6] Gottfried Wilhelm von Leibniz, *Opusculus et fragments inédits de Leibniz*, edited by Louis Couturat (Paris: Félix Alcan, 1903), pp. 614–15, republished in Deleuze, *The Fold*.
[7] We recall here an early example of *objet caché* in the famous work by Man Ray: *L'énigme d'Isidore Ducasse*, 1920.

Taghelmoust: il velo, 2014
Vinyl and sand on lead sheet
42 x 33 cm (16½ x 13 in.)

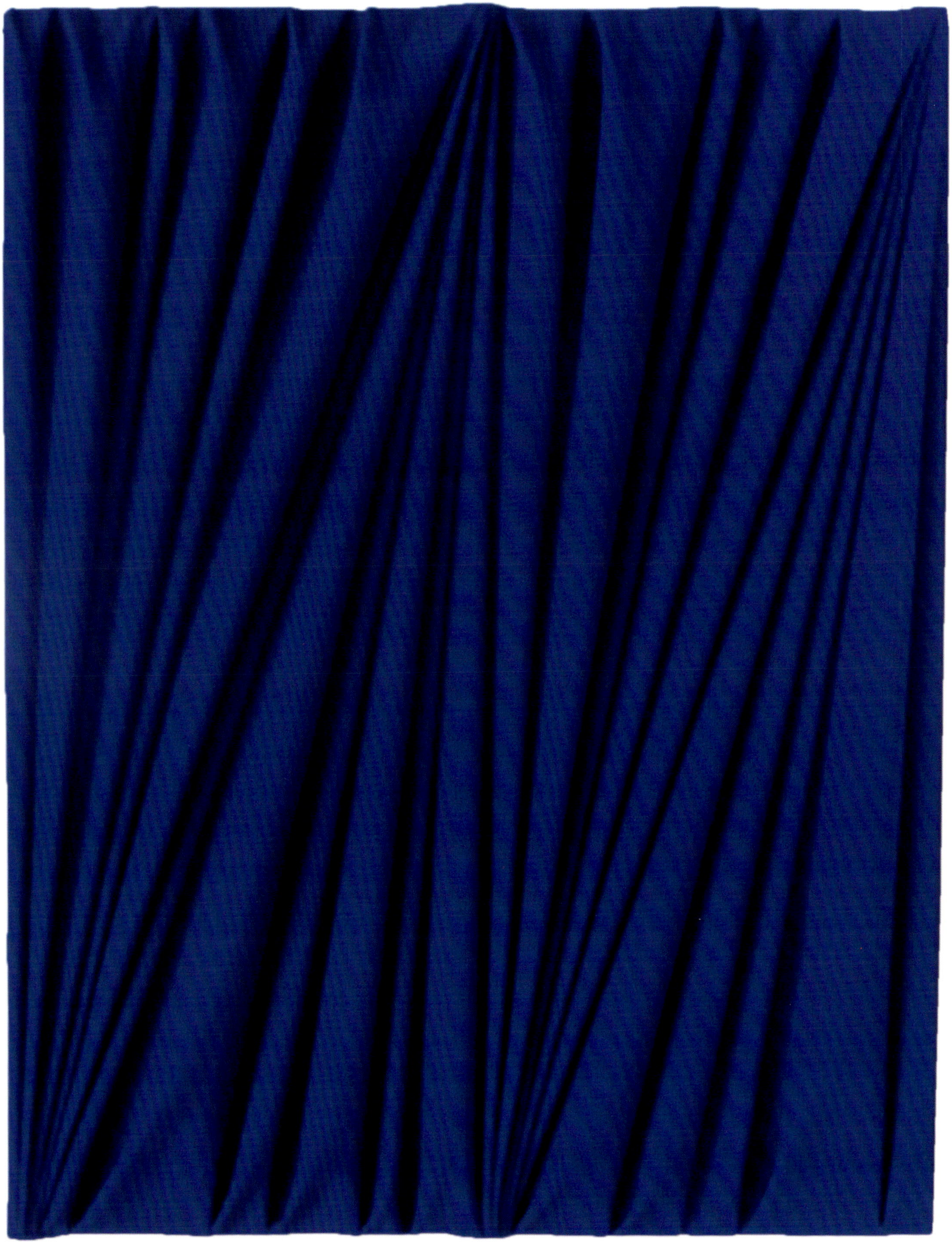

La forma celata, 2008
Vinyl and sand on lead sheet
80 x 60 cm (31½ x 23⅝ in.)

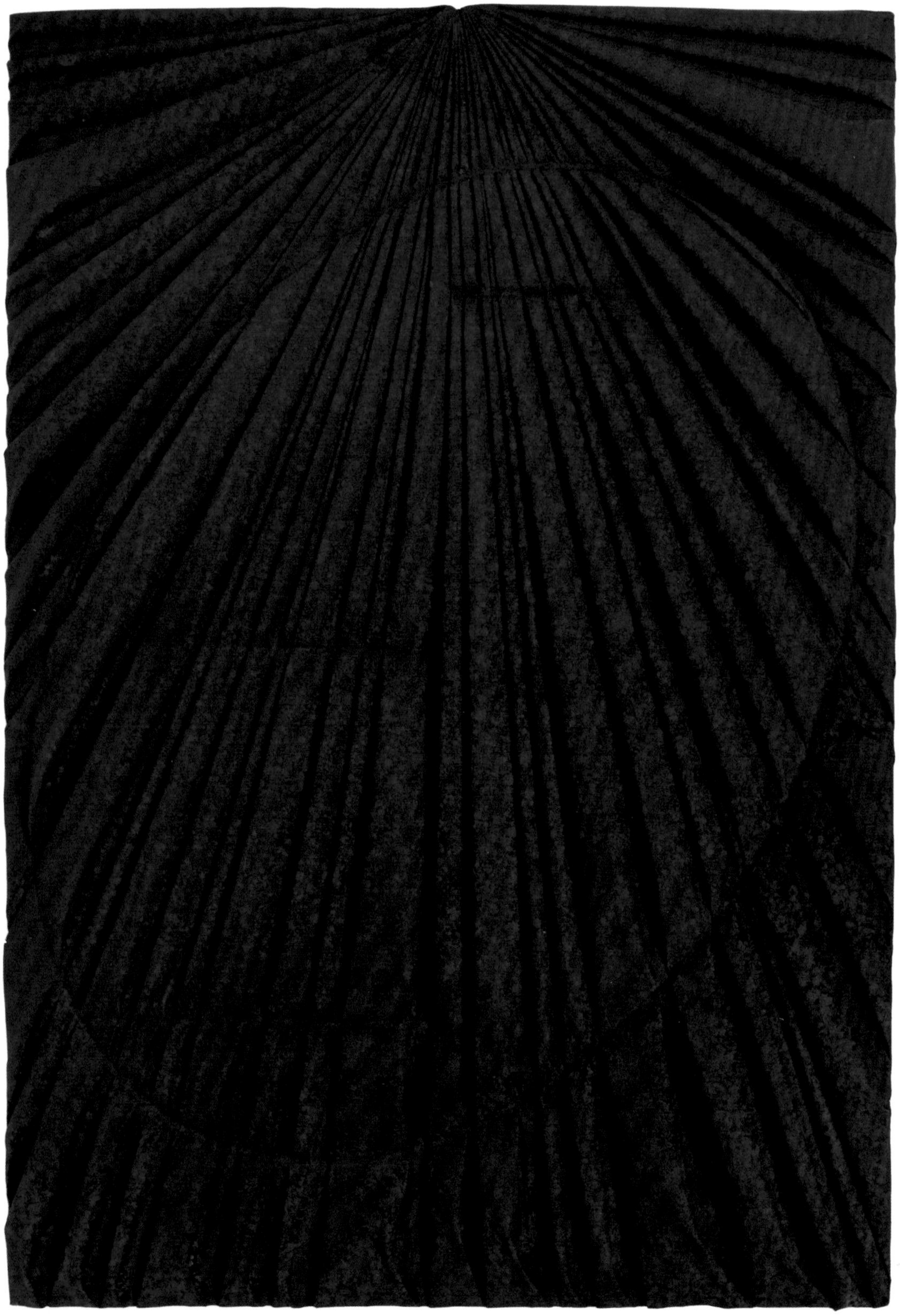

Taghelmoust: il velo, 2013
Vinyl and sand on lead sheet
80 x 60 cm (31½ x 23⅝ in.)

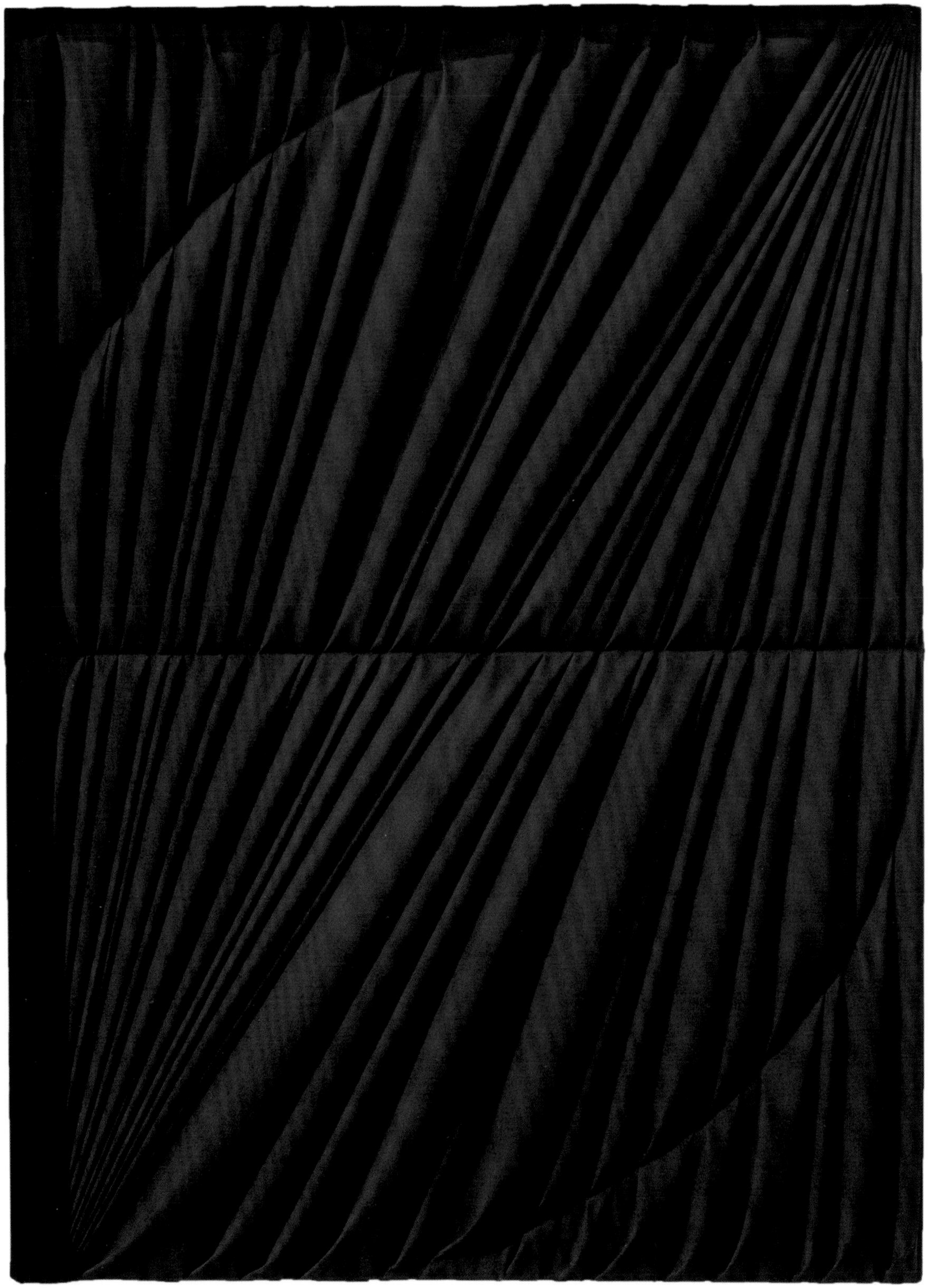

La forma celata: stella di David,
2010
Vinyl and sand on lead sheet
80 x 60.5 cm (31½ x 23¾ in.)

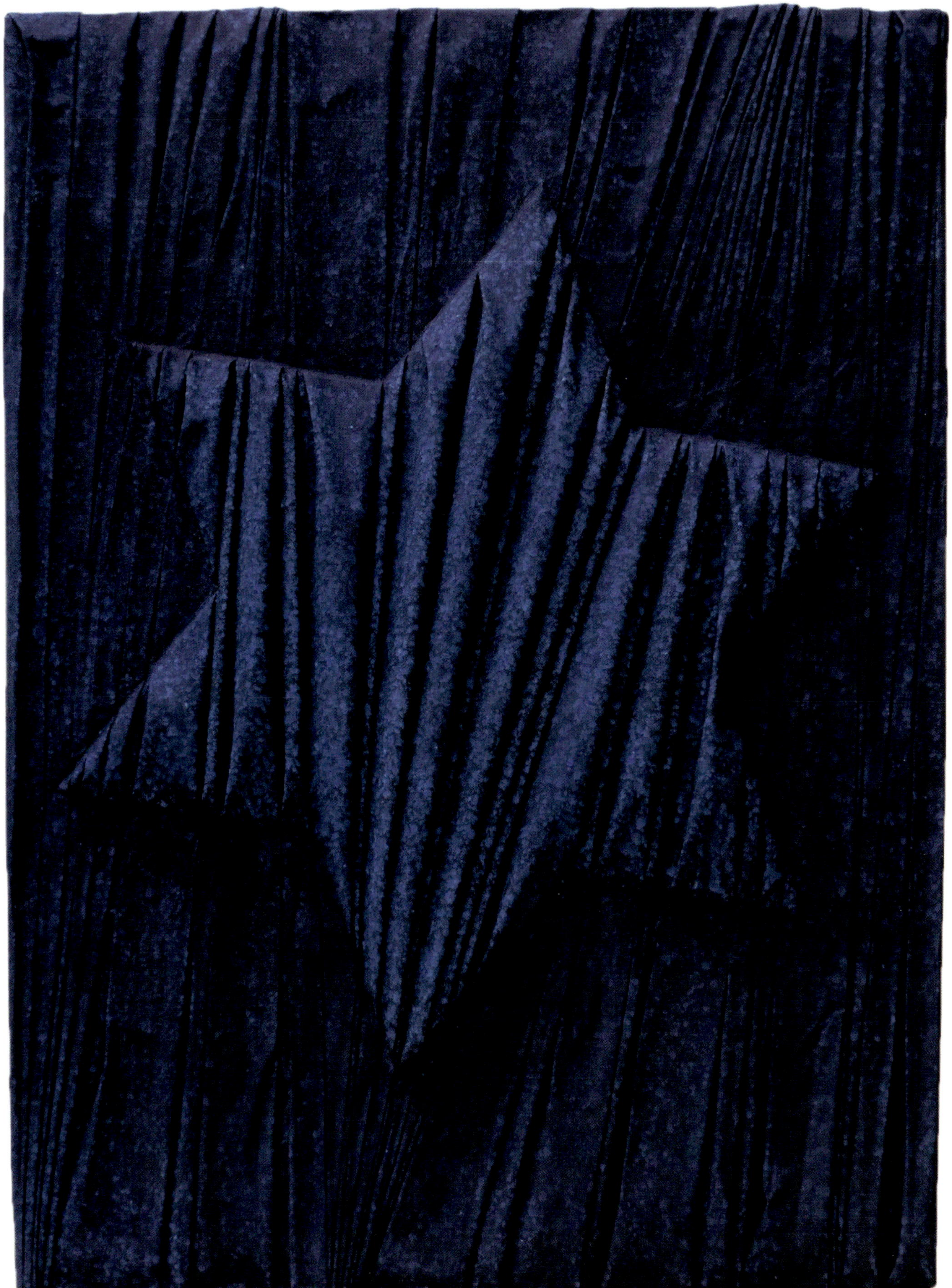

La forma celata, 2014
Vinyl on lead sheet
80 x 60 cm (31½ x 23⅝ in.)

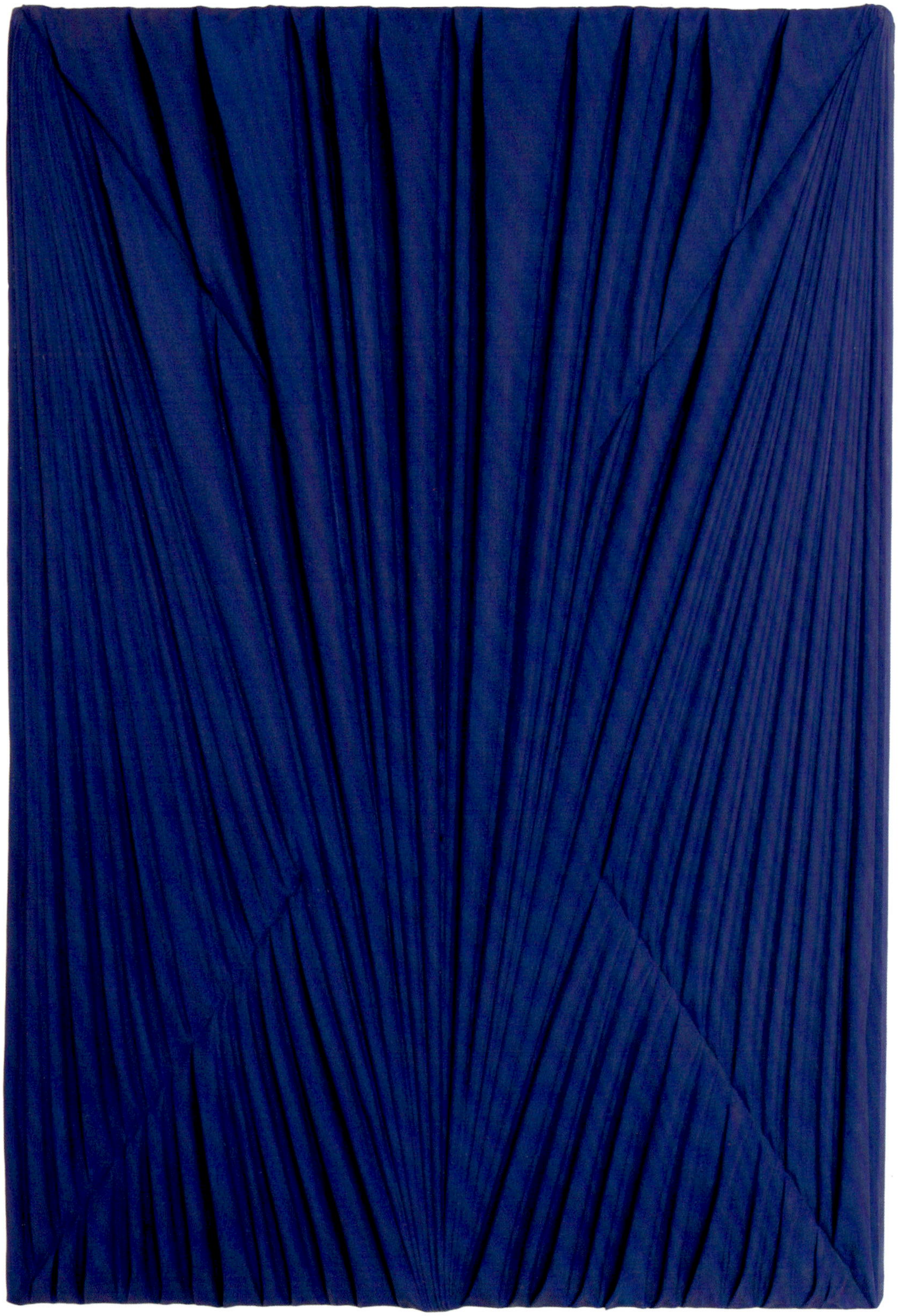

Taghelmoust: il velo, 2009
Vinyl and sand on lead sheet
80 x 60 cm (31½ x 23⅝ in.)

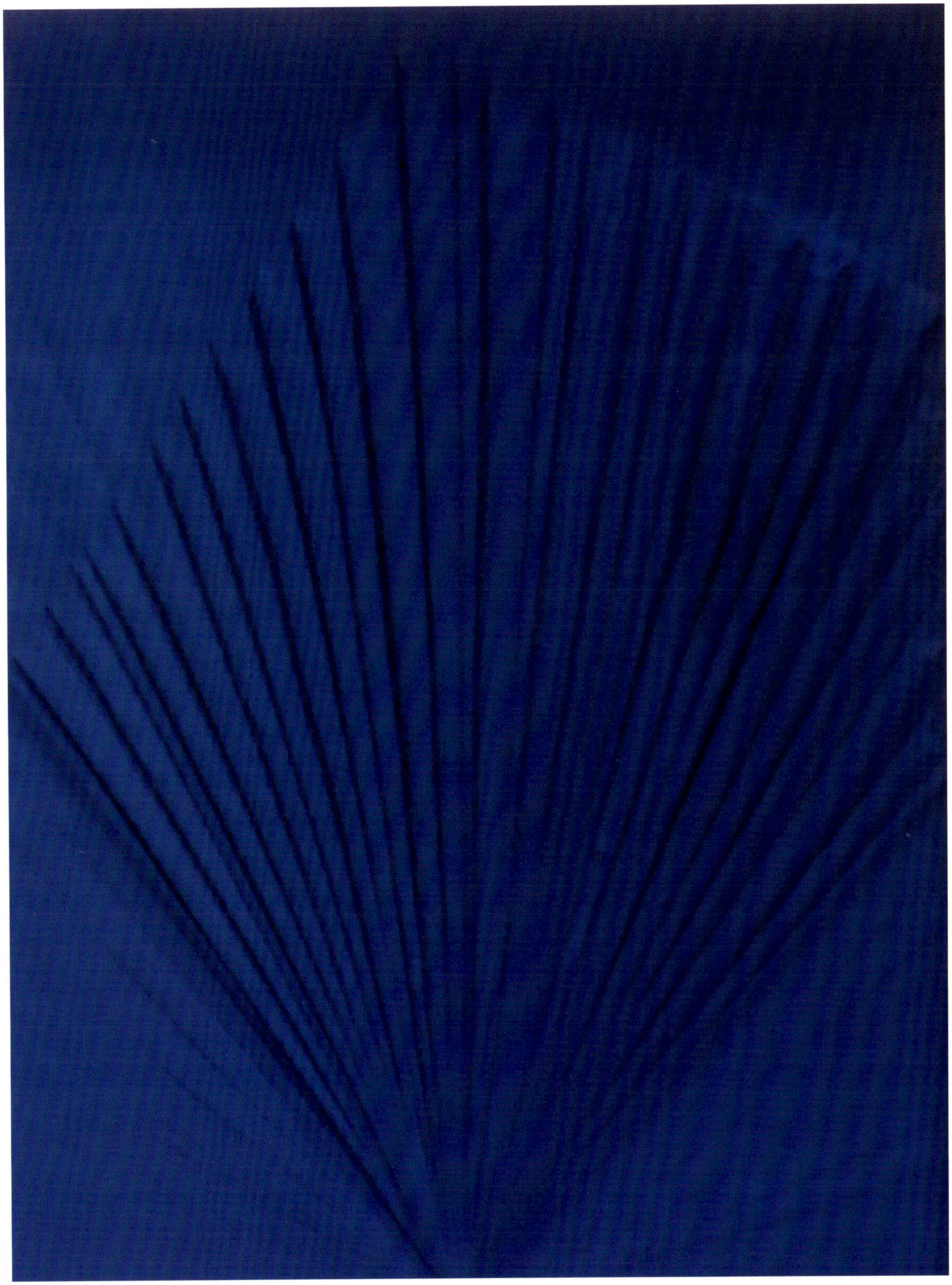

Taghelmoust: il velo, 2000
Vinyl on lead sheet
212 x 177 cm (83½ x 69¾ in.)

Genesi 1 : cielo e mare, 2010
Vinyl and sand on lead sheet
120 x 90.5 cm (47¼ x 35⅝ in.)

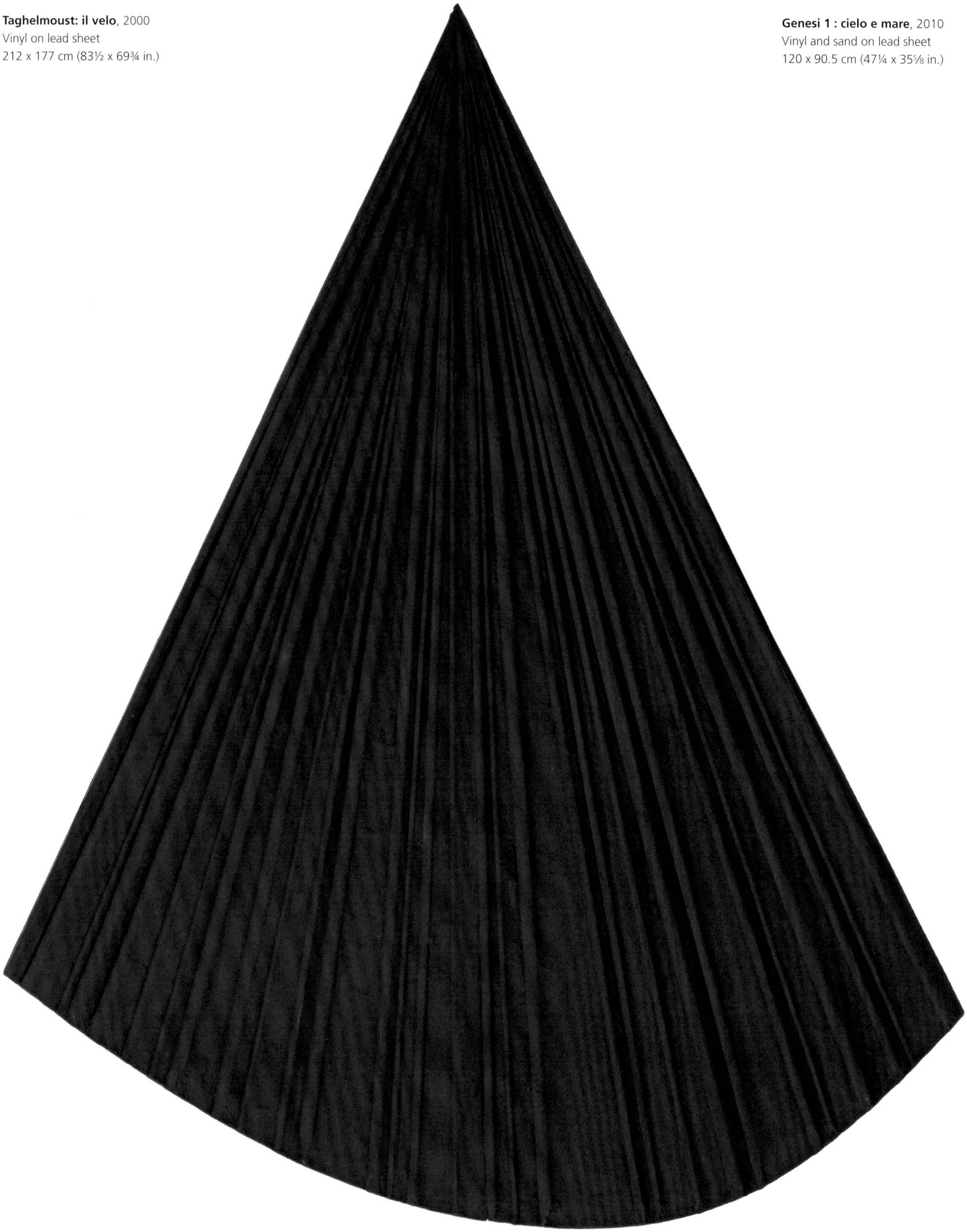

La forma celata, 2015
Vinyl and sand on lead sheet
120.5 x 90.5 cm (47½ x 35⅝ in.)

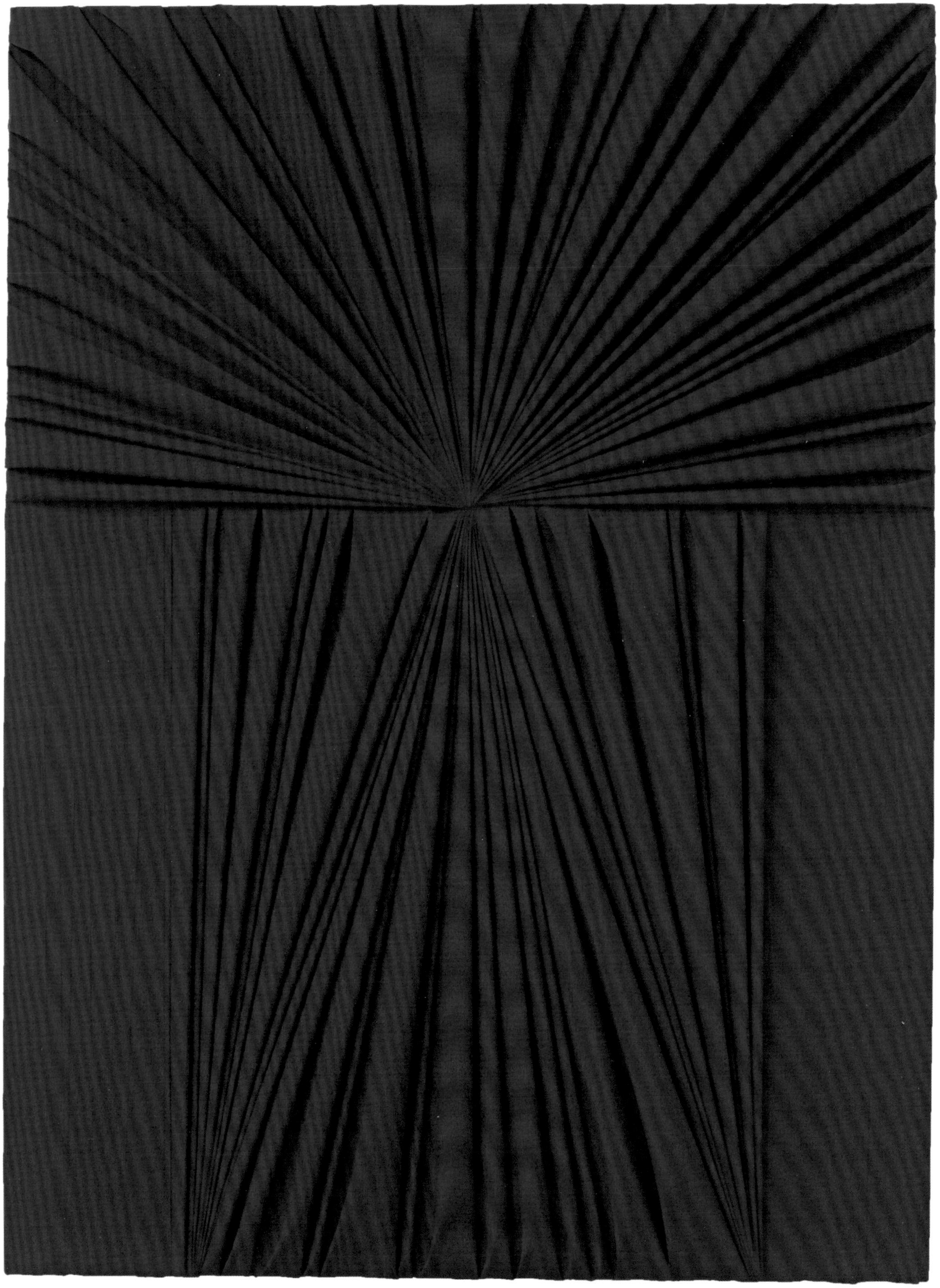

La forma celata, 2015
Vinyl and sand on lead sheet
120 x 90 cm (47¼ x 35½ in.)

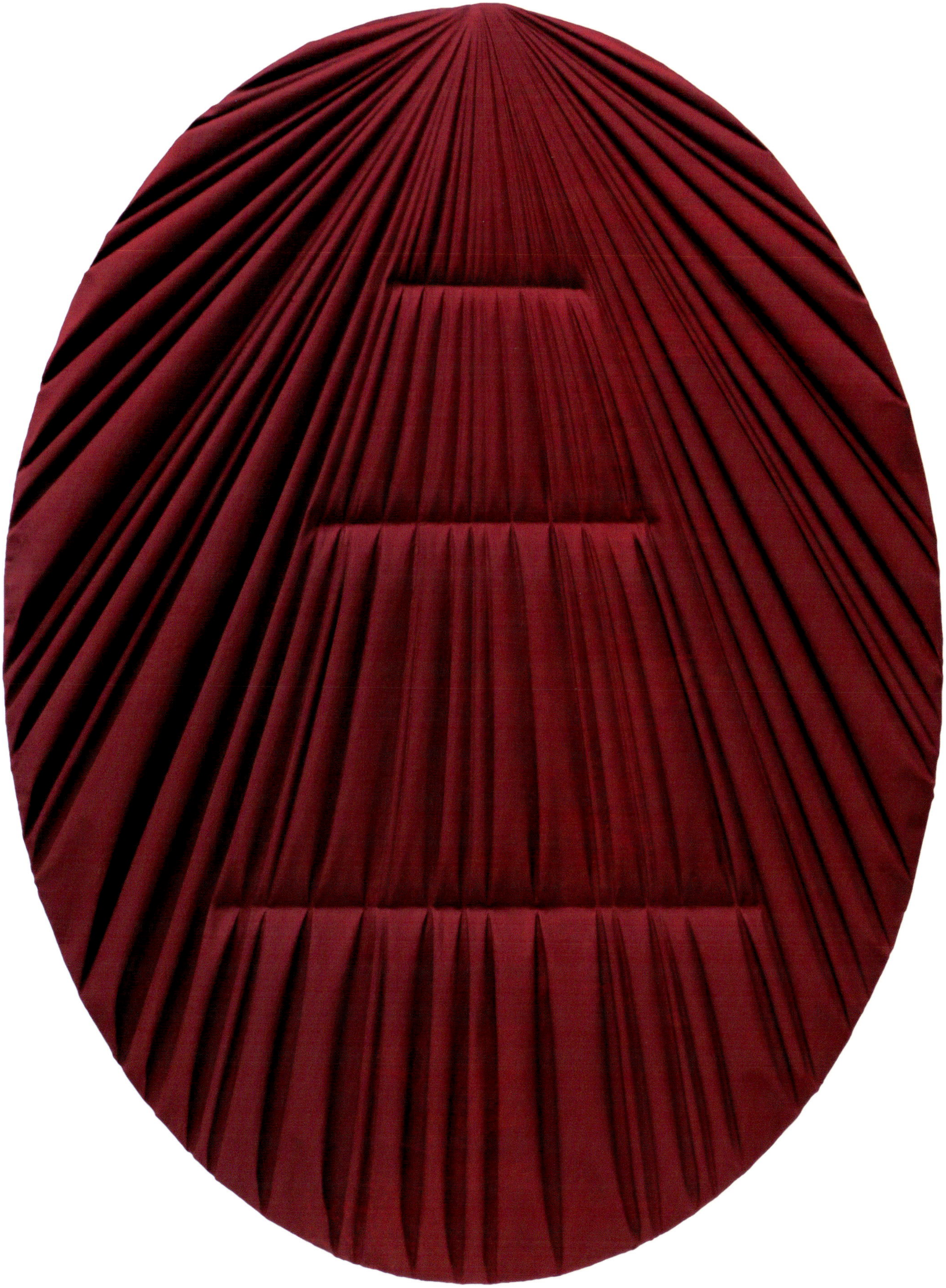

Senza titolo, 2010
Vinyl and sand on lead sheet
121 x 91 cm (47⅝ x 35⅞ in.)

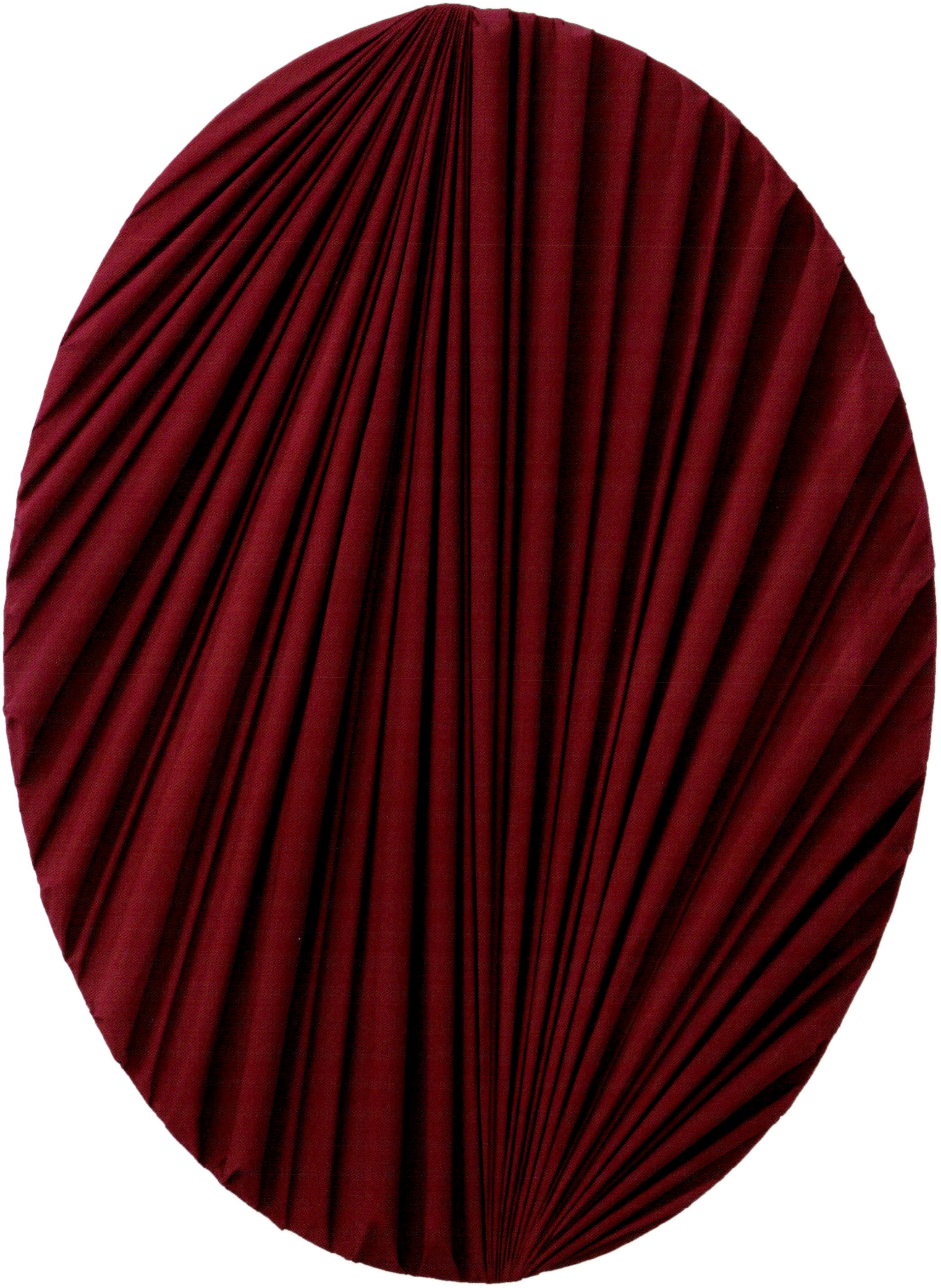

La forma celata, 2008
Vinyl and sand on lead sheet
42 x 33 cm (16½ x 13 in.)

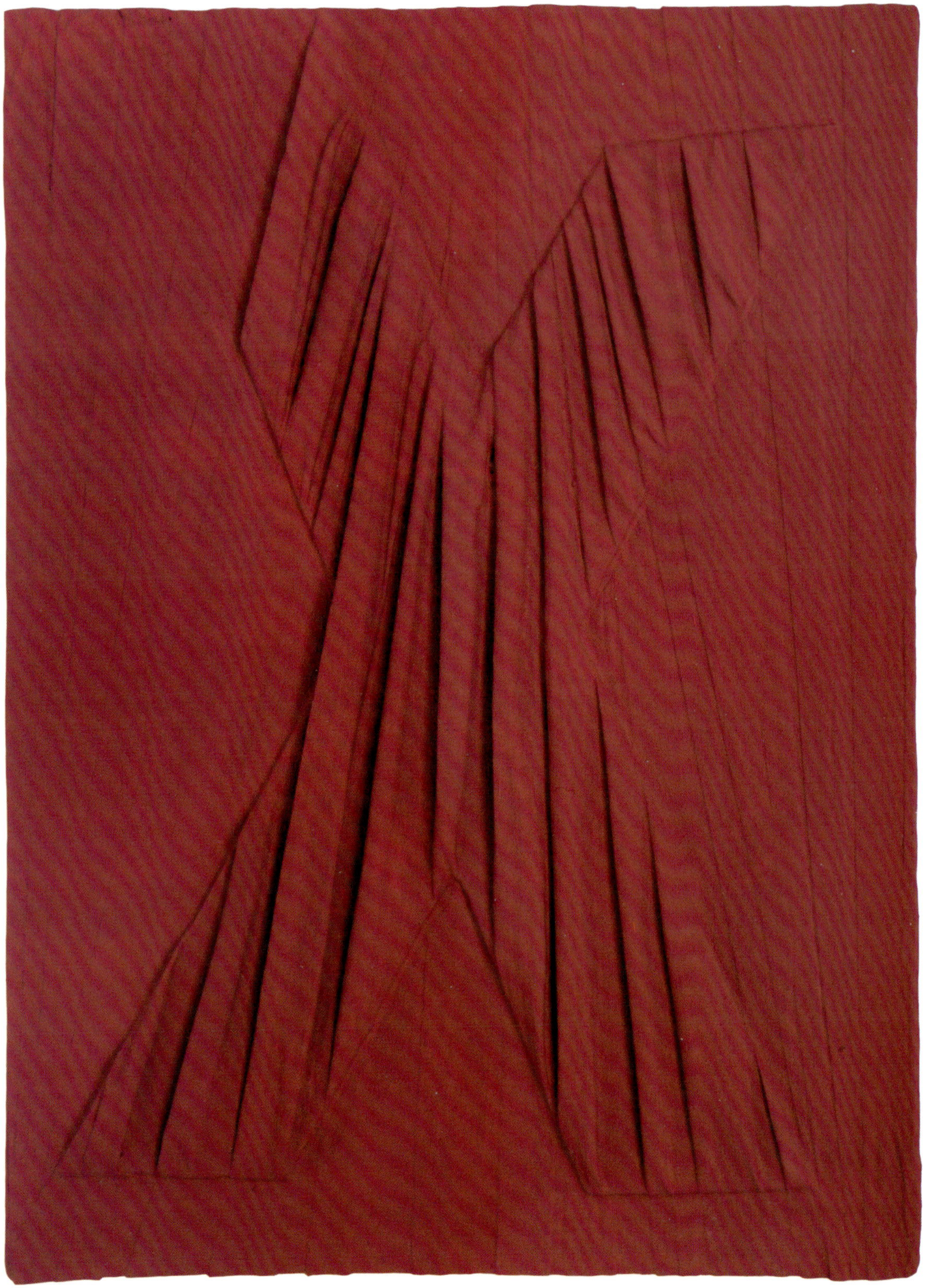

La forma celata, 2008
Vinyl and sand on lead sheet
42 x 33 cm (16½ x 13 in.)

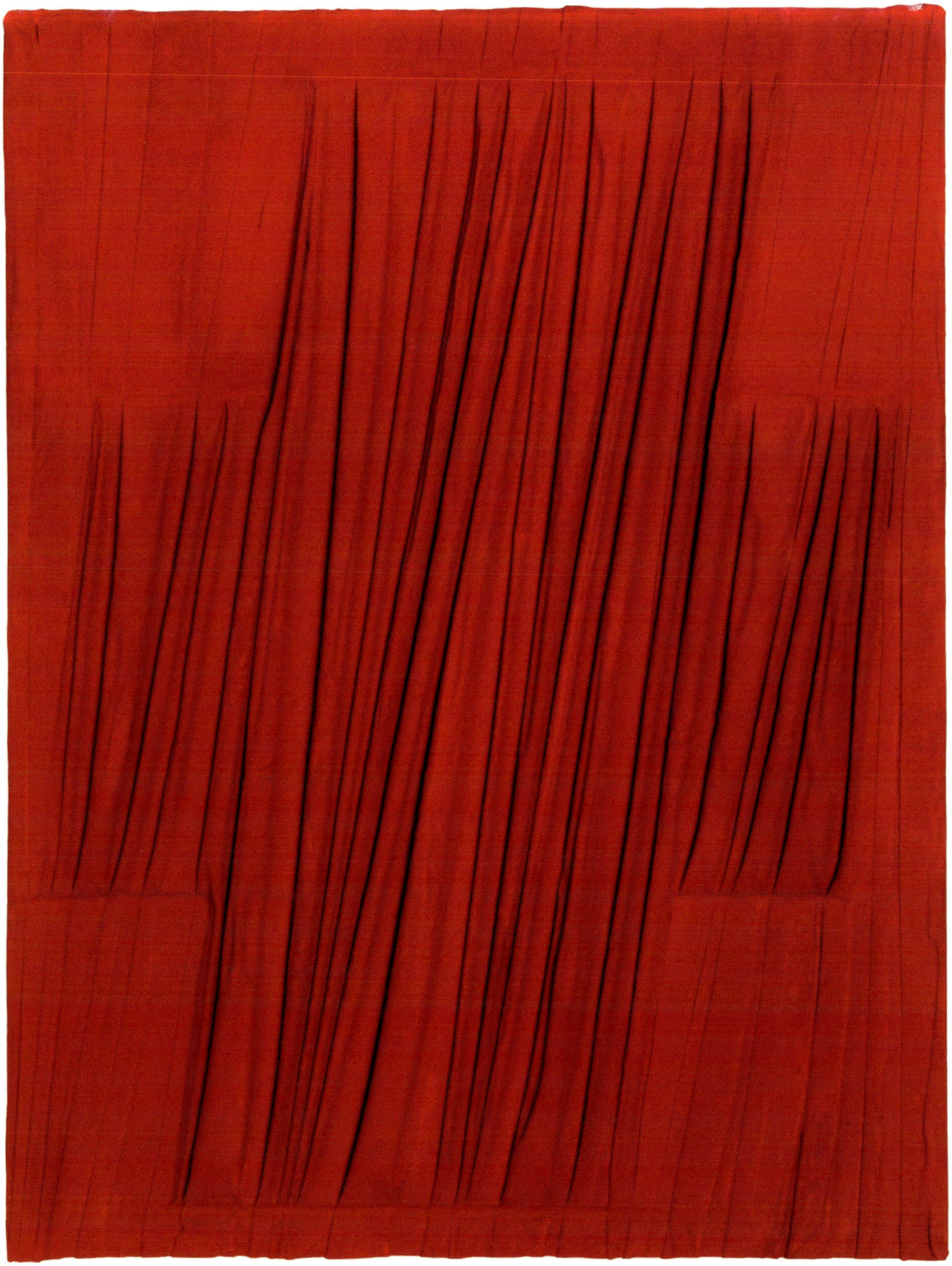

Senza titolo, 2016
Vinyl and sand on lead sheet
120.5 x 90.5 cm (47½ x 35⅝ in.)

Pages 74–75
La forma celata, 2010
Vinyl and sand on lead sheet
121 x 90.5 cm (47⅝ x 35⅝ in.)

La forma celata, 2010
Vinyl and sand on lead sheet
120.5 x 90.5 cm (47½ x 35⅝ in.)

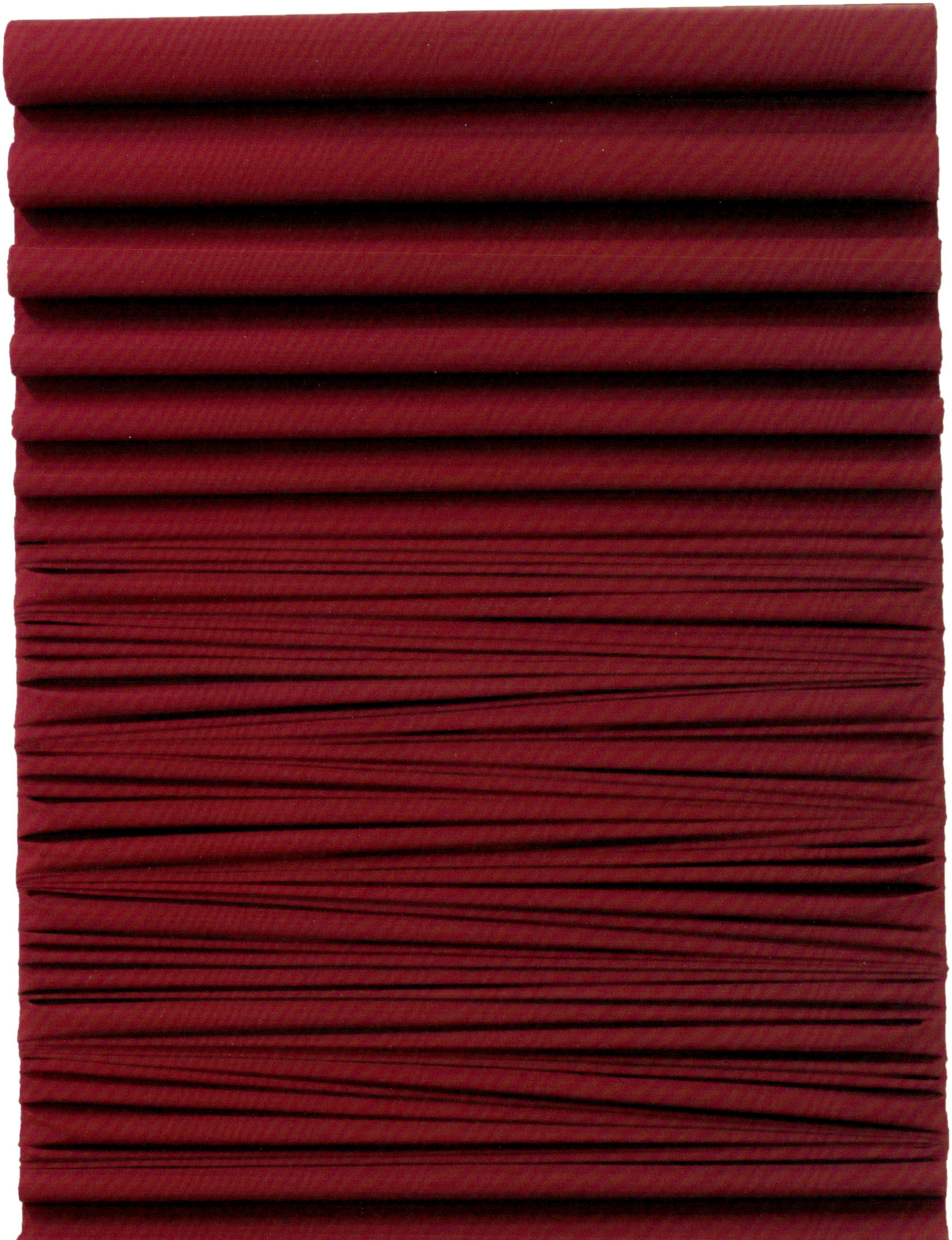

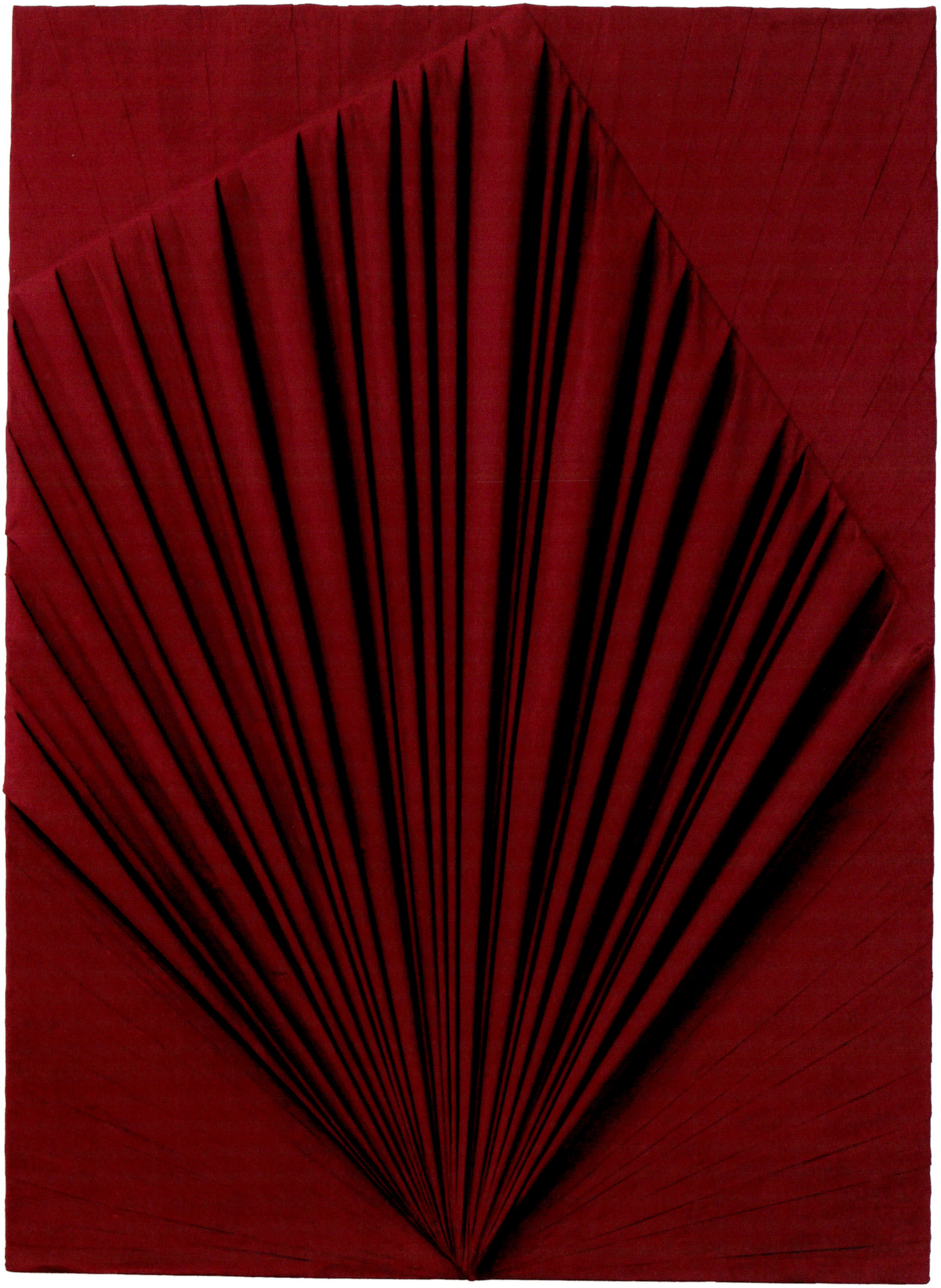

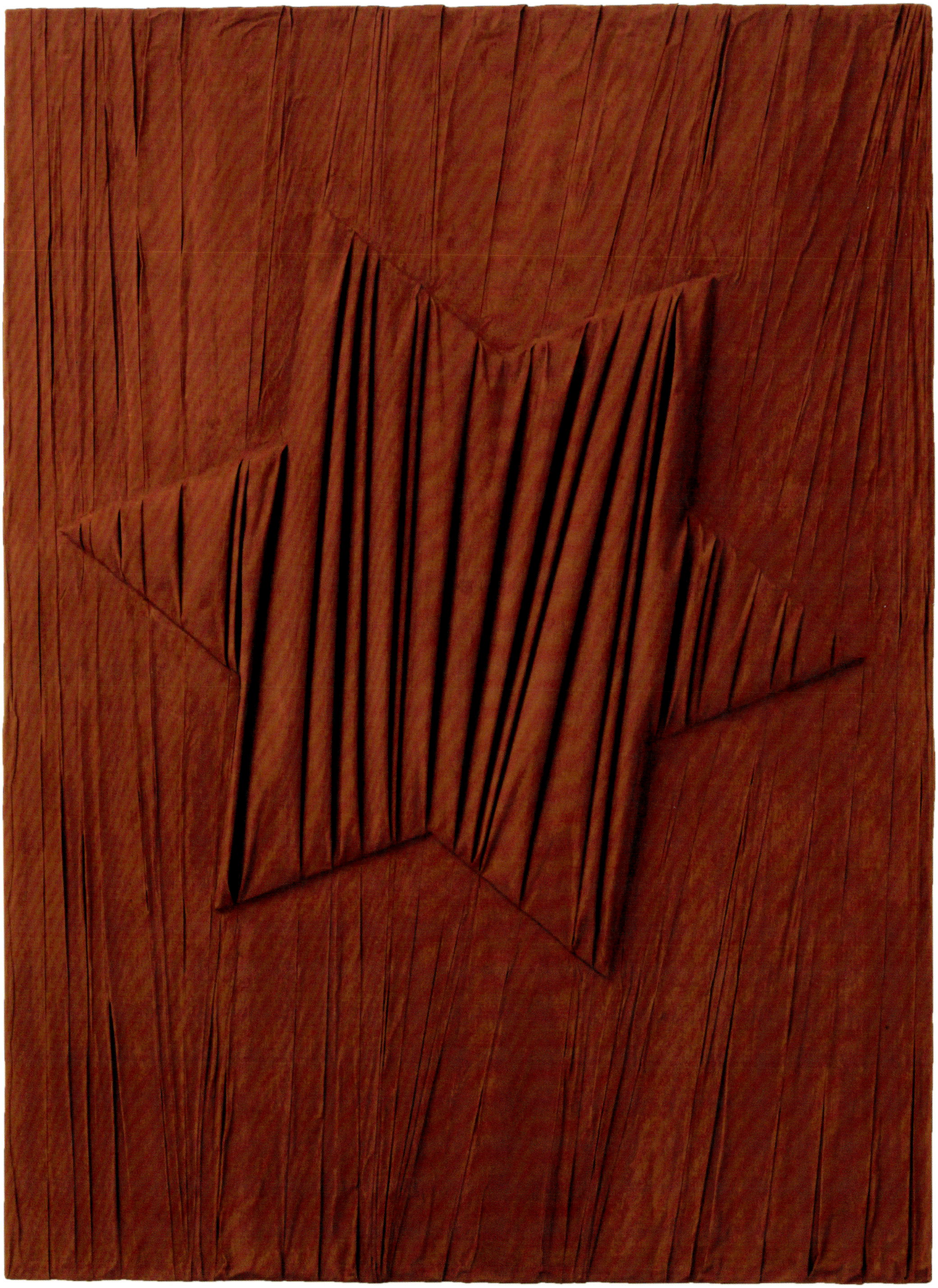

Senza titolo, 2016
Vinyl and sand on lead sheet
120.5 x 90.5 cm (47½ x 35⅝ in.)

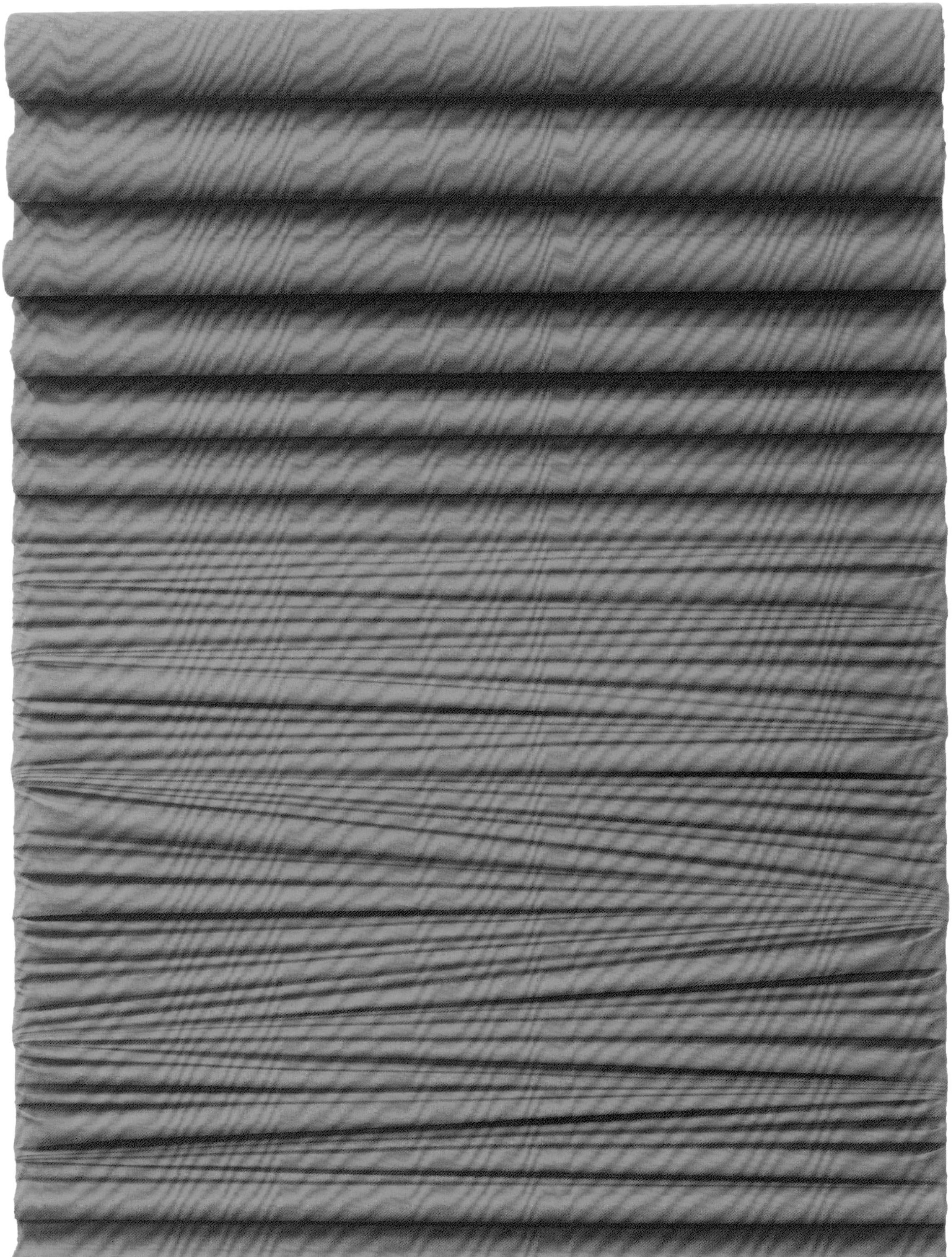

La forma celata, 2014
Vinyl and sand on lead sheet
80 x 60 cm (31½ x 23⅝ in.)

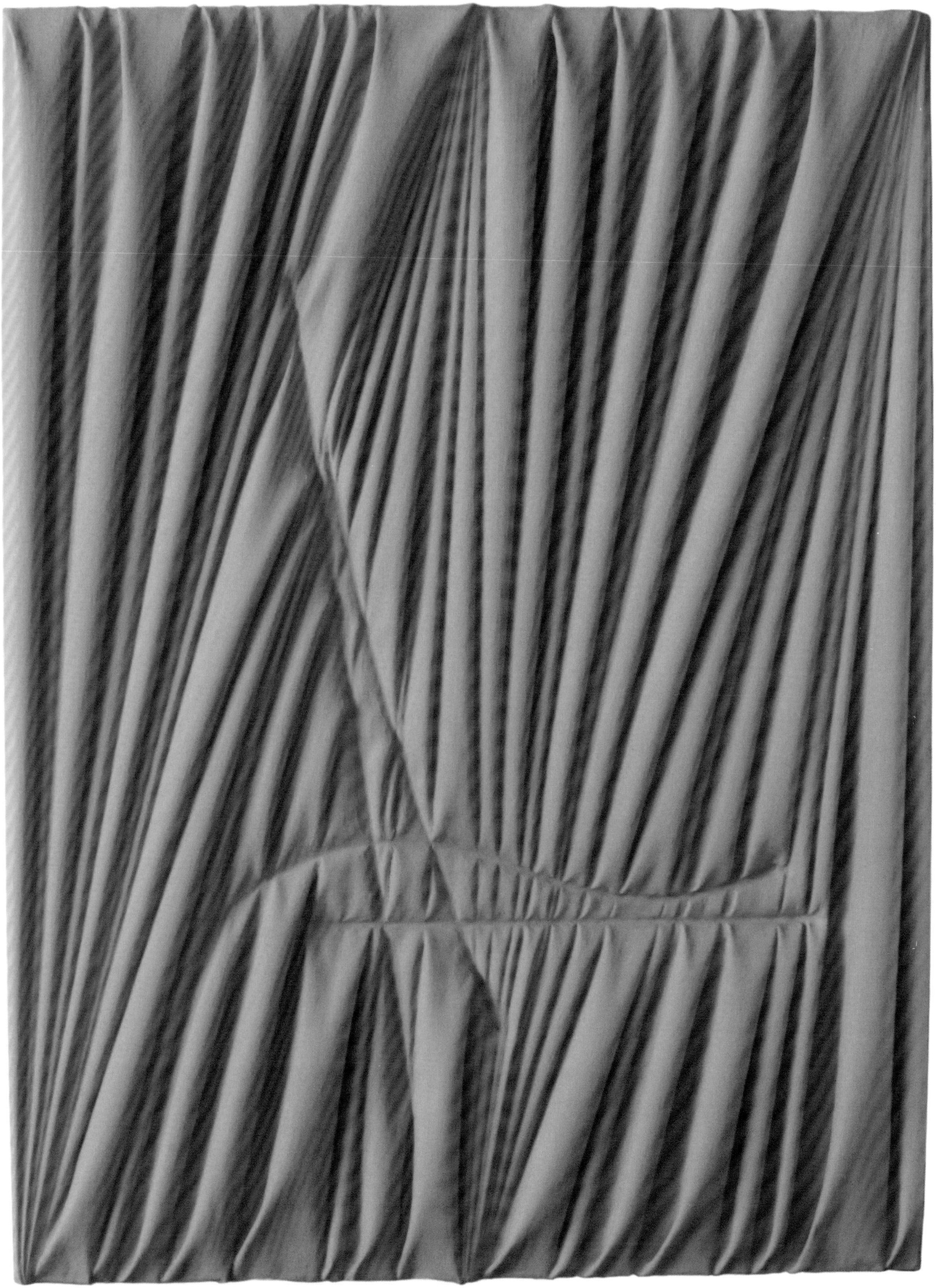

La forma celata, 2013
Vinyl and sand on lead sheet
80 x 60 cm (31½ x 23⅝ in.)

La forma celata, 2013
Vinyl and sand on lead sheet
120 x 80 cm (47¼ x 31½ in.)

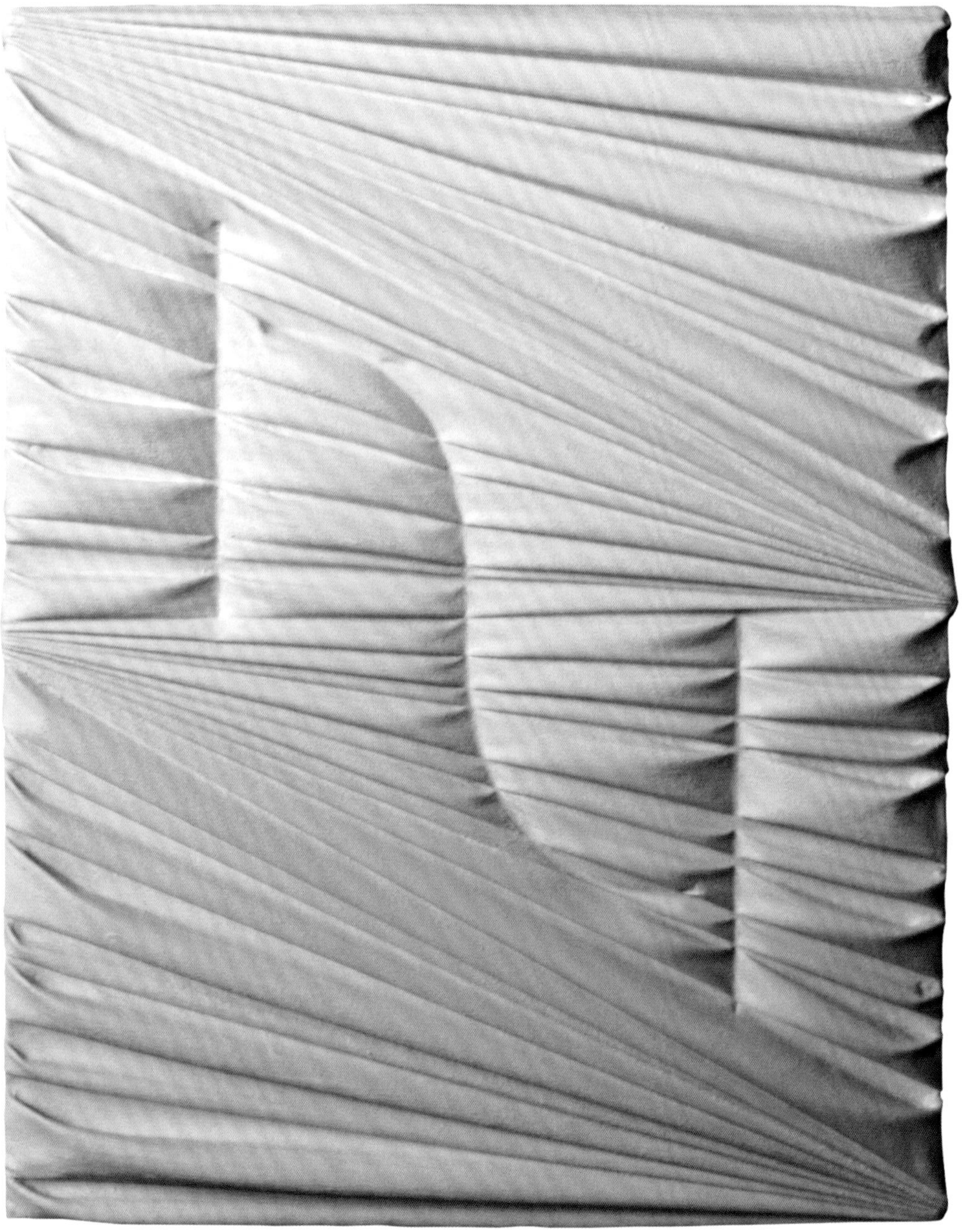

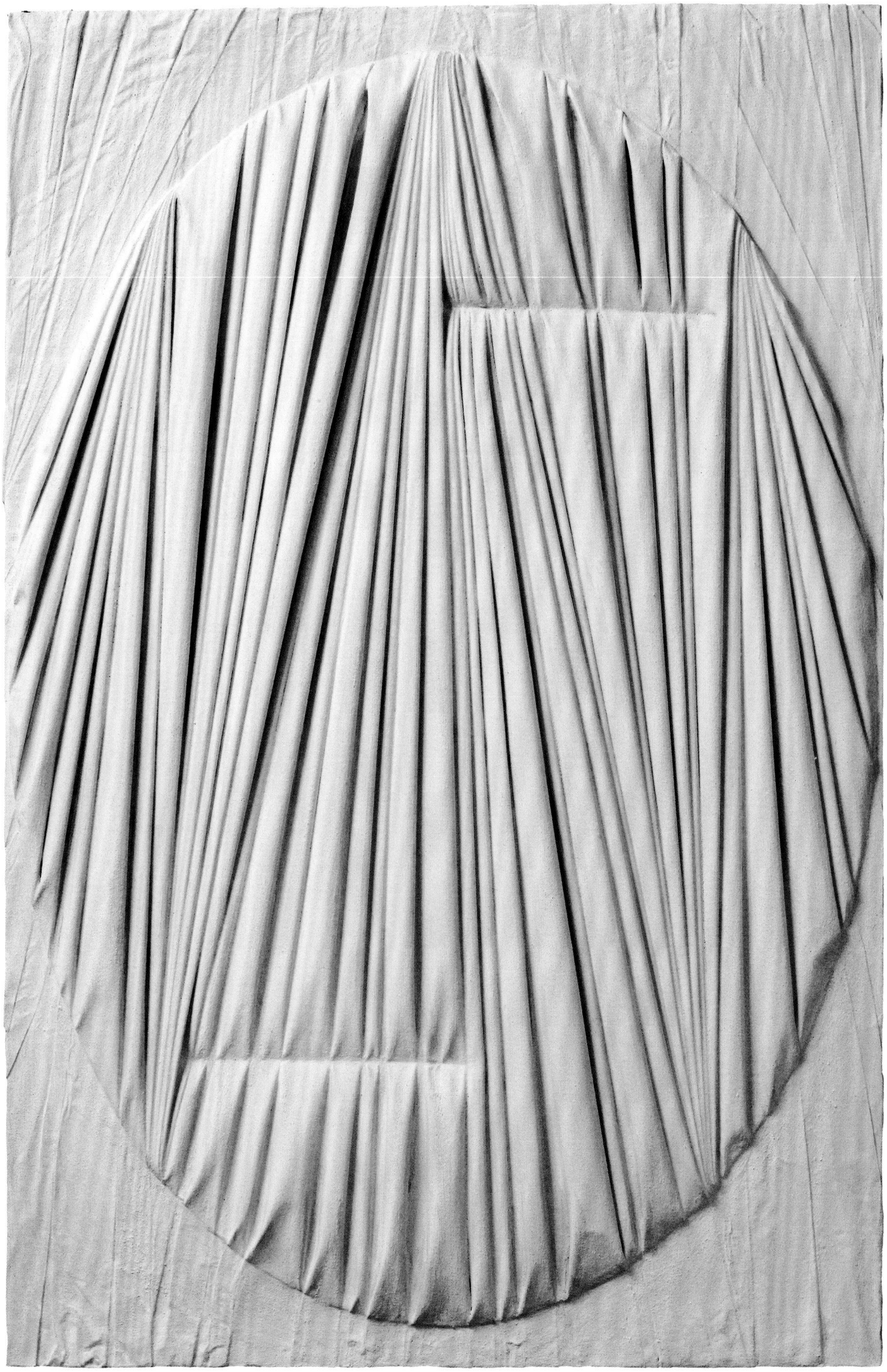

La forma celata, 2010
Vinyl and sand on lead sheet
120 x 90.5 cm (47¼ x 35⅝ in.)

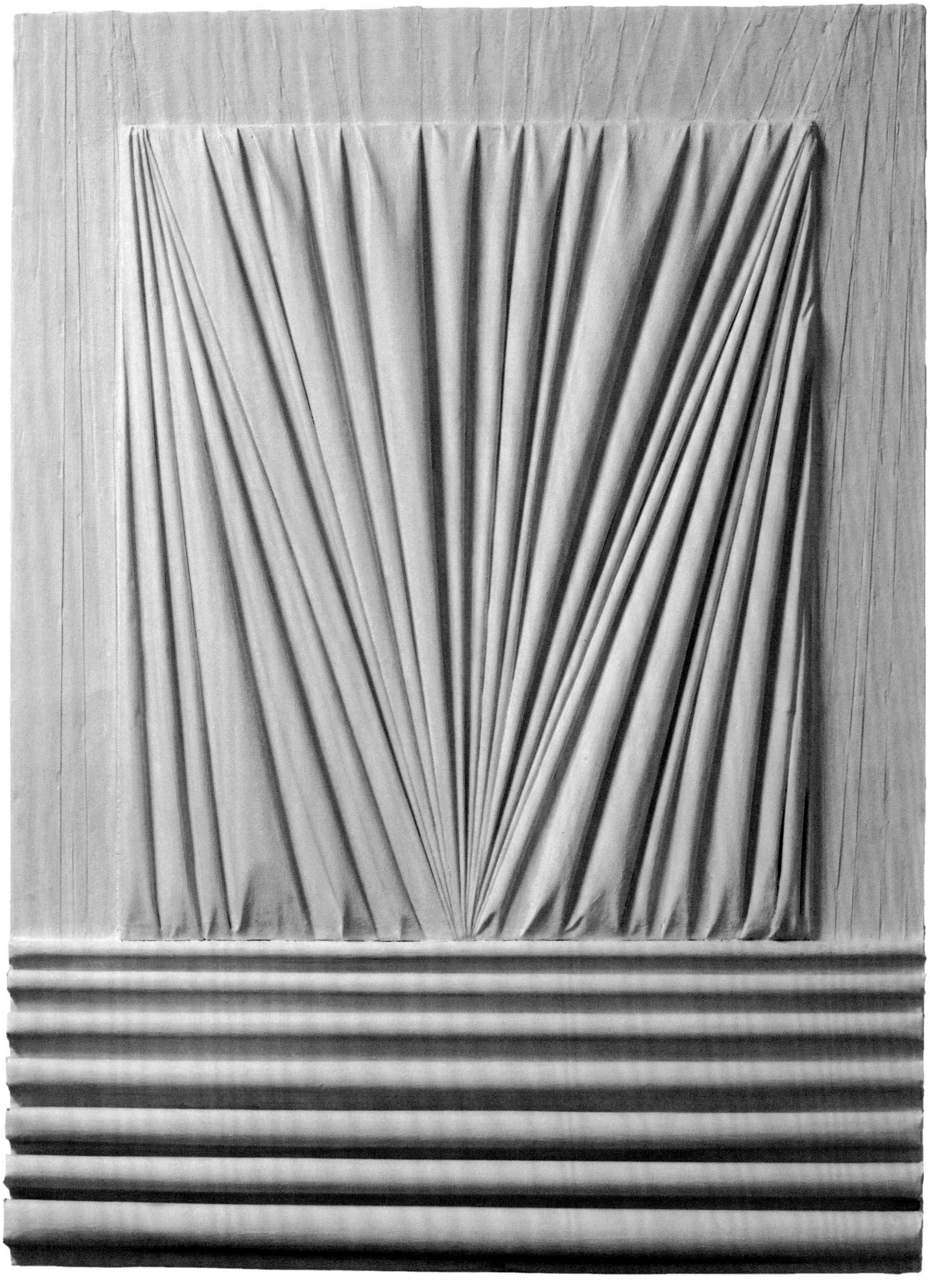

La forma celata, 2015
Vinyl and sand on lead sheet
120 x 90 cm (47¼ x 35½ in.)

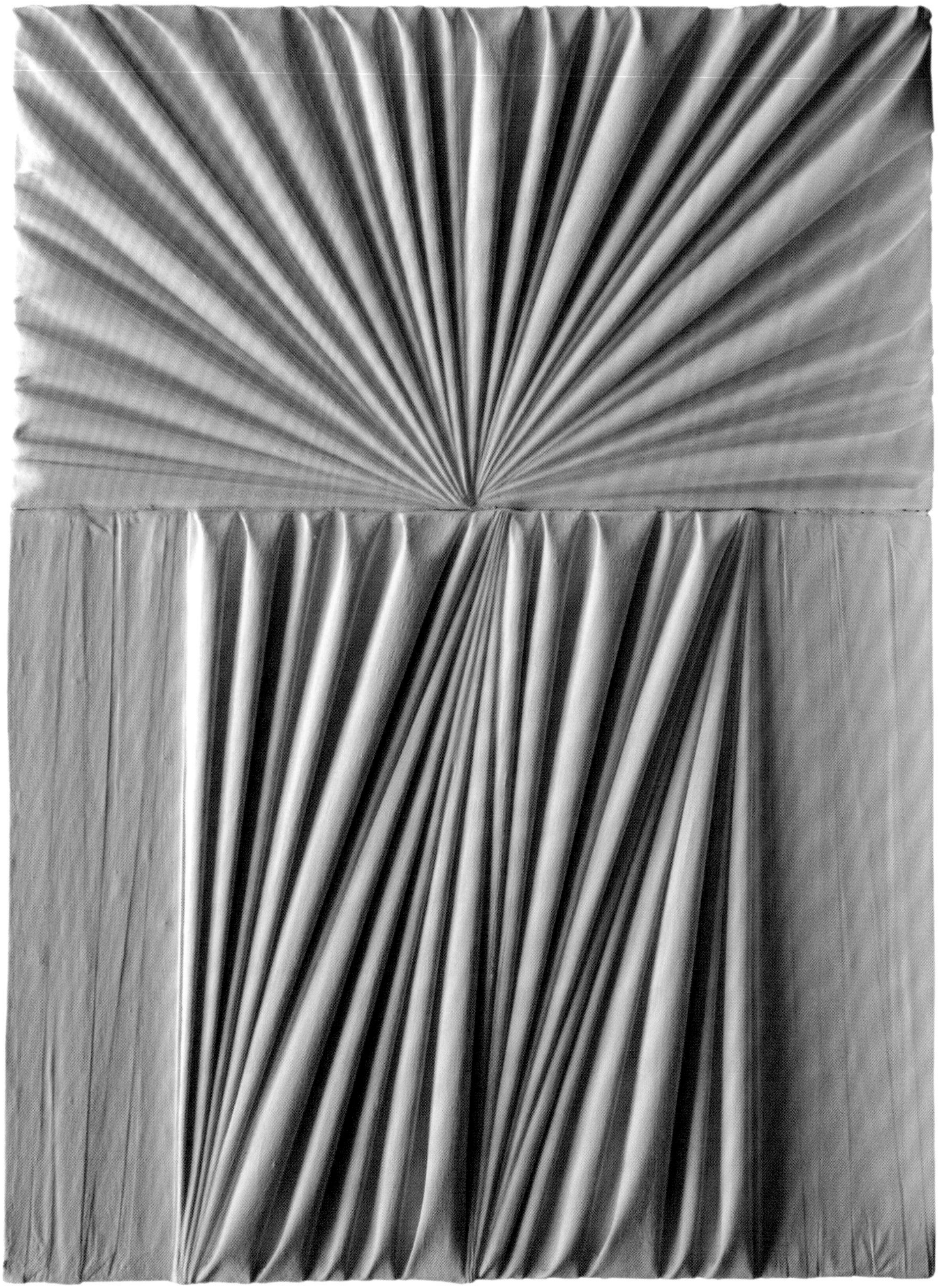

La forma celata, 2015
Vinyl and sand on lead sheet
90 x 120 cm (35½ x 47¼ in.)

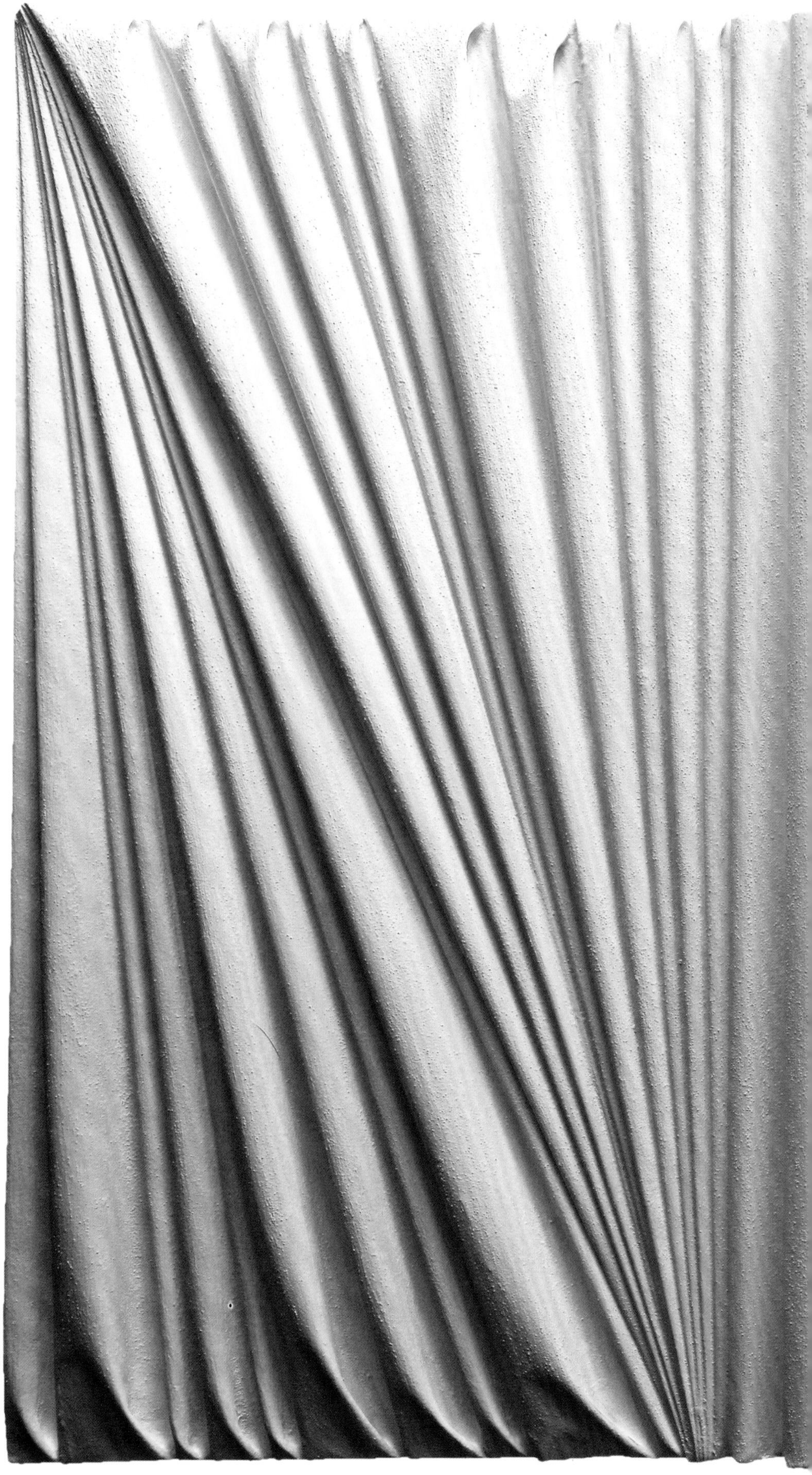

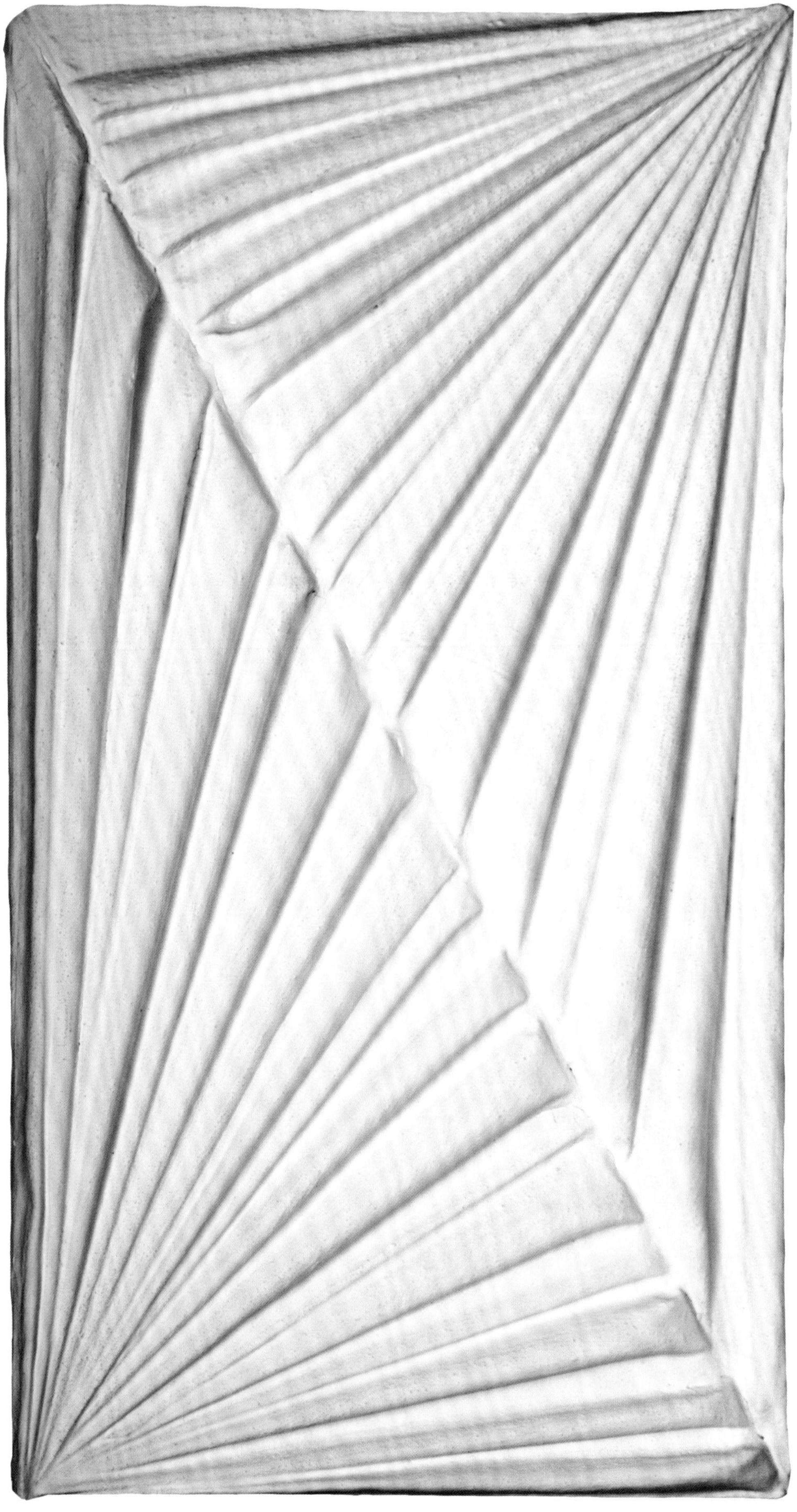

Senza titolo, 2012
Vinyl and sand on lead sheet
40.5 x 21 cm (15⅞ x 8¼ in.)

La forma celata, 2015
Vinyl and sand on lead sheet
121 x 90.5 cm (47⅝ x 35⅝ in.)

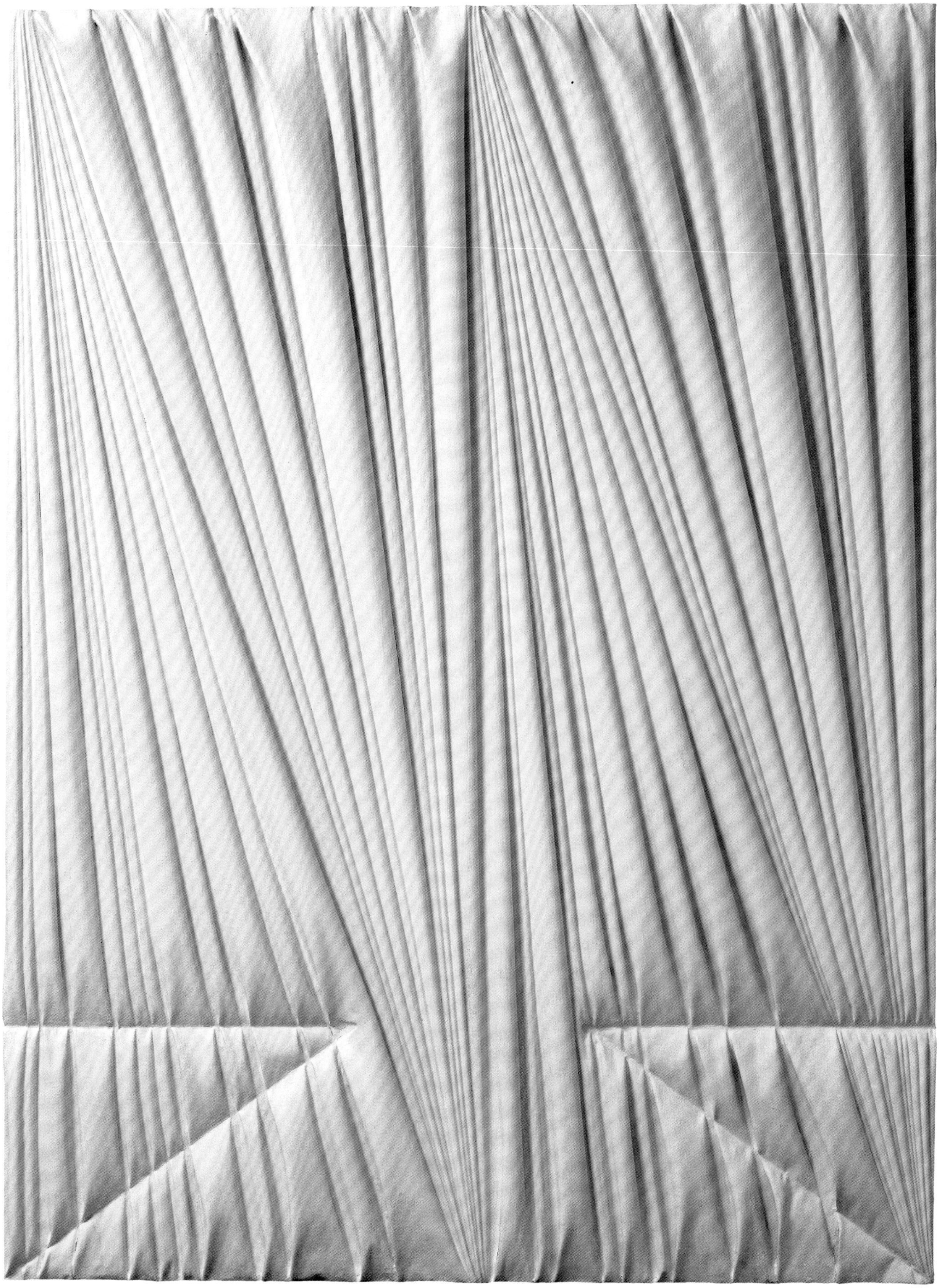

La forma celata, 2013
Vinyl and sand on lead sheet
80 x 60 cm (31½ x 23⅝ in.)

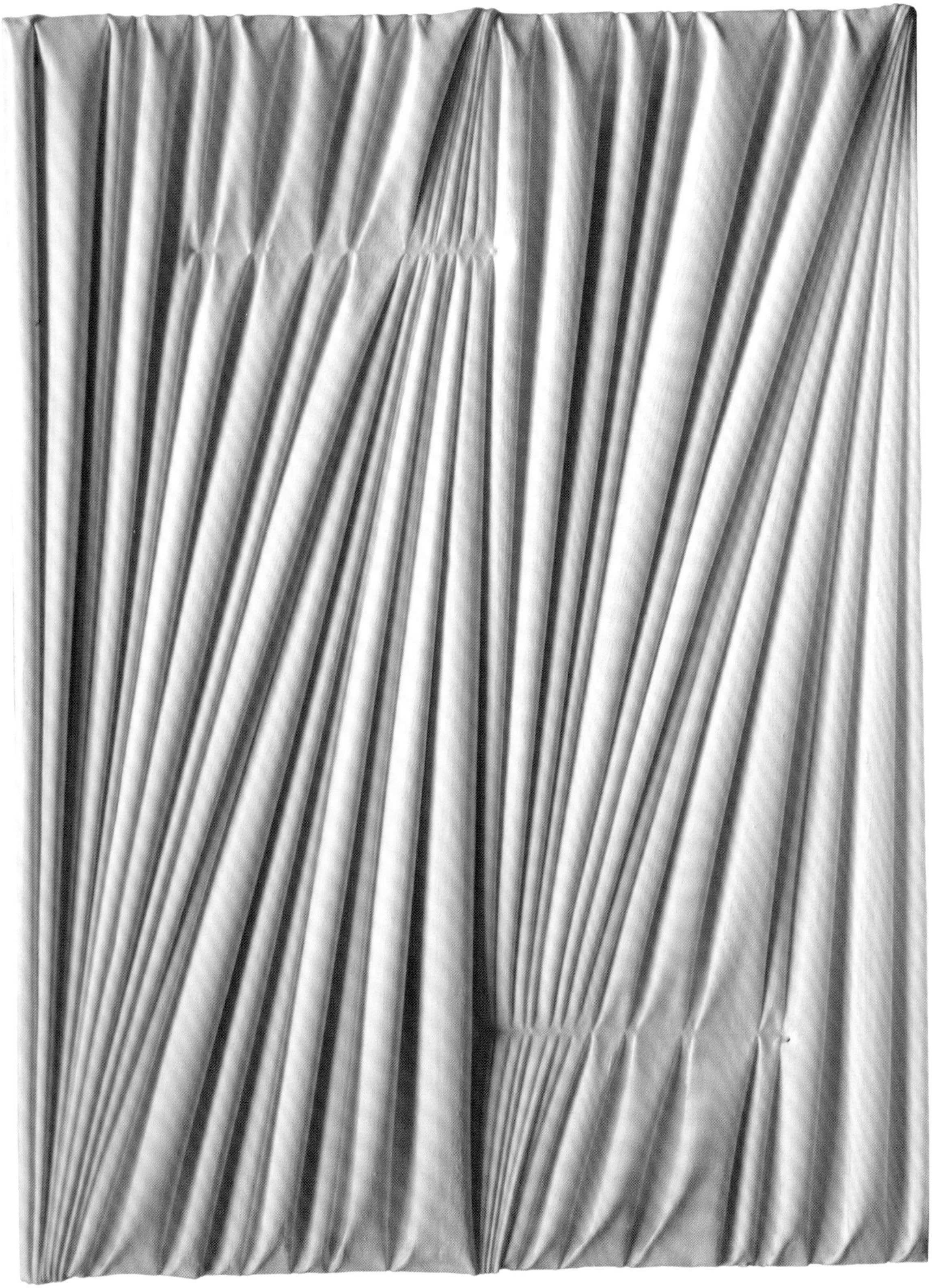

Senza titolo, 2014
Vinyl and sand on lead sheet
80 x 60 cm (31½ x 23⅝ in.)

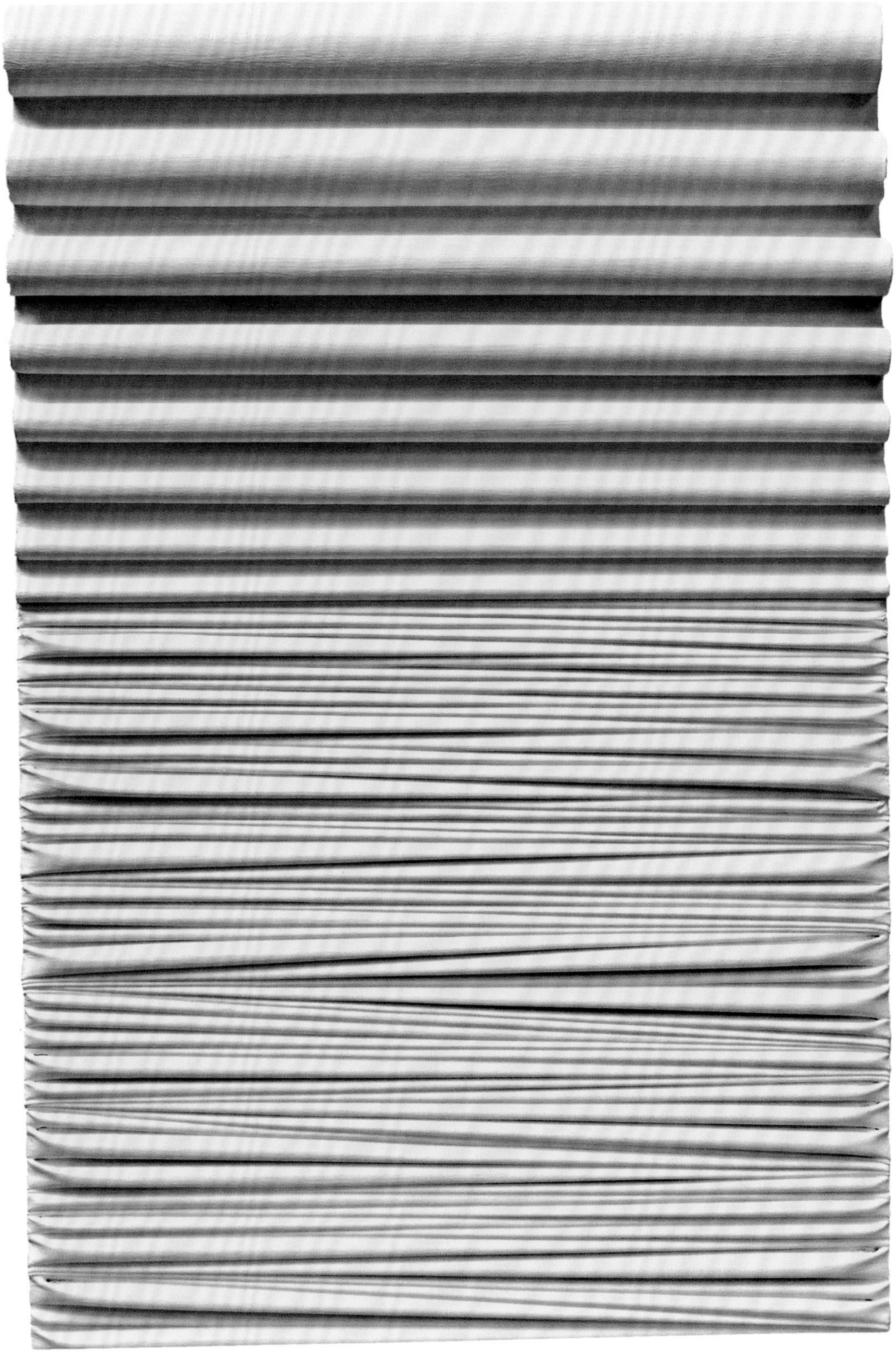

Senza titolo, 2015
Vinyl and sand on lead sheet
120.5 x 90 cm (47½ x 35½ in.)

Senza titolo: piombo, 2015
Shaped lead sheet
120 x 90 cm (47¼ x 35½ in.)

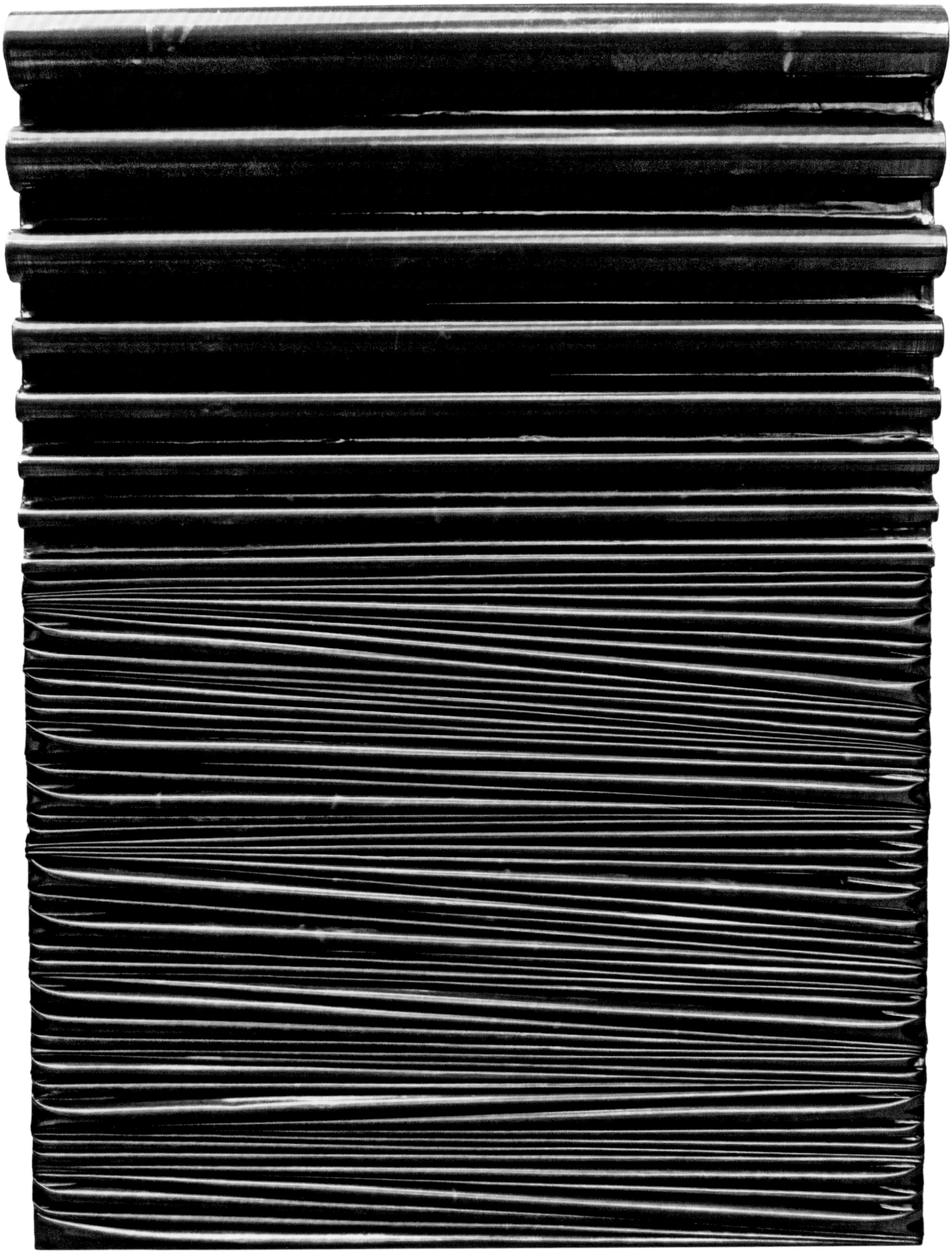

Senza titolo, 2014
Vinyl and sand on lead sheet
42 x 33 cm (16½ x 13 in.)

La forma celata, 2014
Vinyl and sand on lead sheet
80 x 60 cm (31½ x 23⅝ in.)

Senza titolo, 2014
Vinyl and sand on lead sheet
40 x 65 cm (15¾ x 25½ in.)

La forma celata, 2010
Vinyl and sand on lead sheet
121 x 90 cm (47⅝ x 35½ in.)

Senza titolo, 2011
Vinyl and sand on lead sheet
80 x 60 cm (31½ x 23⅝ in.)

Senza titolo, 2013
Vinyl and sand on lead sheet
80.5 x 60.5 cm (31¾ x 23¾ in.)

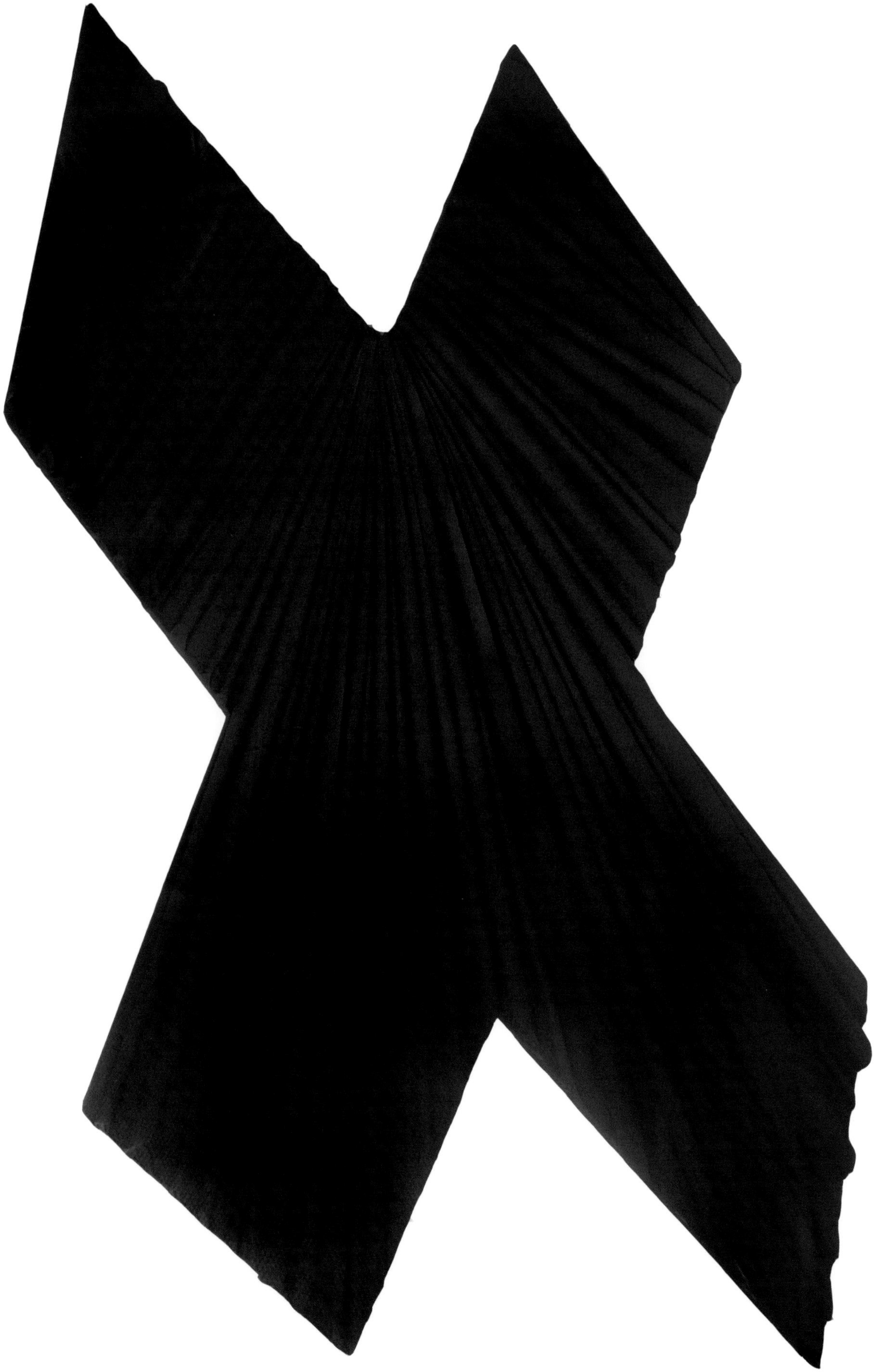

Senza titolo, 2008
Vinyl and sand on lead sheet
185 x 80 cm (72⅞ x 31½ in.)

Senza titolo, 2011
Vinyl and sand on lead sheet
40 x 65 cm (15¾ x 25½ in.)

Senza titolo, 2014
Vinyl and sand on lead sheet
60 x 80 cm (23⅝ x 31½ in.)

La forma celata, 2010
Vinyl and sand on lead sheet
120 x 91 cm (47¼ x 35⅞ in.)

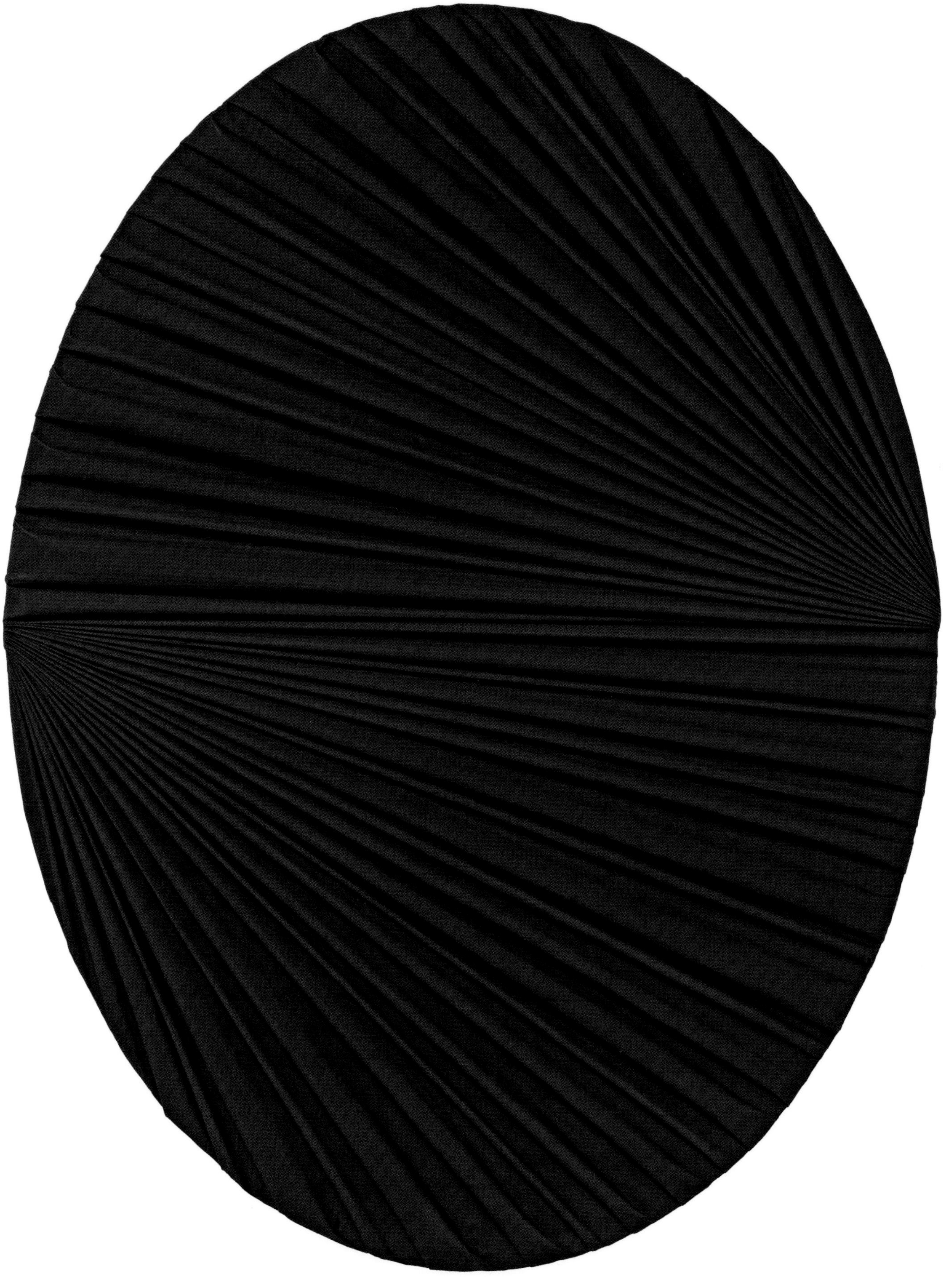

Senza titolo, 2015
Shaped lead sheet
120 x 90 cm (47¼ x 35½ in.)

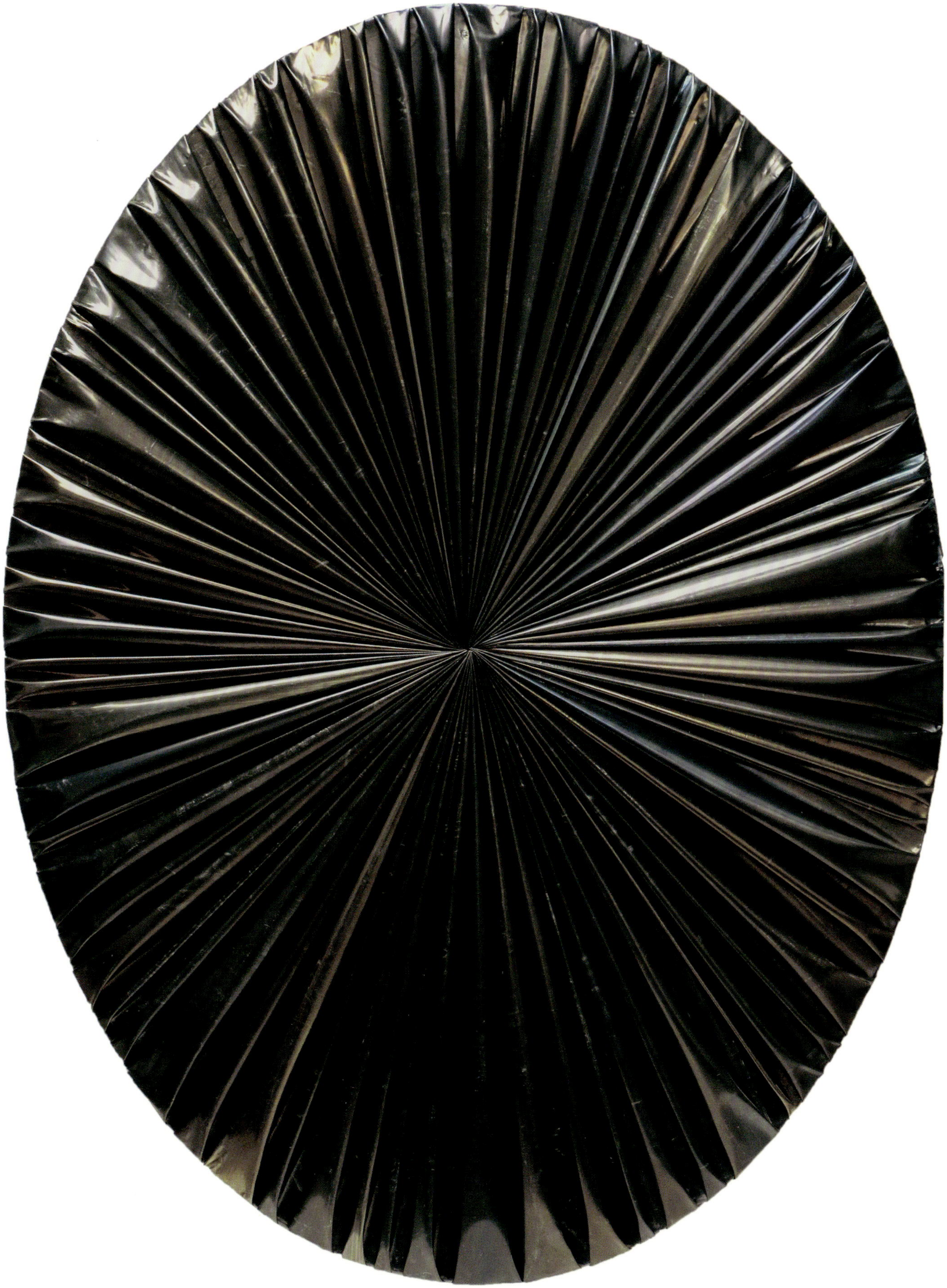

Senza titolo, 2010
Vinyl and sand on lead sheet
91 x 120 cm (35⅞ x 47¼ in.)

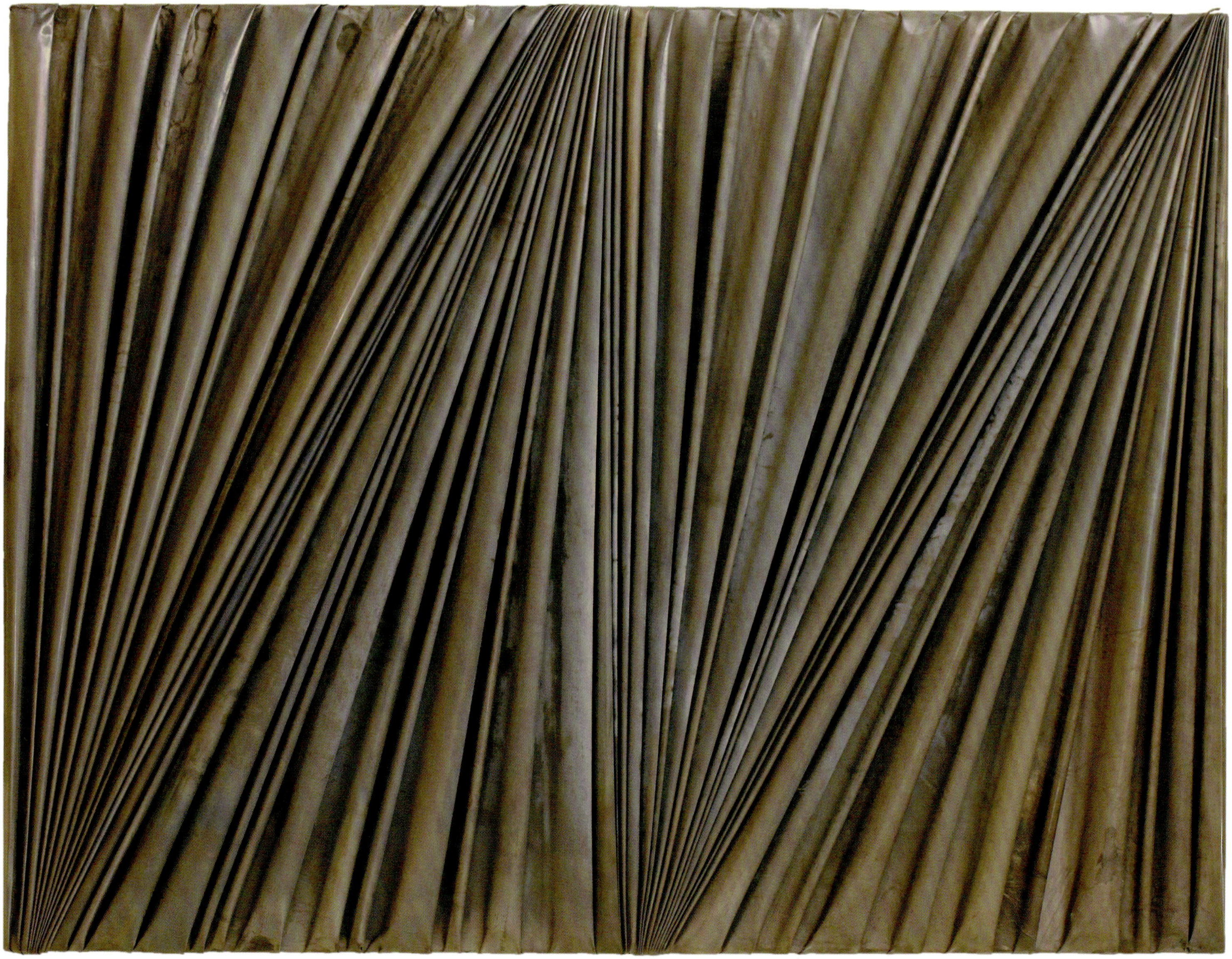

Senza titolo, 2014
Shaped lead sheet
90 x 120 cm (35½ x 47¼ in.)

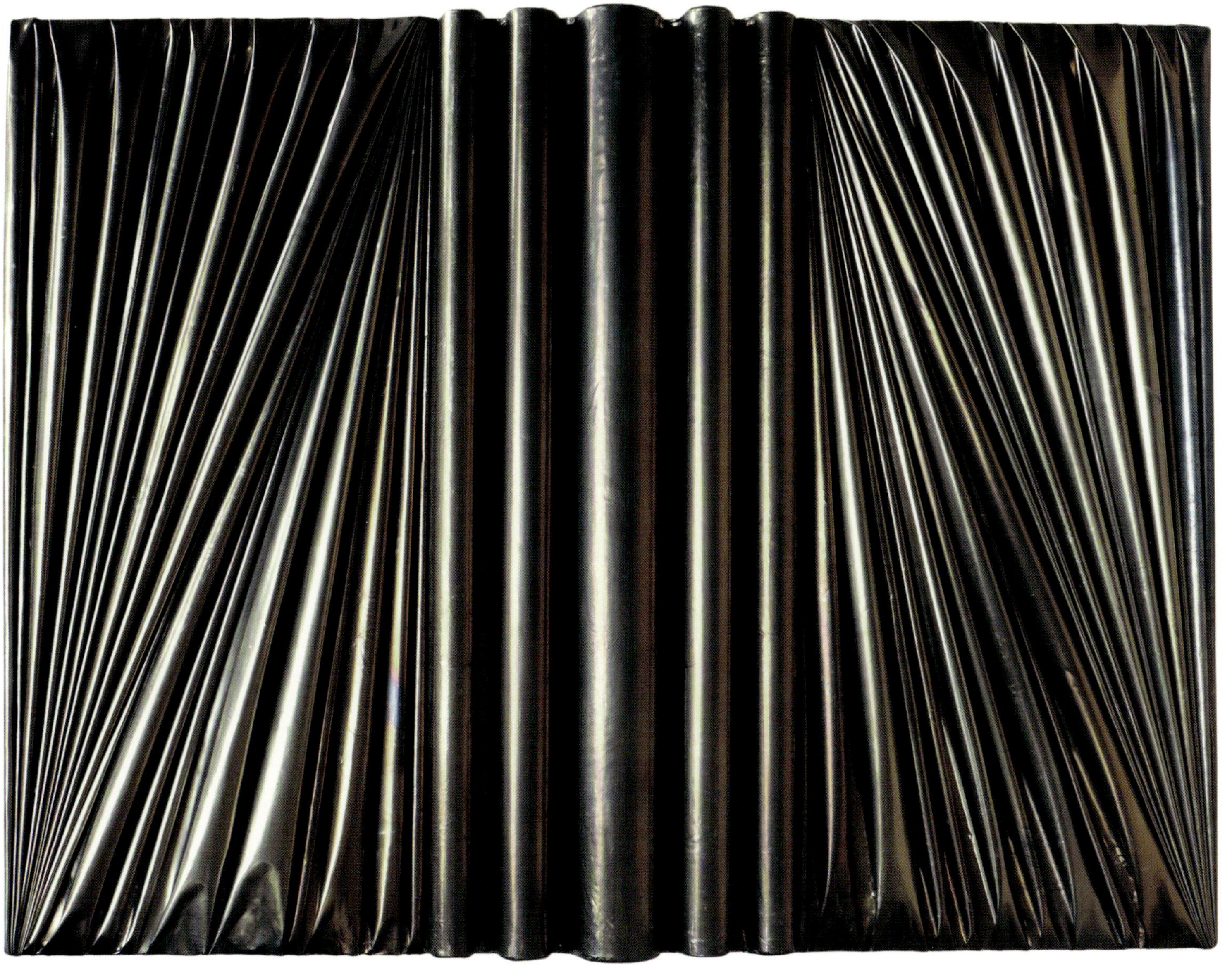

La forma celata, 2010
Shaped lead sheet
149 x 116 cm (58⅝ x 45⅝ in.)

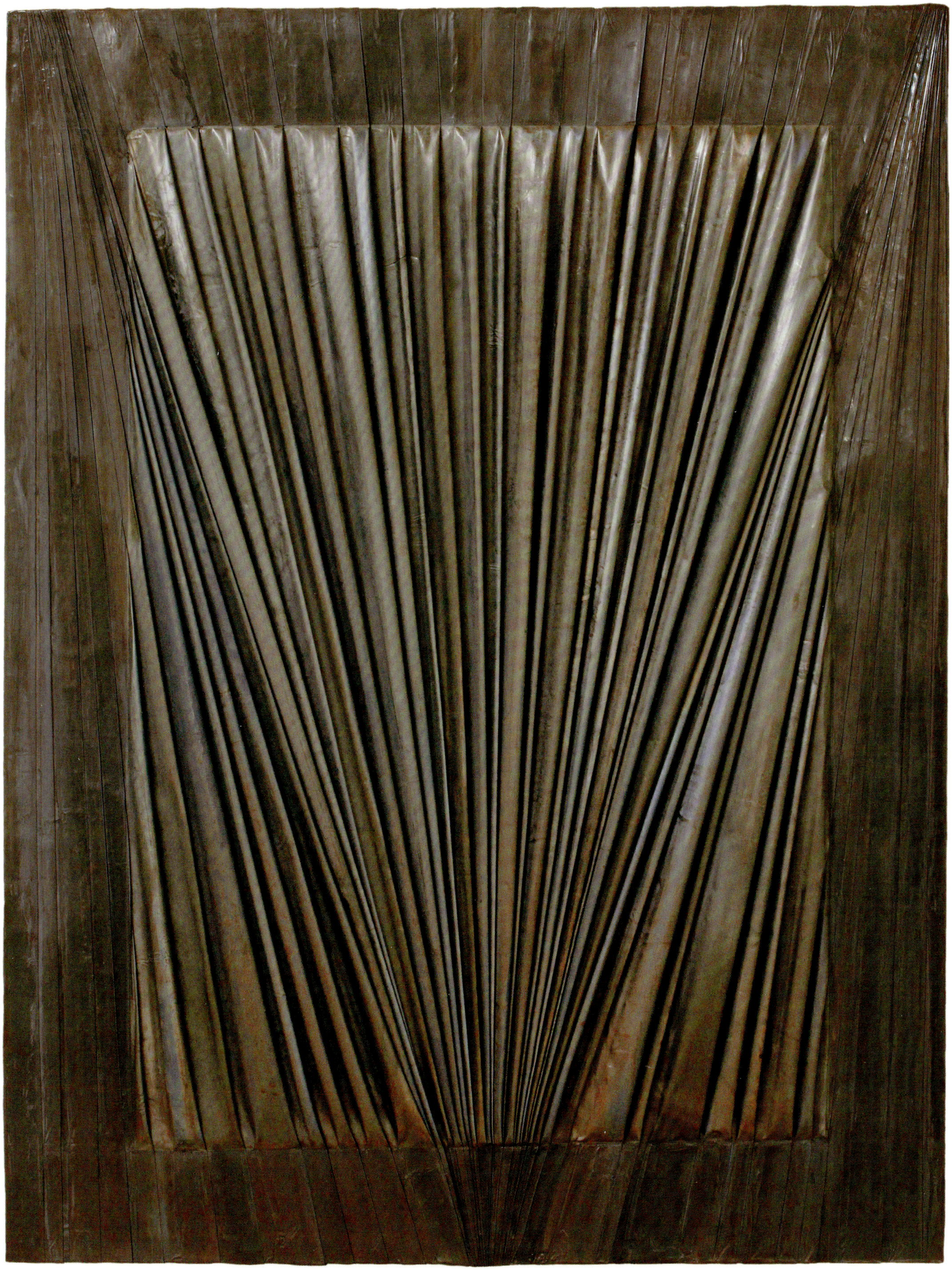

La forma celata, 2011
Shaped lead sheet
120.5 x 90.5 cm (47½ x 35⅝ in.)

Senza titolo: doppio ventaglio, 2014
Shaped lead sheet
120 x 93 cm (47¼ x 36⅝ in.)

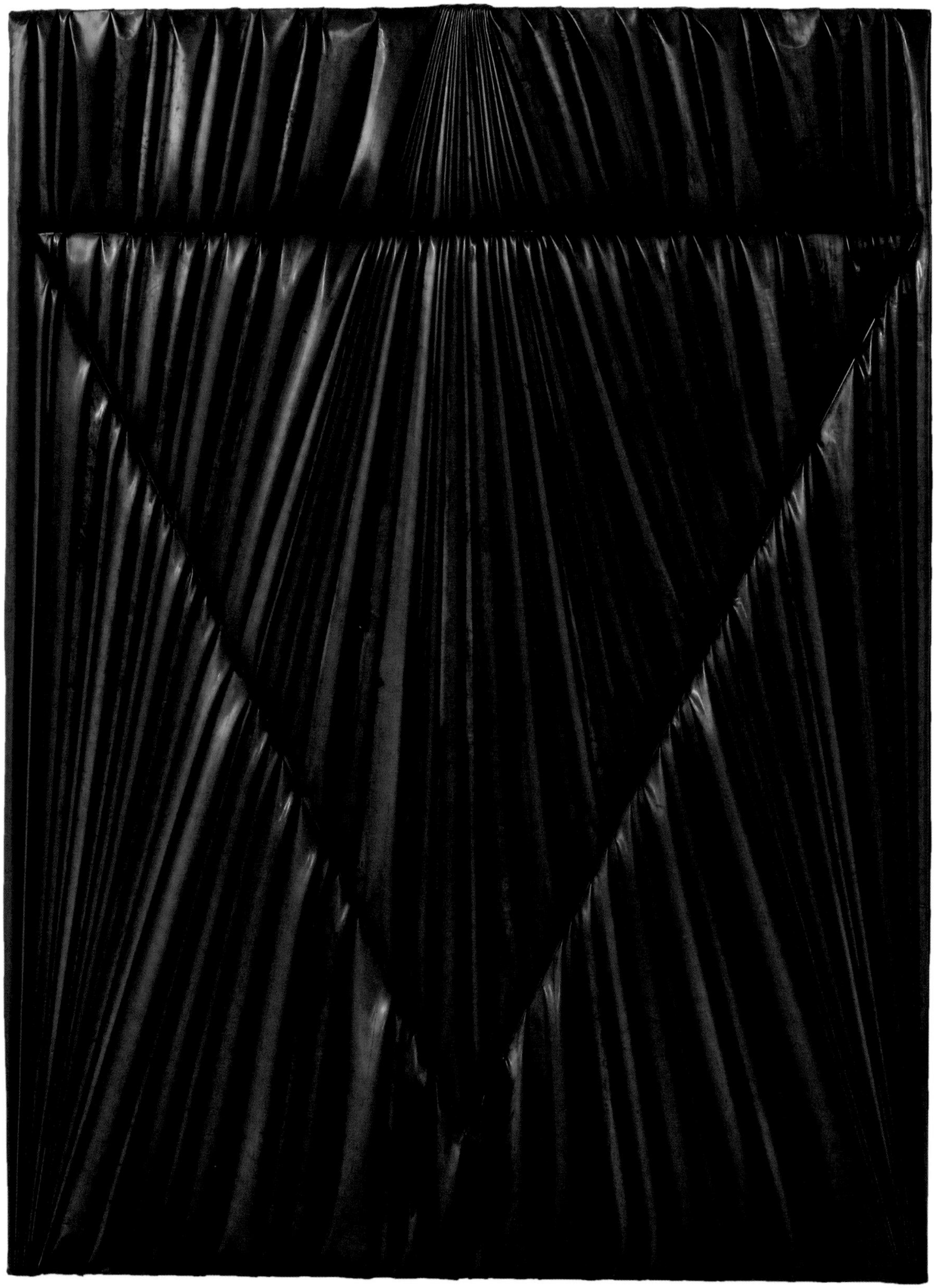

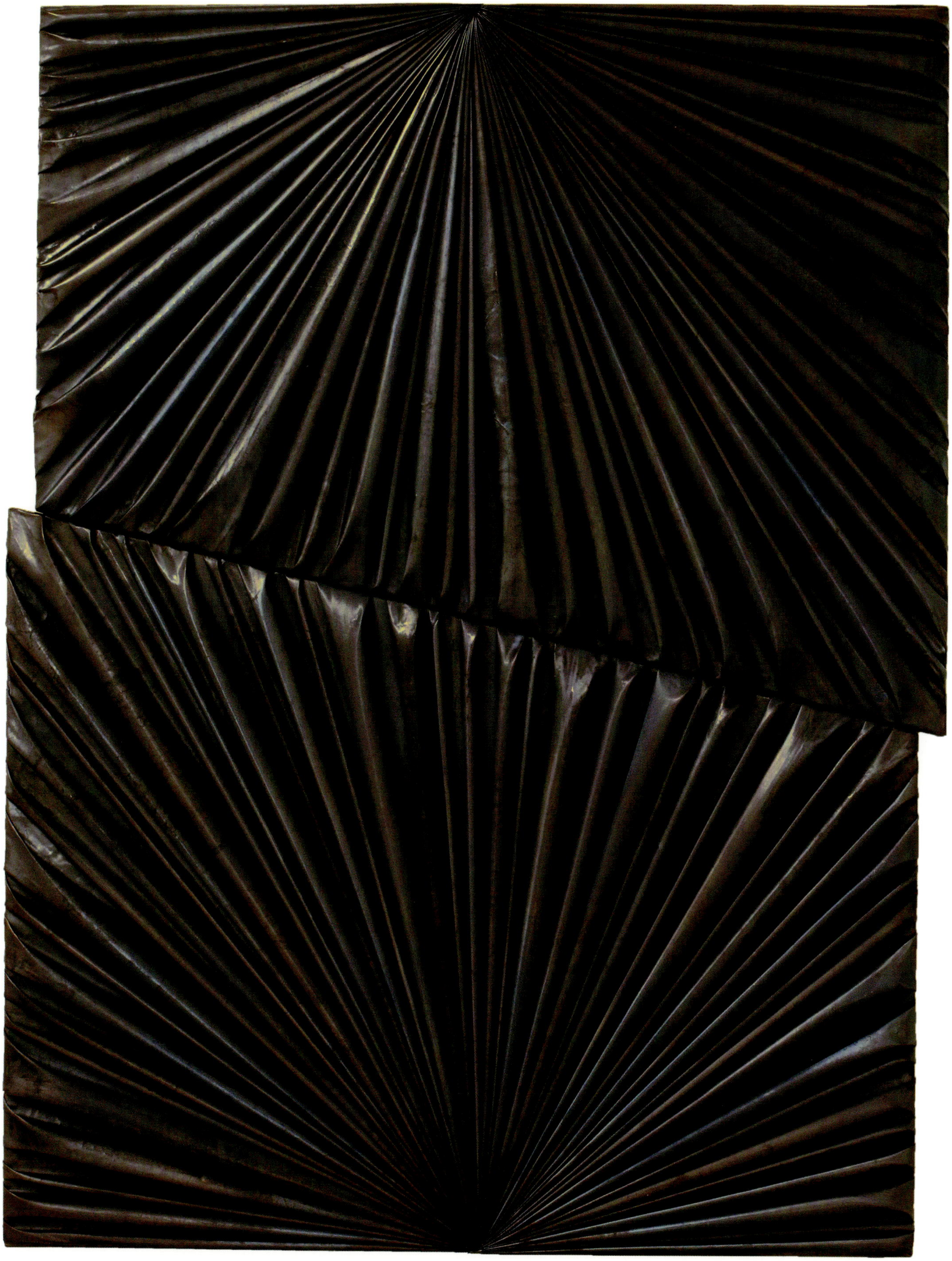

APPENDIX

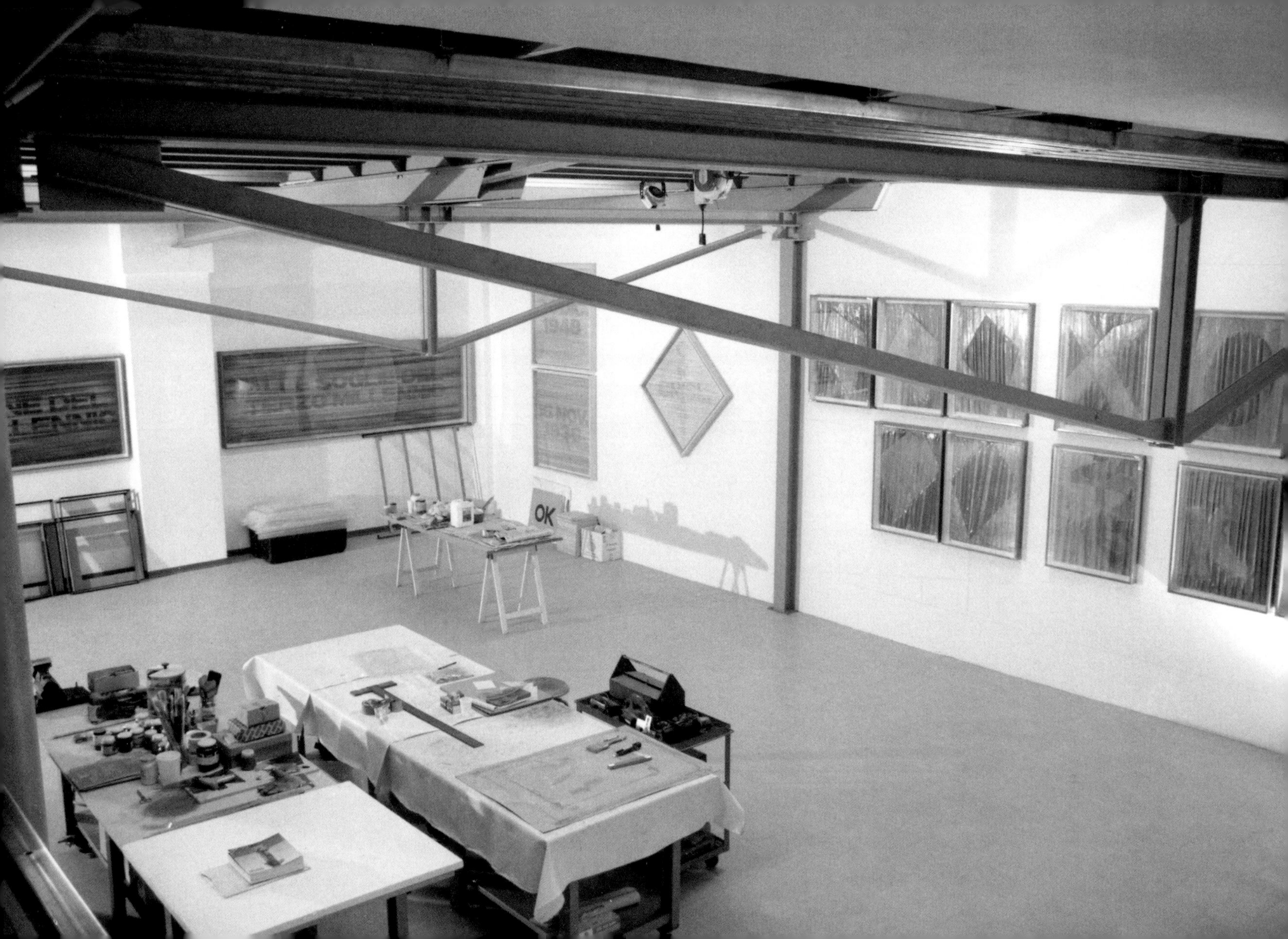
OK

Biography

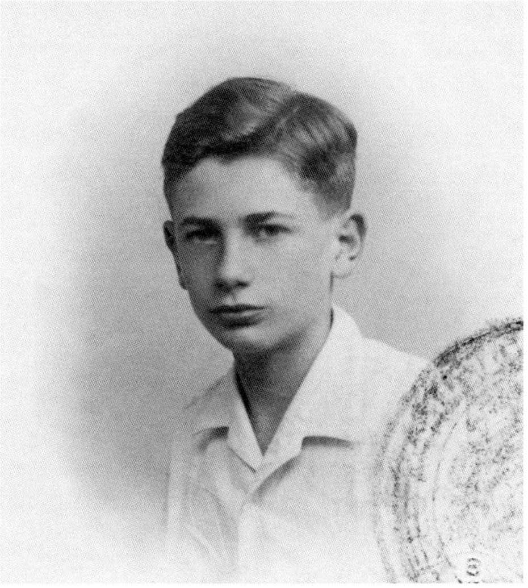

Umberto Mariani at eleven

Mariani's new studio at Via Mecenate in Milan, 1992

Umberto Mariani was born in Milan on 16 November 1936 to a family from Emilia. His father Ugo (Carpi, 1904 – Milan, 1968) and his mother Iole Nizzoli (Reggio Emilia, 1907 – Milan, 1998), respectively an accountant and a primary school teacher, provided a family setting typical of the lower middle-class between the wars, but one strongly permeated by a sense of idealism, something confirmed by his father's active participation in the struggle against Fascism. In the years from 1943 to 1944 their home in Milan served as a refuge for groups of persecuted Jews, protected and assisted by the clandestine organization headed by Fernanda Wittgens. The experience of the war left significant marks on the very young Mariani, especially during the last dramatic months of 1945.

1950

He enrolled in the Brera Art School, passing the rigorous exam of admission with difficulty. He continued with regular artistic studies, attending Achille Funi's school at the Brera Academy from 1954 to 1958. At the same time he became an assistant in his teacher's studio and collaborated on the realization of numerous large frescoes. In 1957 he set up a studio of his own in Milan, in an attic in front of the Polytechnic.

1958

When he received his diploma, he was awarded valedictorian from the Brera Academy and given the chance to travel to the Brussels World's Fair. Here he discovered the work of Constant Permeke and was greatly impressed by it. In the following years, up until the middle of the 1960s, his experiments with free research would be decisively influenced by Permeke's painting, by his epic and dramatic view of humanity and nature.

1959

In the autumn of 1959 he worked with Claudio Nani under the supervision of Funi on the fresco decoration of the chapel of San Carlo Borromeo in the Minorite Basilica of Sant'Angelo in Milan. From November 1959 to April 1961 he did his national service in Bolzano as a mountain artilleryman; this experience allowed him to indulge his great passion for the mountains.
Up until the mid-1960s Mariani would spend a lot of time climbing in the Dolomites and the Western Alps.

1961

Returning to civil life, Mariani resumed his work as an assistant in Funi's studio, an activity that would culminate in the execution of the *Saint Joseph Altarpiece* for the St Peter's Basilica in the Vatican and the imposing fresco and mosaic decoration of the dome and apse in the sanctuary of Sant'Antonio in Rimini. These works, which were carried out from 1963 to 1965, represented the last phase of his collaboration with Funi.
The decision to distance himself from his master stemmed from Mariani's need to develop more personal and up-to-date poetics, if possible in tune with experiences connected to international culture. In 1961 he set up a studio at Via Muratori 50, Porta Romana, Milan.

1963

In Milan he met Ritva Raitsalo, a young Finnish designer whom he would marry in July 1965. During the summer 1964 he went to see Ritva in Helsinki and they travelled through Finland together to the North Cape, following a fascinating route in discovery of the architecture of Alvar Aalto: from Paimio to Rovaniemi, from Jyväskylä to Säynätsalo, Imatra and Otaniemi. They crossed the Russo-Finnish border to visit Leningrad and the Hermitage. Mariani started to exhibit with other artists at provincial galleries (in Cremona, Pistoia and Alessandria, where he met Marisa Vescovo) and in Venice, at the Galleria del Traghetto.

1965

He rented a house and studio at Via Andrea del Sarto 9 in Milan; it was a house with an internal garden and this would be the dominant theme of his pictures for the whole of the following year – *Giardino in città* (*Garden in the City*) and *Serre* (*Glasshouses*).
While on honeymoon with Ritva in Sicily he was invited to enter the competition for the Capo d'Orlando Painting Prize and won. In the autumn he had the opportunity to get to know the work of Graham Sutherland thoroughly through a visit to his major exhibition at the Galleria d'Arte Moderna in Turin.
In Milan he began to frequent the Galleria 32, then in Piazza Repubblica, run by Alfredo Paglione and Renata Usiglio. The climate was that of *Corrente*, steeped in the ideology and political thinking of the Italian left. Here Mariani held his first solo exhibition in October with a series of landscapes based on the theme of Finland, visited the previous year. In Rome he met Enrico Crispolti, who would show a constant interest in his work.

1966

The whole year was devoted to analysis and study of Sutherland's painting (ambiguity between animal and plant worlds: the *Serre* and *Giardino in città*).
From a second trip to Finland he brought back a large number of drawings and pastels that he would work on in Milan during the winter (*Kelohonka*, rocks, sunsets and above all the evocative northern light). He won the San Fedele Prize for young painters. Giorgio Di Genova organized a solo exhibition for him at the Galleria Il Girasole, run by an artists' collective. In Milan he met Vittorio Fagone, recently arrived from Sicily.

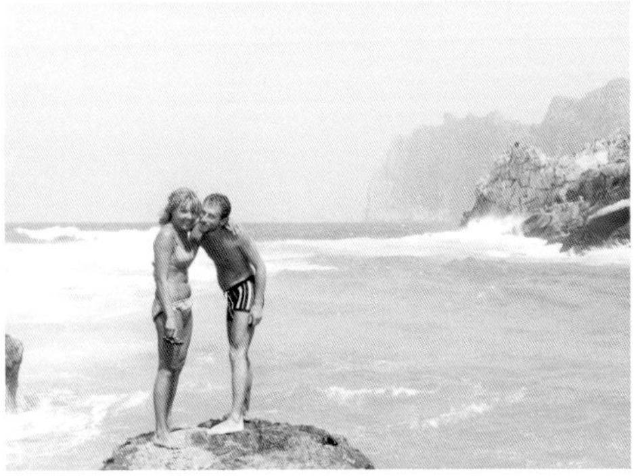
With his wife, Majorca, 1969

1967
This was the year of his maturation as far as themes and language were concerned. Naturalistic motifs were progressively abandoned and the forms became more emblematic. The 'flower' remained a constant feature, but now represented a sort of artificial nature. The structure of the pictures was almost heraldic, with broad parallel bands of tonal colours. He went to Sardinia for a long summer stay. His father fell seriously ill.
At the end of the year he produced the first pictures in the series *Oggetti allarmanti*: *Il castello del pigro*, *Perfettamente alla moda* (*Alarming Objects*: *The Idler's Castle*, *Perfectly in Fashion*). The cushions, armchairs and boots made their appearance, all iconographic elements that Mariani would use constantly until 1973. Fagone invited him to show at the Galleria La Robinia in Palermo together with Paolo Baratella, Fernando De Filippi, Claudio Olivieri and Giangiacomo Spadari: this marked the beginning of an association of Milanese artists that would last for many years. First journey to Paris, where he made contact with French artists of the Narrative Figuration movement: Arroyo, Rancillac, Aillaud, Klasen. He met Gérald Gassiot-Talabot.
1968
He was invited to exhibit at the Salon de la Jeune Peinture in Paris along with Baratella, De Filippi, Spadari and Vittorio Gobbi.
He prepared four canvases measuring 200 x 160 cm (78¾ x 63 in.) on the theme of protest. The May protests broke out in France and the Salon was postponed. Its theme was modified into 'Police et Culture'. With the aforementioned artists he organized an environment made up of five large curtains that could be penetrated as if in an imaginary process of metamorphosis from the figure of a southern man of the people to that of a policeman through six successive images. Mariani joined the collective of Milanese artists who were expressing their disagreement with the way cultural structures were run. The protest would reach its peak with the occupation of the Milan Triennale and the Venice Biennale. He travelled to Yugoslavia.
In September his father died.
The artist was invited by Enrico Crispolti to take part in *Alternative Attuali 3* at L'Aquila, Italy. Enrico Baj introduced him to Edouard Jaguer and he joined the international group Phases. At Jaguer's suggestion, Adolf Kroupa, director of the Dům Umění Města in Brno, Czech Republic, visited Mariani's studio and plans were made for an exhibition in Czechoslovakia.
1969
The Salon de la Jeune Peinture postponed from the previous year was held in Paris. The Italians' environment stirred keen interest. The magazine *Phases* published a series of Mariani's works and Jaguer organized a solo exhibition of his work at the Galerie Arcanes in Belgium. He met Jean Dypréau and Jean-Pierre Van Tieghem. He was invited by Aligi Sassu to spend the summer months on Majorca, where he painted several canvases. He won the Alcudia Painting Prize. On his way back from Majorca with Ritva, he stopped briefly at Calice Ligure and made contact with the community of artists that frequented the village.
He got to know Théodore Koenig, publisher of *Phantomas*, and for two years was a guest at his house. He met Gianfranco Bellora and began his collaboration with the Studio Santandrea in Milan. Crispolti organized a solo exhibition for him at Bruno Piattelli's studio in Rome, at the time fitted out as a gallery as well. The *Phases* magazine in Paris devoted its cover to him and published *L'osservatore mondano* (*The Worldly Observer*).
1970
The Dům Umění Města in Brno held a solo exhibition of Mariani's work that stirred enormous interest as it was the first exhibition by a Western artist in Czechoslovakia after the Soviet invasion. He visited Milan Grygar's studio and encountered the work of Jiří Kolář, practically unknown at the time in Italy. Third trip to Finland, where with Ritva he met the painters Jalavisto and Osipow. He signed a contract with the Studio Santandrea, where in May he showed for the first time a series of works from the cycle *Oggetti allarmanti*.
1971
The Nykytaiteen Museo in Tampere staged a solo exhibition of his work alongside those of his Finnish friends Jalavisto and Osipow.
He met Sara Hilden, who bought one of his paintings. He travelled to Lapland with Ritva, who was writing an autobiographical book. He stayed on Lake Inari. The collaboration with the Studio Santandrea in Milan continued. Dypréau invited him to take part in the 6th International Exhibition in Knokke-Heist, where he was awarded the Grand Prix.
He moved home and studio to Via Andrea del Sarto 11. He began the series of paintings *Daumier: andata e ritorno* (*Daumier: There and Back*), referring directly to the political and social satire of the great French painter and caricaturist. This series represented the moment of Mariani's greatest adherence to post-1968 ideology. After the terrorist attack on the Banca Nazionale dell'Agricoltura (December 1969), Milan had become the centre of conflict between the institutions and forms of protest by the youth. Mariani formed ties with the

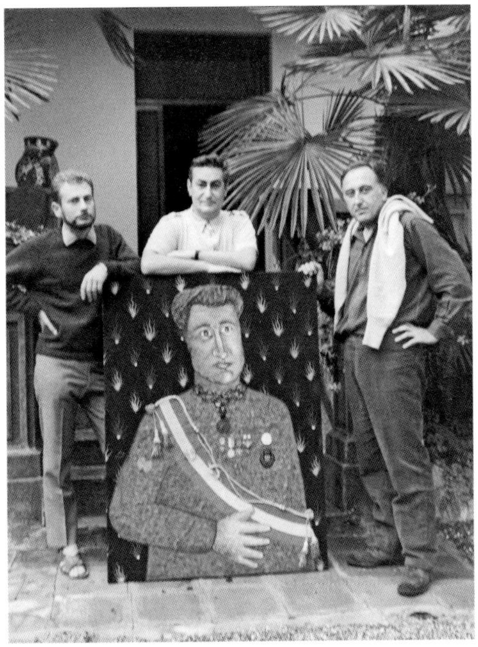

With Paride Accetti and Enrico Baj in Baj's studio at Vergiate, 1969

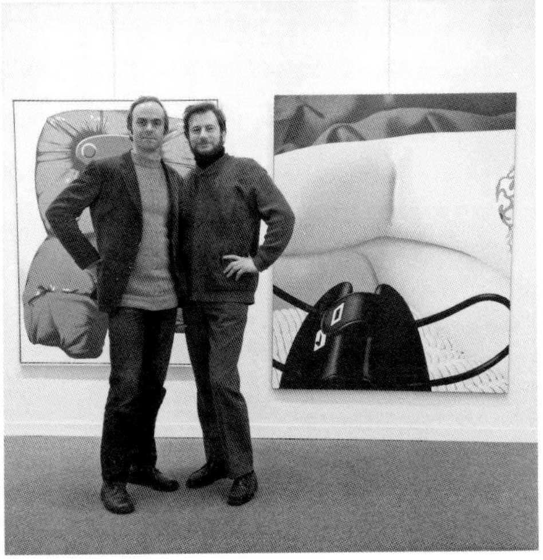

Exhibition *Klasen – Mariani – Schlosser*, Studio Soldano, Milan, 1972

Milanese artists of his generation most committed to tackling themes of social and political life: among them, Baratella, De Filippi, Spadari, Mauro Staccioli and Alik Cavaliere.

1972

The Studio Soldano, Milan, staged the exhibition *Klasen – Mariani – Schlosser*. Mariani continued the *Daumier: andata e ritorno* series. He painted, among others, *Ritratto del questore G.* (*Portrait of the Chief of Police G.*), *Il giudice imparziale* (*The Impartial Judge*) and *Le président général Napo(litain) Leon*. During the summer he found a new house at Calice and made friends with the artists Emilio Scanavino, Tino Stefanoni, Renato Mambor and Paolo Icaro. In November he presented his new works at the Studio Santandrea in Milan in the exhibition *Nove personalità – Daumier: andata e ritorno*. In August he made a journey to Turkey with Ritva: Istanbul, the Aegean coast, Cappadocia.

1973

Dypréau and Van Tieghem invited the 'Milanese group' to show at the Palais des Beaux-Arts in Brussels. The catalogue of the exhibition, entitled *Quatre peintres et une ville : Milan*, included texts by Dypréau himself and Crispolti. Brussels reacted with indignation to the themes tackled in the works on display: a resounding flop on moralistic grounds.
At Ritva's behest the couple decided to separate. His mother Iole suffered a serious disability and spent many months in hospital.
For Mariani this was the year of the short series *La citazione differente* (*The Different Quote*): *Ritratto di Piero Manzoni* (*Portrait of Piero Manzoni*), *Ceci n'est pas un Magritte* and *Le lacrime della signora Jones* (*Mrs Jones's Tears*). It was a moment of reflection and inquiry; drapery became a central motif.

1974

The exhibition *Quatre peintres et une ville : Milan* had a prestigious sequel. Pierre Gaudibert, director of the Musée d'Art Moderne de la Ville de Paris (ARC 2), wanted to stage the show. The catalogue was supposed to include a text by Vittorio Fagone, but a technical hitch prevented the translation from arriving in time. In the meantime the director of the museum had been forced to resign. He was replaced by Suzanne Pagé, who honoured the commitment and opened the exhibition in June. A month earlier the Studio Santandrea had presented a preview of Mariani's works in Milan.
In September the artist planned the first painting of the *Alfabeto afono* (*Aphonic Alphabet*) series. It consisted of two draped letters, 'S' and 'A': the initials of the Saint Andrews restaurant in Milan, where the work was hung. Other businesses and companies would follow the example, as would some collectors: Zucchi, Beolchini, Griffin, Franchi, Dossi, Benuzzi, etc. Mariani travelled to Kenya and Tanzania. Jaguer organized a major exhibition of *Phases* at the Musée d'Ixelles (Brussels), to which Mariani was invited to show two imposing canvases. He met Franca Speranza and took a short holiday with her on Corfu.

1975

He worked intensely on the theme of the *Alfabeto afono*. He staged an exhibition with this title at the Studio Santandrea in May. He produced works on a large scale as well, often in two versions, one in white and another in black, a sort of positive and negative. He signed a contract with the Galerie Bellechasse in Paris. In the summer he went to Portugal with Franca: it was the year of the Carnation Revolution. The country was passing through an extraordinary period of change and the general atmosphere was one of great but non-violent exhilaration. Much more dangerous was his return through the south of France, where a revolt by winegrowers obliged them to travel at night, under police escort. Koenig organized a *Phantomas* exhibition at the Musée d'Ixelles, to which Mariani was invited to take part. The brief and intense relationship with Franca came to an end.

1976

Alfabeto afono proved a success and the artist developed the theme, although new issues emerged; the illusory play of the presence and erasure of the word stimulated Mariani to take the experiment in the direction of more complex forms. Invited to the United States by Icaro, he stayed at his friend's house in Woodbridge. He visited New Haven and New York and then, with Icaro and his wife Nancy, travelled south, passing through Philadelphia, Washington, the Tennessee, Memphis, the Mississippi region and New Orleans. He played host to Costas Tsoclis, living in Paris at the time, in his Milanese studio and through him met Christos Tzivelos (Tsoclis prepared an exhibition of his own at the Studio Santandrea). Invited by Tsoclis to Hydra for the summer, he made a second journey to Greece. On Hydra with Tino and Mariola Stefanoni, he met Anneta Mylonogianni, ceramist and director of the Monastiraki Museum in Athens. This was the start of a long connection with Greece. He got to know Flavio Caroli.

1977

The Galerie Paul Facchetti in Paris presented four large paintings by Mariani at its stand at the Bologna Arte Fiera, including the first work in the *Teorema* (*Theorem*) series, in which two large carpenter's vices grip the ends of the painted canvas: the dialectic relationship between the virtual painted form

Studio Santandrea, Milan, 1972: from left, Nino Soldano, Enrico Baj, Renato Volpini and Umberto Mariani. Solo exhibition *Daumier: andata e ritorno*

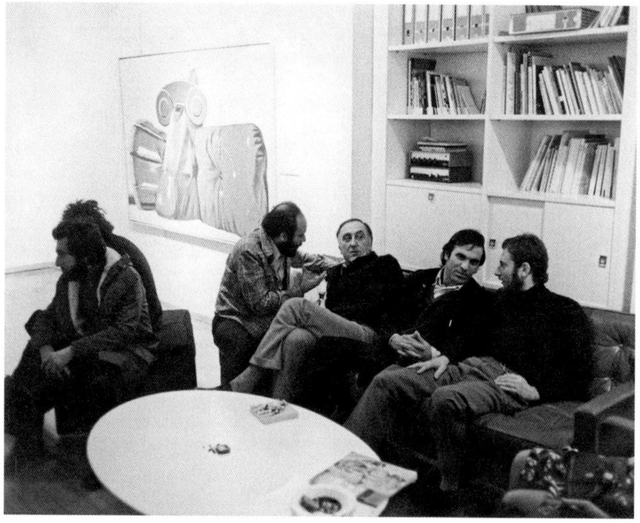

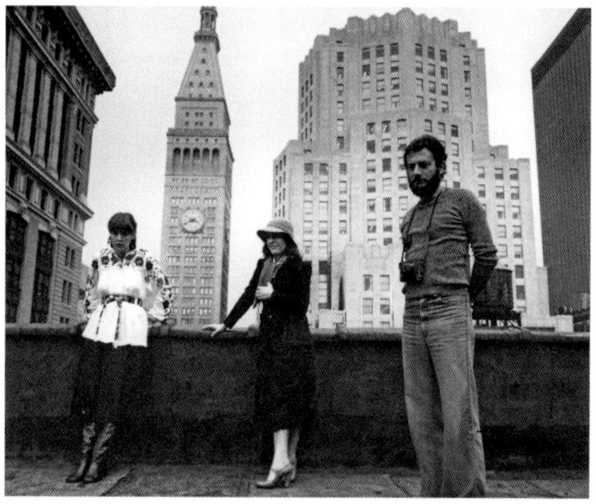

On the roofs of New York with Camilla Adami and a friend, 1974

and the real physical object was introduced into Mariani's work. For the whole year the artist developed the *Teorema* series, using canvases of the same dimensions of 80 x 195 cm (31½ x 76¾ in.), or multiples of them) on which different materials interfere with the painted drapery. Anneta came to Italy and the two formed a strong sentimental relationship. They spent the summer together on Hydra, Santorini and Spetses. Mariani met Pavlos, Takis and Iolas.
He was invited to take part in the *Mythologies quotidiennes* exhibition at the Musée d'Art Moderne de la Ville de Paris.
He worked for more than a month in Tsoclis's studio in Paris, painting three canvases for the show: the pictures measured 150 x 300 cm (59 x 118 in.) each and a special space was prepared inside the museum where they could be hung on three walls. He was also invited to exhibit at the Salon de Mai. Marisa Vescovo staged a solo exhibition of his work at the Sala Comunale in Alessandria; the catalogue had texts by her and by Bruno Corà. Caroli reviewed the exhibition in a long article published on the literary page of the *Corriere della Sera*.

1978

He worked on the completion of the *Teorema* cycle. Franco Farina invited him to Ferrara, where, in November, he opened an exhibition at the Padiglione del Parco Massari with forty works. Some of them belonged to the *Alfabeto afono* series while eighteen represented the complete series of *Teorema* realized up to then. The text in the catalogue was by Vittorio Fagone. He spent the summer at Calice Ligure.
The international recession had a strong effect on the art market and the Studio Santandrea annulled its contract with Mariani.

1979

It was a year of reflection. Mariani developed themes that were still similar to those of *Teorema*, without notable innovations. Only at the end of the year did he start to realize large installations with a markedly theatrical accent. He travelled to Egypt with Stefanoni, Bertini, Sarri and Marisa Vescovo on the occasion of an exhibition at the Italian Institute of Culture in Cairo. He returned to Athens for a brief visit and met up with Anneta. Caroli invited him to take part in *Testuale: parole e immagini* at the Rotonda di Via Besana in Milan.

1980

At the beginning of the year he was contacted by Omar Ronda, who visited the exhibition in Ferrara; Ronda gave concrete form to his interest with a long-term proposal of collaboration and bought several large works from the *Teorema* series. He carried on with the creation of installations referring explicitly to the theatre: the series *Il luogo dell'illusione* (*The Place of Illusion*) and *Relitti di scena* (*Stage Wrecks*) were begun. They were clear citations of de Chirico and Magritte, but with a more 'broken-up' spatiality. At the same time a precise interest in the baroque emerged. The installations were shown for the first time in April at the castle in Portofino in an exhibition presented in the catalogue by Mirella Bentivoglio. With Staccioli, Stefanoni and Giovanni Lucci he showed at the Galerie Studio in Warsaw. Through Ronda he met the gallery owner from Geneva Marie-Louise Jeanneret, who took an immediate interest in his work and invited him for a year to her Centre International d'Expérimentation Artistique at Boissano.
The summer was devoted entirely to Greece. He visited Crete with Anneta and then, as a guest in Tzivelos's studio, worked on large canvases. *Dechirichiana: le spiagge d'Italia* (*Dechirichian: the Beaches of Italy*), *Strumenti e altro per una deposizione in rosso* (*Instruments and Other Things for a Deposition in Red*) and other minor works were created in Athens.
He remained very close to Tsoclis. In Brussels he met Zaira Mis, who bought several of his works and introduced him to Florent Bex. With Stefanoni he proposed a project to the Internationaal Cultureel Centrum (ICC) in Antwerp that would take shape the following year.

1981

Baratella, Mariani and Stefanoni were the protagonists of the exhibition *Het verhaal, de illusie, de symbolen* hosted by Bex at the ICC in Antwerp; the text on Mariani in the catalogue was written by Luisa Somaini. The Gordon Matta-Clark Foundation acquired one of his installations entitled *Il luogo*

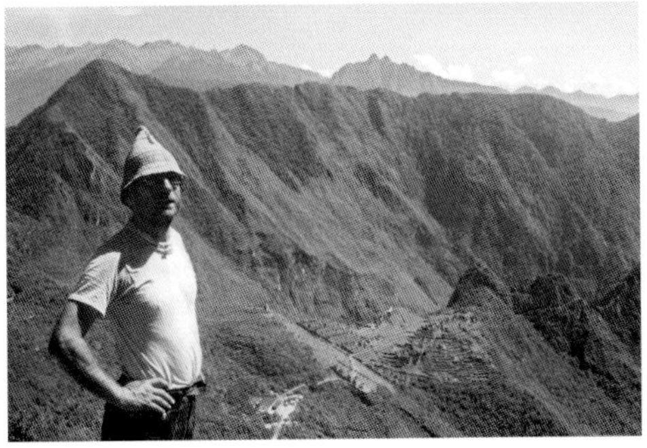

Peru, Inti Punco (The Sun Door), 1984:
the entrance to Machu Picchu

dell'illusione. Rossana Bossaglia invited him to contribute to the exhibition *Lombardia: vent'anni dopo* at the Castello Visconteo in Pavia. He continued working on theatrical themes and executed the series *Relitti di scena*, a metaphor derived from Magritte's *Epaves de la mémoire*. He gave up teaching at state school and at the invitation of Guido Ballo became a teacher of painting at his Nuova Accademia in Milan.

1982

Ugo Carrega invited him to hold a solo exhibition at the Mercato del Sale gallery in Milan, where he presented four installations. The Galleria Dossi in Bergamo put on *Verum factum*, an exhibition on the theme of perceptive deception conceived by Luisa Somaini, who also wrote an essay in the catalogue, with works by Pietro Coletta, Tim Head, Tsoclis and Mariani. He worked in Athens on the preparation of works for the exhibition at Vicky Drakou's Oraisma gallery. In July he presented works created expressly for the eccentric spaces of the Galerie Fabien de Cugnac in Ostend. He spent the summer at Calice working on pastels and drawings. In October the Galerie Jeanneret exhibited three works by Mariani at the FIAC in Paris that would be bought by the Kennedy family.

1983

The Galleria Dossi in Bergamo presented the works created for the *Alfabeto afono* series from 1974 to 1979 in a solo exhibition (catalogue with critical anthology). Rossana Bossaglia chose two of his works from the 1960s for the exhibition *Il pop art e l'Italia*, staged at the Castello Visconteo in Pavia. During the summer he travelled in the north of India, Kashmir and Ladakh. Zaira and Marcel Mis commissioned from him an installation for the Philippe Demar showroom in Brussels. He started to work on the plans.

1984

The installation for Demar was finished and mounted. He worked in Athens on a second exhibition for Vicky Drakou (Omega gallery) that proved a great success; all paintings were sold. He prepared pictures and a large installation for an exhibition at Marie-Louise Jeanneret's gallery in Geneva, which opened in October with a text in the catalogue by Guido Ballo. In the summer he travelled in Peru and Bolivia: he reached Machu Picchu after walking for three days through the Andean passes on the ancient Camino Real, navigated the Urubamba on launches and climbed to the Chalcantaya at a height of 19,000 feet. At the end of the year he was invited by the Galerie Graff in Montreal to realize a series of graphic works and gave a lecture at the local university.

1985

His interest in theatrical subjects was fading while he started to focus on less descriptive baroque forms. He began the series of the *Specchi* (*Mirrors*), elliptical shapes from which broken pieces of frame emerged. The gold, lead and paint established a very lively dialectical relationship. The allusion to the dynamism and vitalism of the baroque was evident. Illusion, as crux of the work, was now proposed in a highly metaphorical key. These new works attracted the attention of some collectors, but the market appeared totally uninterested. The plan for an exhibition with ten *Specchi* animating a single large space was unable to get off the ground. Ronda organized an exhibition at Biella, showing a *Specchio* and other works of the last five years. Mariani made a brief journey to the East: Sri Lanka and Nepal.

1986

He developed the theme of the *Specchi* further and with the publisher Giampaolo Prearo planned a book that would bring together several chosen works on this subject. The idea took form as a book-object, in which photographs of the installations were accompanied by an original made with different media, exemplifying directly the nature and materials of the works reproduced. In the end fifty copies would be produced, containing five hundred bronze casts, collages, drawings and frottages. Mariani travelled to North Yemen with Anneta. He began a close collaboration with the Galleria Millennium, at that time located in Lausanne, prior to its transfer to Milan. The Musée d'Art Contemporain in Montreal organized a major exhibition to celebrate the twenty years of the Galerie Graff: Mariani was invited to show two installations from the series of the *Specchi*.

1987

The Milan Trade Fair placed at his disposal a spacious stand in which to exhibit a series of large works. He acquired the studio at Via Mecenate 76 in Milan, located in one of the former buildings of the Caproni company; his neighbours were Lucrezia De Domizio and Fernando De Filippi. He met the architects Salvati and Tresoldi, who helped him with the renovation. He carried on with the work on the book *Specchi*, which would be completed in December. In the summer he travelled with Anneta in Pakistan; they followed the Karakorum Highway through the mountains between the Himalayas and the Hindu Kush to the land of the Hunza and all the way to the border with Chinese Xinjiang.

1988

The work on the new studio was unable to proceed due to financial difficulties. The Galleria Millennium assembled a certain number of his works from the 1970s, with which it organized an exhibition at the Studio Col di Lana in Milan.

During the summer he travelled with Anneta in Armenia and Kurdistan. They found superb vestiges of the Armenian culture. Unfortunately Mariani contracted a serious form of hepatitis. During the forced period of rest he planned a return to the themes of the *Alfabeto afono*, characteristic of his work in the 1970s.
The dynamic and vitalistic moment of the baroque was over.
In the autumn he started to realize a long series of works (*Untitled*) where the painted drapery entered into a dialectic relationship with the superimposed outlines of letters and numbers cut out of sheet metal. The elliptical shape persisted as a constant element derived from the *Specchi*.
He was invited to take part in *Textilia*, an exhibition held at the Basilica Palladiana in Vicenza: he showed an installation from 1984, the expression of a marked theatricality, in which a piece of real fabric used as a curtain held a dialogue with the illusion of the painted drapery.

1989

He developed the theme of the *Ferri* (*Irons*), outlines of letters of the alphabet and numerals in rusty or silvered sheet metal. He also created a series of small works using thin sheets of lead as a fabric with stiff folds on which it was possible to leave an impression: the 'hidden form' (*forma celata*). They were a success. He sent the book *Specchi* to the Biblioteca Nazionale in Florence for the exhibition *Pagine d'artista*. One copy would remain in the permanent collection of the library. Caroli invited him to participate to the exhibition *Italian Contemporary Art* at the National Taiwan Museum of Fine Art in Taipei. The work on the studio progressed slowly.
In the summer he travelled in the eastern part of Canada and Alaska, visiting the legendary towns of the gold prospectors in the Yukon and admiring the immense expanses of wilderness, the mountains, the rivers, the wild animals. Angelo Colella proposed the realization of a sculpture in glass to the FIAM in Pesaro. The project was accepted and work began.

1990

The realization of the sculpture presented more technical problems than expected, but Vittorio Livi refused to give up and wanted to find the best solutions. The trials continued. During the year Mariani worked on both the 'iron' and the 'lead' series. He also returned to the theme called *Autobiografico* (*Autobiographical*): the first, isolated works had been presented in Ferrara in 1977.
He now worked regularly with the material Kristall: words and numbers that are citations of facts and dates related to Mariani's life were wrapped in this transparent plastic; the colour partly obliterated the visual message. At last work on the studio was able to progress more rapidly, as his economic situation had improved. Exhibition in Biella with Ronda (*La macchina dell'arte*).
In the summer he went to Brittany with Anneta. Tino Stefanoni introduced him to Edoardo Manzoni of the Galleria La Polena in Genoa; in June the gallery would show one of his *Specchi* at Art Basel.

1991

The Galleria Millennium presented again the Milanese group of the 1960s and 1970s (Mariani, De Filippi, Baratella and Spadari) at the Kunstmesse in Frankfurt. In March an exhibition entitled *Specchi* was put on in the ample spaces of the Galleria La Polena: it included four of Michelangelo Pistoletto's large mirror pictures and four of Mariani's installations with the same title.
The Fondazione Mudima in Milan planned a retrospective of the Milanese group for 1993, to mark the twentieth anniversary of the exhibitions in Brussels and Paris. Cesare Marraccini and Antonio Tancredi came up with the project for an anthological exhibition in Teramo. Work on the studio came to an end and the space was inaugurated in October at the same time as the Galleria Millennium exhibition. Lucrezia De Domizio organized the *Luogo del desiderio*, a cultural project linked to the common spaces in Via Mecenate. Mariani worked intensely on the installations planned for Ronda's new gallery in Biella. The space was large and fascinating, and needed to be managed with care. At the end of November Mariani's exhibition opened at the Galleria Atrium. During the summer he travelled in the north of Greece and Thrace, where he visited Edirne, the ancient Hadrianopolis. The glass sculpture was finished.

1992

In May the anthological exhibition opened at the new Museo Archeologico in Teramo, where fifteen rooms housed eighty works covering a period of twenty-five years (1966–1991). The catalogue, edited by Enrico Crispolti, also included a poem by Miklos Varga and a critical anthology with texts by E. Jaguer (1969), G. Gassiot-Talabot (1975), M. Bentivoglio (1980), L. Somaini (1982) and G. Ballo (1984). The Galleria La Polena presented a large installation of a markedly theatrical character, dating from 1979, at Art Basel. In November the same gallery in Genoa held a solo exhibition entitled *Arte come spettacolo* (works from 1970 to 1980): it comprised five installations with explicit titles, such as *Relitti di scena*, *Il luogo dell'illusione* and *Sipario* (*Curtain*); Elena Pontiggia wrote a long review of it in *Il Giornale*. During the summer Mariani was Tsoclis's guest in Tinos, where he produced several works for the *Autobiografico* series. The exhibition at the Fondazione Mudima was postponed, and never took place. The book *Specchi* published by Prearo was shown at the Museum of Modern Art of New York as part of the exhibition *The Artist and the Book in 20th-Century Italy*, with a catalogue published by Allemandi, Turin. The Gordon Matta-Clark Foundation exhibited one of Mariani's installations at Turnhout, Belgium.

1993

Zaira Mis commissioned around twenty works from him for an exhibition in Brussels in June. The exhibition received extensive coverage in the newspapers and on the radio and the television. He spent the summer in Greece again, where he went back to working on the *Autobiografico* cycle. The Galleria La Polena presented three of his 'lead' pieces at Art Basel. The magazine *Art in Italy* devoted its cover to him; inside there was a long feature with an article by Enrico Crispolti.

1994

Mariani's production was centred on the theme of the 'Hidden Form', i.e. the 'lead' series. In February the Galleria La Polena organized a solo exhibition in Genoa entitled *Piombi*. In March the artist left his old home for good and moved into Via Mecenate. After twenty-five years he also gave up the house at Calice Ligure. Nino Soldano staged a series of small thematic exhibitions at the Lord Byron Café in Milan and Mariani participated with an installation bearing the words 'Lord Byron'. At Arte Fiera in Bologna five galleries presented works by Mariani: Annunciata, showing the installation *Grande piombo* (*Large Lead*), La Polena, Steccata, Millennium and Fioretto. In the summer he was back to Greece, staying on Anafi. Anneta's mother, who was suffering from a serious illness, died at the end of August. In December the Ammiraglio Acton gallery in Milan organized a meeting-performance with the title *Tra le pieghe del pensiero*. Toti Carpentieri chose Mariani for the cover of an issue of *Arte & Cronaca* in which a long dialogue between him and De Domizio was published. The book *Specchi* was shown at the Guggenheim Foundation in Venice. A six-page feature on the artist's studio-home was published in the December issue of the magazine *Abitare*. He met Demetrio Paparoni in Basel.

1995

In May the Galleria Eos in Milan opened a major solo exhibition: four installations – *Grande ferro* (*Large Iron*), 1995, 280 x 460 cm (9 x 15 ft); *Relitti di scena*, 1994, 303 x 245 cm (10 x 8 ft); *Grande piombo*, 1993, 245 x 200 cm (8 x 6.5 ft); *Anamorfosi della lettera E* (*Anamorphosis of the Letter E*), 1991, 290 x 460 cm (9.5 x 15 ft) – along with the glass sculpture and twenty-eight 'leads'. The publisher Adriano Parise of Verona brought out the lavish volume *Mariani-Vandrasch* with a poem by Giancarlo Majorino and critical essay by Elena Pontiggia. Over the course of the exhibition the volume was presented by Demetrio Paparoni, Mauro Staccioli and Emilio Tadini. In the autumn the same book was presented by De Filippi, Majorino and Pontiggia at the solo exhibition held at La Crocetta Arte Contemporanea in Gallarate. The artist started to work on the project of a large sculpture to be realized at Tortolì, in Sardinia. In the summer he returned to Sicily with Anneta to see his friends at Capo d'Orlando and then stayed at Soligo's beautiful house on Stromboli.

1996

In January the book *Mariani-Vandrasch* was presented by Giorgio Celli and Paola Serra Zanetti at the Saletta del Circolo Artistico Iterarte in Bologna. Roberto Peira invited Mariani to show at his galleria in Bra: title of the exhibition, *Piombi*. On this occasion the same book was presented in the rooms of the Banca Popolare di Novara, with commentaries by Marco Rosci, Vanna Pescatori and Maurizio Sciaccaluga. Edoardo Manzoni expanded the programme of the Museo d'Arte Contemporanea Su Logu de s'Iscultura at Tortolì: after the works by Mauro Staccioli, two important sculptures by Pietro Coletta and Ascanio Renda were unveiled and the sketches and plans for Mariani's *Grande sipario* (*Large Curtain*) presented; Sciaccaluga prepared the text for the Mariani exhibition. In July Mariani made a trip to Iceland; he saw the great geysers and crossed the volcanic deserts of the interior. The magazine *Ottagono* devoted four pages to a feature on the artist's house.

1997

In January he set off for India with Anneta and they travelled through Rajasthan to the Thar Desert, going on to visit the cave temples of Ellora and Ajanta. In February Mariani opened an exhibition at the Centro Arte in Milan with works dating from 1972 to 1996. At the Bogani plant in Limbiate work began on *Grande sipario*, a sculpture in Cor-ten steel measuring 3.8 x 8.9 metres (12.5 x 29 ft). It was presented in Piazza Racugno at Tortolì on 31 May. Rossana Bossaglia, Fabio Cavallucci, Lucrezia De Domizio and Giannella De Mure spoke at the unveiling ceremony. In the same period the artist won, in collaboration with De Filippi, the national competition for the realization of the monumental *Via Crucis* (*Stations of the Cross*) in Carrara marble, 3 x 18 metres (10 x 59 ft), for the church of the new district penitentiary in Sanremo. The work was completed in September. In the

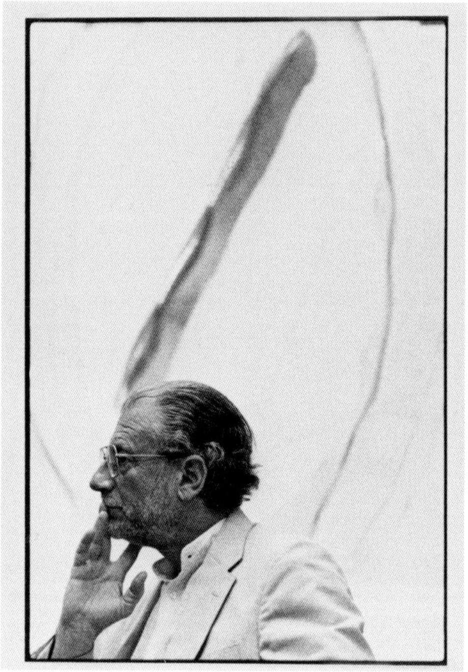

During the exhibition at the Galleria Eos, Milan, 1995

summer he went to Namibia, where he met the indigenous Himba tribes.

1998

Again in collaboration with De Filippi he won the national competition for a monumental sculpture to be placed in the barracks of the Carabinieri at Amelia (Terni). In May he was invited by the Municipality of Milan to hold a solo exhibition at Palazzo Reale. Over the course of the summer he travelled through the highlands of Bolivia, visiting the salt flats of Uyuni and their astonishing coloured lagoons at an altitude of nearly 13,000 feet. The magazine *Art & Life* devoted the cover of its January issue to the *Grande sipario* sculpture. In the same month the German magazine *MD* dedicated five pages to Mariani's studio-home. At the end of the year the artist made a journey to Mali. For four days he visited the villages of the Dogon people along the Bandiagara Escarpment on foot. He crossed the swamps of the Niger River and arrived at the mythical city of Timbuktu, encountering the Tuareg peoples and the architecture of their mosques. The journey made a strong impression on him that was reflected for the first time in his work.

1999

He began the series of works entitled *Taghelmoust: il velo* (*Taghelmoust: the Veil*): this is the name in the Tuareg language for the piece of cloth that men use to cover their head and face. Forms and materials already utilized in earlier years now reappeared in the deep indigo blue colour characteristic of the Tuareg. But there were also new forms derived from the mud and dung architecture of their mosques. Invited to participate in the 13th Rome Quadriennale, he showed the large sculpture *Patroclo* (*Patroclus*). He was asked by Frette, the famous textile manufacturer, to design the logo of the company; he created fifty-four works on a large scale – *tondi* with a diameter of 200 cm (78¾ in.) – using the media of painting, sculpture and silk-screen printing, that would be placed in their sales points around the world (Los Angeles, San Francisco, London, Paris, Chicago, Rome, Milan…). Lucrezia De Domizio commissioned a work from him for the collection of her house at Bolognano; it would be unveiled in September. He spent New Year's Day 2000 in Niger and travelled 1,500 miles across the desert of the Ténéré in search of the ancient salt pans of Bilma and the ruined cities of Djama and Djado.

2000

The journey in Niger brought new motivations to his research. He developed and added to the *Taghelmoust: il velo* series and opened a solo exhibition at the Caltex gallery in Biella with the same title in November. In collaboration with De Domizio, he designed an environment on a triangular plan with the title *Suoni del tempo* (*Sounds of Time*). During the summer he paid a visit to Tibet. He joined thousands of pilgrims on the circumambulation of Mount Kailash, the sacred mountain of the Buddhists and Hindus. In the winter he returned to the Sahara: in the south of Algeria he walked across the plateau of Tassili n'Ajjer in search of its many caves filled with rock paintings (Saharan Neolithic era). He encountered the Tuareg peoples again. In various chapters of his vast work on the history of 20th-century Italian art Giorgio Di Genoa spoke of Mariani's work at length and with accuracy.

2001

In March the Galerie Artiscope in Brussels opened his solo exhibition *Taghelmoust (le voile)*, which was made up of about twenty wall-mounted reliefs and four models on a scale of 1:10 of the same number of environmental sculptures planned in the previous months. As usual Zaira Mis publicized the exhibition very well, and among others it was reviewed by Gilles Sorel in the magazine *Déco Idées*, by Colette Noël in the financial newspaper *Het Financieele Dagblad* in Amsterdam and in Italy by Laura Dago in *Gioia*. The Museo d'Arte delle Generazioni Italiane del Novecento at Pieve di Cento acquired three of his major works. At the end of the year he returned to Nepal with Anneta and spent five days trekking among the hills and villages at the base of Annapurna, in the Pokhara region.

2002

At the end of February Mariani opened an exhibition at the Spazio Annunciata in Milan. This was the fulfilment of an old project of Sergio Grossetti's, who was now able to present large-scale works in the rooms of his new gallery. The title was again *Taghelmoust: il velo*, and for the first time it included a sculpture related to that title of optimal dimensions: over three metres in height and two and a half in depth (10 x 8 ft). The exhibition also provided an opportunity to catch up with Elio Marchegiani and his wife Carola Pandolfo, whom he had not seen since the 1970s when they were all part of the small group in the orbit of the Studio Santandrea. Edoardo Manzoni, present at the opening, proposed taking an expanded version of the exhibition to the Time in Jazz festival at Berchidda, in Sardinia. A passion for jazz was something that Mariani and Manzoni had in common. The theme of the 2002 festival was 'In the Sign of Art'. In collaboration with the PAV (Progetto Arti Visive) of Sassari, Mariani created four environments in a former cork works that evoked forms and impressions of Africa through

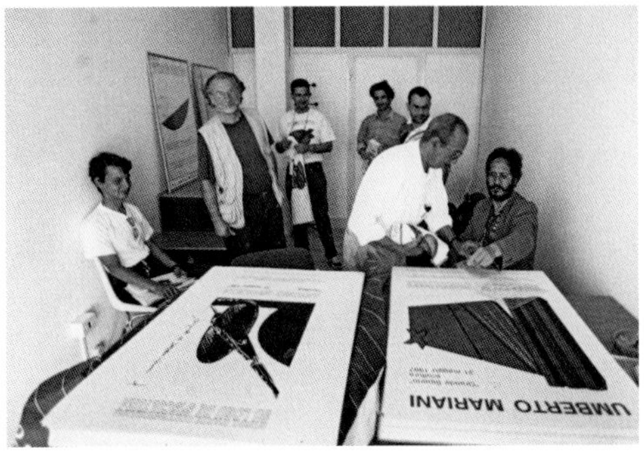

The signature of the posters, Tortolì, Sardinia, 1997

sculptures and lighting. He also created the scenery for the concluding evening of the festival, headlined by the Farafina group from Burkina Faso: the encounter between the two cultures was an exciting one. He took part in the exhibition *Hommage aan Mondrian* organized by the Galerie Conny van Kasteel first at the Mondriaanhuis in Amersfoort and then at the Kunstcentrum in Zaanstad. He planned a trip to the Acacus Mountains in southern Libya at the end of the year, but a banal bureaucratic hold-up stopped him from going.

2003

The *Terzocchio* magazine of Bologna devoted its cover to Mariani. In February he opened a solo exhibition in the rooms of the Galleria Comunale at Castel San Pietro Terme. The project was coordinated by Carola Pandolfo on the initiative of the councillor Bruno D'Amore. The title was again *Taghelmoust: il velo*, and the text in the catalogue was by Flaminio Gualdoni. In addition to an environment of great emotional force called *Notturno* (*Nocturne*), he showed for the first time the forms inspired by 'Tuareg crosses', i.e. the silver necklaces worn mostly by the men that Mariani, blowing them up in size, paradoxically called 'jewellery of sand'. In April he held his first solo exhibition in the Netherlands, at the Galerie Conny van Kasteel at Egmond aan Zee: the gallery presented its special programme that had always entailed coupling the work of an Italian artist with that of a Dutch artist; after Del Pezzo, Staccioli and Castellani, it was now the turn of Mariani's wall reliefs and the sculptures of the Dutchman Peter Jansen. The combination worked well, with the indigo blue forms of Mariani inspired by the head and face coverings worn by the Tuareg alongside the bronze shapes derived from the dance of the Whirling Dervishes presented in the exhibition by Jansen. He was invited by De Domizio to place a 'work-sign' in the Piantagione Paradise at Bolognano as part of the *First Free International Forum*, but unfortunately it was postponed due to economic problems. During the summer he returned after twenty years to the north of India, to Kashmir and Ladakh. He ascended the Zanskar Valley, visiting remote Buddhist monasteries. He crossed valleys and passes at over 13,000 feet. In winter he travelled to southern Libya and saw the famous rock paintings in the Acacus desert. Once again he encountered Tuareg tribes.

2004

At the end of May he opened a solo exhibition entitled *Relitti di scena* in Florence, under the auspices of Etoile Toy / Visual Art Florence and held on the premises of the Florence Dance Centre. The exhibition, organized by Giuliano Serafini, presented five large installations with a strongly theatrical flavour created in the 1980s and 1990s that fitted in well with the activity of the centre, a school of classical dance. On the day of the vernissage a group of students staged a performance choreographed by Keith Ferrone with music by Pankow FM. The event was part of the cultural week promoted by the Ministry for Cultural Activities. In October the same exhibition would be put on at the Spazio Cesare da Sesto in the Palazzo Comunale of Sesto Calende. In March the Spazio Hajech of the Brera Art School presented a solo exhibition by Mariani referring to the years in which he was a teacher, from 1967 to 1982. At the RAI Convention Centre in Amsterdam, Galerie Nine presented a wall with seven works by Mariani (three were sold). The magazine *Italia Imballaggio* devoted the cover of its March issue to him. In May the Galerie Malichin in Baden-Baden organized a show entitled *Skulptur und Malerei – Dialog mit afrikanischer Kunst* with works by Iginio Balderi, African sculptures and seven pictures by Mariani dating from between the 1970s and the early 2000s. During the summer the artist left for Pakistan with the ambitious aim of climbing the Baltoro Glacier as far as the base camp of K2, but unfavourable weather thwarted his plans. In November he received an invitation to the 14th Rome Quadriennale and Claudio Cerritelli included him in the exhibition *L'incanto della pittura*, housed in the Casa del Mantegna in Mantua.
In the winter he visited southern Ethiopia, meeting the remote Mursi and Karo peoples.

2005

In agreement with Luciano Caramel, commissioner of the Rome Quadriennale, Mariani planned a free reconstruction of a typical mud building of the desert, a structure measuring 4 x 4 metres (13 x 13 ft). The work stirred keen interest among the critics and public. On the opening day the physical presence of a Tuareg in traditional dress was the focus of attention. The national television broadcast images of the work on several news programmes. He met Mara Coccia, who showed a great deal of interest in his work, as did the daily press and the specialist magazines. Invited to participate in *2005 Miniartextil – Como*, he presented a large installation from 1980 with the title *Il luogo dell'illusione* in the deconsecrated church of San Francesco in Como, in which an intriguing comparison was made between painted fabrics and real ones.

2006

The Galerie Malichin in Baden-Baden showed twelve works by Mariani dating from 1968 to 2001 in its stand at the Karlsruhe

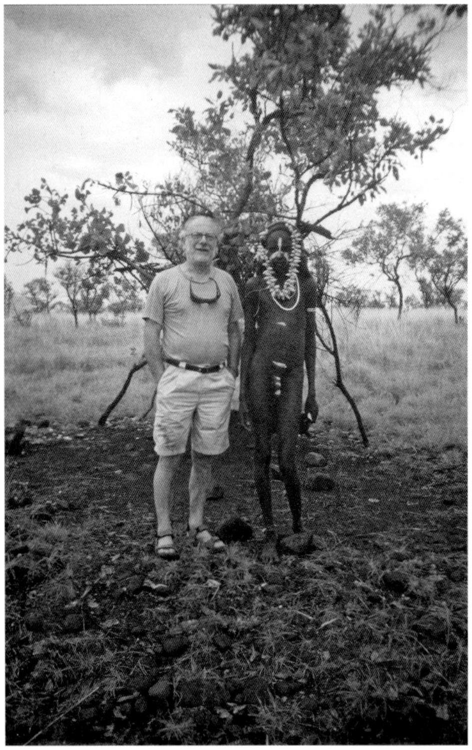

In the south of Ethiopia with a member of the Karo tribe, 2004

Art Fair, which were then put on display at the gallery itself. In the summer the artist went to the north of Pakistan and reached the base camps of Rakaposhi and Nanga Parbat. Then, across the Chinese border, in Xinjiang, he climbed in four days to the base camp of Muztagh Ata. Invited to take part in the Suzzara Prize, he endowed the local museum with a large work. In October the Galleria Annunciata in Milan presented four of his works from the 1960s at the exhibition *L'immagine critica. Milano negli anni sessanta – Tra pop art e contestazione*. The critical text was by Walter Guadagnini: an account of artistic life in Milan between the 1960s and 1970s. The artist then realized a sculpture in Carrara marble and Cor-ten steel measuring 4 x 4 metres (13 x 13 ft) for the barracks of the Carabinieri at Bono, in Sardinia. Through his collector friend Gian Carlo Rotta of Lecco, he showed his works to the new Progettoarte Elm gallery in Milan and the Galleria Orler in Venice, and the two galleries immediately put them up for sale, with very positive results. The Milanese gallery went on to present his work at a series of art fairs, including those of Genoa, Bergamo, Verona and Milan.

2007

The publisher Gabriele Mazzotta, in collaboration with the Meeting Art auction house, brought out a volume of 142 pages with the title *Autobiografico – Un po' dappertutto* and a text by Remo Bodei. The book contained sixty reproductions of works from the *Autobiografico* series that referred to sixty places around the world visited by Mariani in the course of his travels. Presented first at the Fondazione Mazzotta by Claudio Cerritelli, Angela Madesani and Paolo Rosa, the book accompanied also the solo exhibition at the Galerie Conny van Kasteel at Egmond aan Zee in May, where twenty pictures from the *Autobiografico* cycle were on display. The Galerie Malichin exhibited fourteen of Mariani's works at the Karlsruhe Art Fair. Orler in Venice and Progettoarte Elm in Milan took an interest in his work, with notable results at the national and international level. In summer he went to the Svalbard Islands, reaching as far north as 80° of latitude. The Galleria Annunciata in Milan staged a solo exhibition with the title *Milano anni sessanta – Mariani ieri e oggi*: it consisted of twenty-two pictures that covered the entire course of his work from 1968 to 2007. The text in the catalogue was by Angela Madesani. He was invited by De Domizio to take part in the event *Joseph Beuys – Defence of Nature* at the 52nd Venice Biennale. At the end of the year he went to Mauritania and walked for five days through the desert to reach the legendary caravan city of Chinguetti.

2008

He was invited to take part in the Campigna Prize at Santa Sofia in Romagna on the fiftieth anniversary of its institution. The Galerie Malichin presented ten more works by Mariani at the Karlsruhe Art Fair that aroused considerable interest. The same happened at the Verona Art Fair with the 'lead' pieces presented by Progettoarte Elm. In May a televised special on the Galleria Orler had a sensational outcome: all the works shown were reserved. His collaboration with Progettoarte Elm became closer and a solo exhibition in Milan was planned for January 2009. His friend Marraccini persuaded two companies in Abruzzo and the Marche specializing in the sale of furnishing products by prestigious designers to hold exhibitions with paintings from the 1960s and 1970s belonging to the series *Oggetti allarmanti*: the direct confrontation of painted objects and real objects was a stimulating one. Over the course of the summer he visited Ecuador and the Galápagos Islands. At the end of the year he went to Uganda where he followed trails on the border with the Congo. He met a community of pygmies and went to see mountain gorillas in the jungle.

2009

In January Mariani's solo exhibition organized by Francesco Tedeschi opened in the spaces of the Progettoarte Elm gallery in Milan. It consisted of ten triptychs of different dimensions. It received highly good reviews. The Dellapasqua boatbuilding yard at Marina di Ravenna planned celebrations of its fifty years of activity for the summer. For the occasion the management expressed the desire to hold an exhibition of Mariani's work at their commercial offices at Marinara. The project took shape with the help of Giampiero Lami. The introduction to the catalogue was written by Giuliano Serafini. Over the course of the year the 200-page volume *Umberto Mariani: Opere 1991-2009* produced at the behest of the Galleria Orler took shape, with texts by Gérard-Georges Lemaire, Elena Pontiggia, Marco Rosci, Flaminio Gualdoni, Giuliano Serafini and Angela Madesani. One of Mariani's works appeared on the cover of the November issue of the medical review *Prevenzione Tumori*. For Mariani this was the year of the poles. During the summer he went on a cruise to the far north of Canada, reaching the Inuit village of Qaanaaq (Thule) in Greenland, one of the world's northernmost inhabited centres.
In December he first visited Easter Island and then circumnavigated the Antarctic continent aboard the Russian icebreaker *Kapitan Khlebnikov*. The same month, on 13 December, the printing of the book for Edizioni Mazzotta was finished. Orler presented the volume on the *Speciale TV* programme. Mariani was still sailing on the *Kapitan Khlebnikov*, but he made a satellite telephone

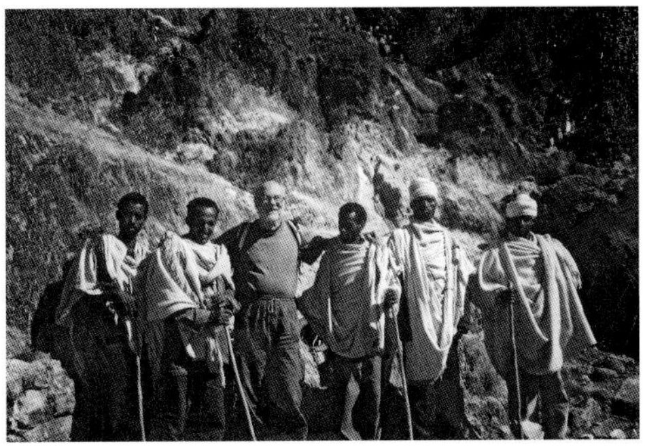

Among the pilgrims of the Coptic Christmas, Lalibela, Ethiopia, 2007

call during the broadcast. The voyage in the Antarctic lasted for a month. His encounter with hundreds of thousands of penguins at Cape Adare: unforgettable.
The Galerie Malichin of Baden-Baden showed more than ten works by Mariani at the Karlsruhe Art Fair. A notable sales success. Gérard-Georges Lemaire invited him to show three works at the exhibition *Le noir absolu et les leçons de ténèbres* staged in the majestic spaces of the Centre d'Art Villa Tamaris at La Seyne-sur-Mer (Toulon) in the south of France. The same exhibition will also be held in the vicinity of Paris and at Mont-de-Marsan in the Landes.

2010

He was invited by Pontiggia to hold an exhibition in the hall of the Bocconi University in Milan. For the occasion he realized fifteen works of the *Autobiografico* series relating to his recent voyage in the Antarctic. Each work was accompanied by photographs taken on location. The exhibition was introduced by a long text by Lucrezia De Domizio. She also invited him to participate in the *Fourth Free International Forum – In Defence of Nature* that was held in the hypogeum at Bolognano. He presented a video illustrating the strict laws protecting the environment on the continent of Antarctica. Bruno Corà wanted one of his works from the 1960s for the exhibition *Il grande gioco – Forme d'arte in Italia 1947-1989* that opened in February at the Rotonda della Besana in Milan. During the summer he travelled in the unspoiled nature of Kamchatka, among volcanoes and the nomadic Korjak tribes that follow the great herds of reindeer. Through his friend Tino Stefanoni he met Armanda Gori and her husband, owners of the gallery of the same name in Prato. They immediately took an interest in his work and organized an exhibition in their gallery for December. Excellent results. At the same time the date (16 June 2011) was set for him to hold an exhibition at the prestigious venue of Palazzo Medici-Riccardi in Florence. The historic Biblioteca Riccardiana would present a copy of the book *Specchi* published by Prearo in 1987. The Studio Lattuada in Milan planned an exhibition documenting the origins and developments of Spatialism. It opened at the beginning of December with a text by Massimo Donà in the catalogue. Mariani was present with five works. The Portuguese Post Office dedicated a 20 euro cent stamp to Mariani with a reproduction of one of his works. For several months he devoted himself to the realization of more than thirty works in lead for an exhibition in Florence coordinated by Giuliano Serafini.

2011

Francesco Tedeschi invited him to take part in the exhibition of works inspired by Genesis, *In principio... Origine e inizio dell'universo* that was held in March and April in the cloister of the Catholic University of Milan. He was invited to contribute a work to the exhibition on the history of the fan that would be held in 2012 at the Museo Archeologico in Florence.

2012

At the start of the year the artist travelled over the deserts of western Egypt bordering with Libya and Sudan to visit the rock paintings dating from the Saharan Neolithic era. The Schless Art space in Bergen aan Zee, The Netherlands, staged a special joint show, *Umberto Mariani, Mauro Staccioli, Anthonie Sas*. And the artist took part in two exhibitions held at the Galleria Annunciata, Milan, titled *Ritorno alla pittura* and *Anni sessanta. Come eravamo*.

2013

In January Mariani was invited by Francesco Poli to contribute to the exhibition *1966-1976 – Milano e gli anni della grande speranza* for the Fondazione Roberto Franceschi staged in the halls of the Bocconi University in Milan. In March-April Fabio Migliorati organized jointly with Armanda Gori Arte (Prato) an exhibition titled *Opere recenti – Piombi*, held in the beguiling setting of the deconsecrated church of Sant'Ignazio in Arezzo. Mariani entered a large-format work for the exhibition *Alchimia del silenzio* curated by Ninni Esposito and Lucrezia De Domizio at the Art Fair in Bari. That summer he was invited by Claudio Cerritelli to the International Sculpture Show held in the grounds of the castle at Racconigi, Piedmont. In July the Armanda Gori gallery mounted a personal exhibition of Mariani's work in their Pietrasanta branch. In October the artist was contacted by Opera Gallery, a multinational art organization with twelve branches in every continent, and an exclusive world contract was signed. Again in October the artist exhibited sixty works covering the years 1966–2013 in the Cloisters of San Domenico (Reggio Emilia); this broad anthology, curated by Sandro Parmiggiani, was expressly requested by the artist in memory of his mother Iole Nizzoli, born in Reggio Emilia in 1907 (catalogue by Allemandi, Turin). In November Opera Gallery mounted a personal exhibition of Mariani's work in their Hong Kong branch.

2014

Mariani was invited to take part in the Paris Biennale; he spent the summer in Valle d'Aosta, where he alternated outings across the glacier of Mont Blanc with intense spates of creativity. Opera Gallery began compiling a monograph on Mariani's work (Skira Editore). Inspired by Titian's portrait of the Italian poet Ludovico Ariosto

La realtà dell'illusione, Milan, 1995

(1474–1533), Mariani created a new work requested by Sandro Parmiggiani, which would be shown at the exhibition *Ludovico Ariosto e l'Orlando Furioso* mounted in Palazzo Magnani, Reggio Emilia (accompanied by a rich exhibition catalogue edited by Parmiggiani). Meanwhile, first the Parma branch and then the Reggio Emilia branch of the Contemporary Art Fair, jointly with the Armanda Gori Arte (Prato), invited Mariani to organize a retrospective as part of the *Mostre Evento* art programme.
In October the artist took part in the exhibition *Nati nel '30 – Milano e la generazione di Piero Manzoni* mounted at the Palazzo della Permanente, Milan. That year various galleries put on shows of Mariani's work during art fairs. Opera Gallery presented a solo show of Mariani's work in their Hong Kong gallery.

2015

In April Opera Gallery inaugurated its new Paris branch with a show entitled *Grand Opening* in which Mariani's contribution was also used for the printed invitation.
He took part in the exhibition *Bianco* organized by the Galleria L'Incontro in Chiari (Brescia). Subsequently the artist was invited by Costa Rica to contribute to the Peace Pavilion at the Venice Biennale, but he withdrew after clashes with the organizers.
In September he held an exhibition with works dating from 1968 to 2015 at the Museo di Pittura Murale in Prato. He created an environmental work measuring 200 square metres (2,152 square feet) entitled *Plutone e Dioniso* (*Pluto and Dionysus*) and dedicated to the theme of peace, in memory of Dag Hammarskjöld, winner of the 1961 Nobel Prize.

2016

In March and April, at Villa Bardini in Florence, he staged an exhibition, *Mariani* chez *Capucci*, curated by Giuliano Serafini and with a catalogue published by Skira. The show, presented in the rooms of the Fondazione Capucci, set out to underline the remarkable affinities between the creations of the great fashion designer and Mariani's work.
It was a great success, receiving favourable reviews in the press all over the world. The Xinhua news agency devoted a long article to it that came out in the *People's Daily* of Beijing.
At the end of the year, Opera Gallery put on a solo exhibition by Mariani with works from the last five years; the show was presented in conjunction with the *Panorama of the Italian Monochrome of the 20th century*.
In November the Fondazione Mudima in Milan presents an anthological exhibition of Mariani's work. A volume edited by Gérard-Georges Lemaire with ample documentation of the artist's life and worki is published to coincide with the event.

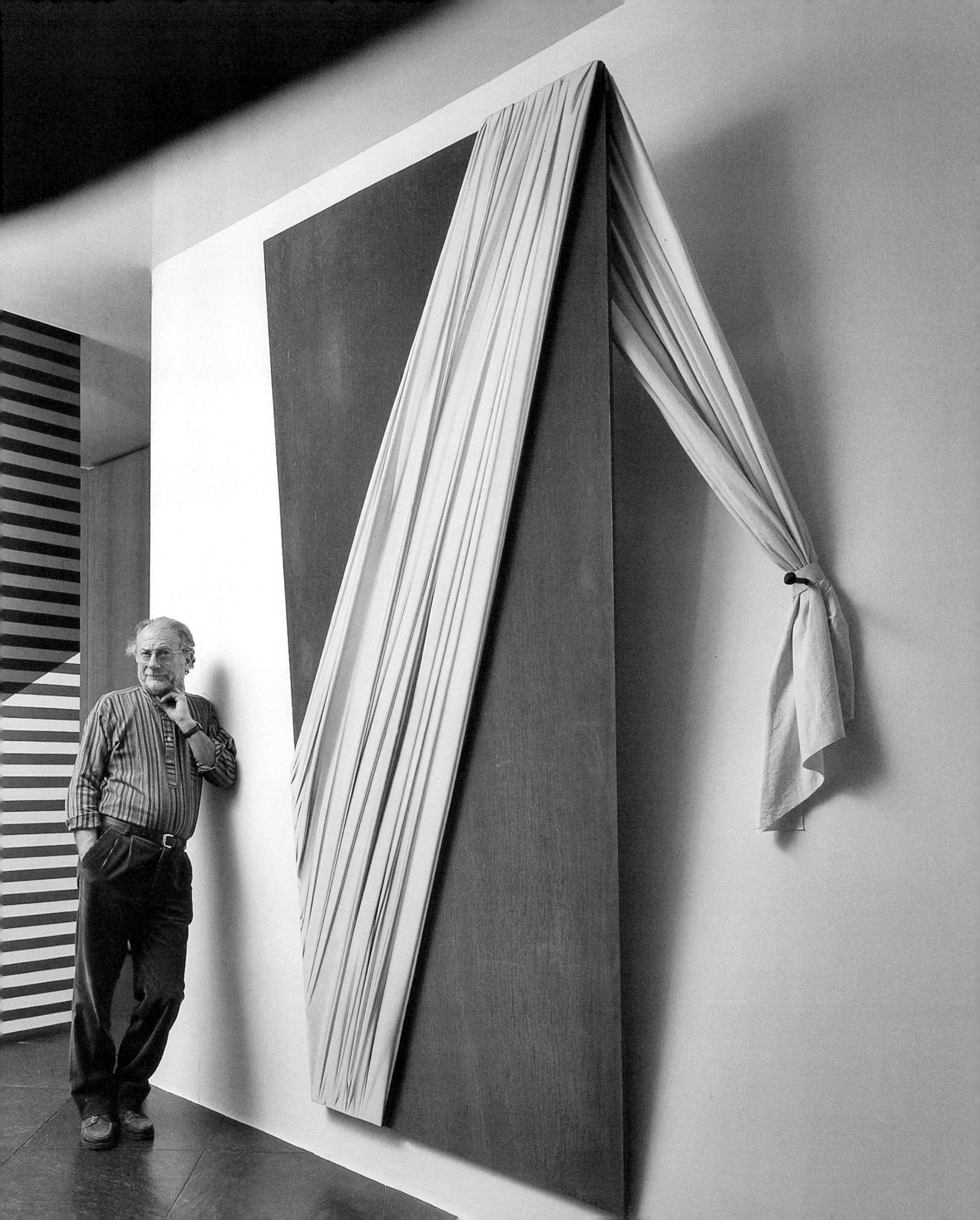

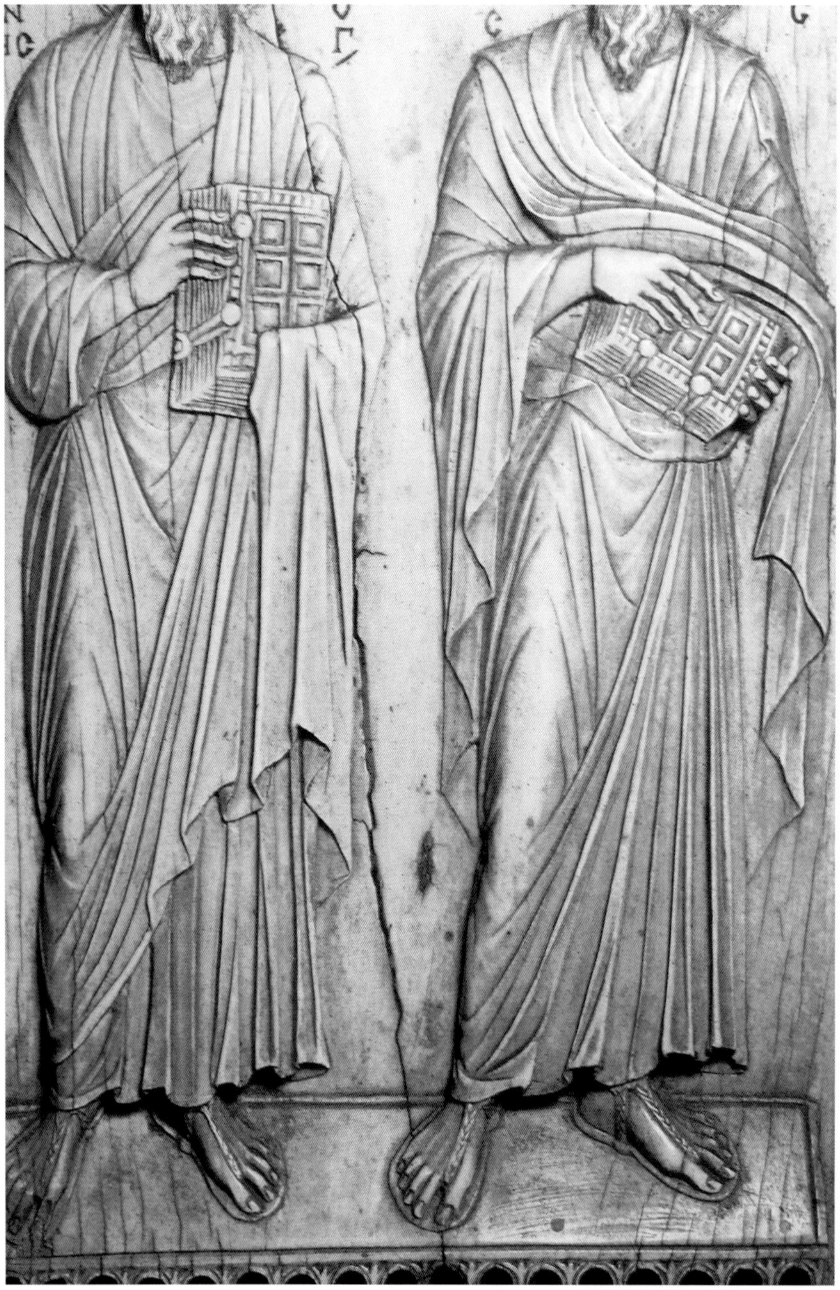

La grande bellezza, o la vita nelle pieghe
A proposito di Umberto Mariani

David Rosenberg

Byzantine bas-relief, tenth century

In matematica, si giudica una dimostrazione in termini di coerenza e di eleganza. Se si applicano questi due criteri all'opera di Mariani, ci troviamo certamente dinanzi a uno dei pezzi forti della scacchiera dell'arte moderna e contemporanea. Dietro l'evidenza e la soggiogante bellezza delle sue opere c'è un'intera vita di lavoro e di riflessione, ma anche, sullo sfondo, tutta la storia dell'arte moderna e contemporanea in Italia e in Europa a partire dagli anni sessanta. E al di là ancora, una riflessione e una serie di pratiche che si inscrivono nell'ambito più vasto della storia dell'arte occidentale e delle culture arabo-musulmane e orientali.

Benché sia nato, viva e lavori a Milano da numerosi anni, Umberto Mariani non si definisce un milanese puro, poiché la sua famiglia è originaria di Reggio Emilia. Umberto nasce nel novembre 1936, due anni dopo il fratello maggiore. I suoi genitori si erano conosciuti qualche anno prima. Come numerosi giovani di quel tempo, si incrociavano lungo la via principale di una piccola città dove gruppi di ragazze e ragazzi passeggiavano osservandosi da lontano. Un giorno, si ritrovano tutti e due in fondo a un tram. Fanno conversazione. Si piacciono, si rivedono spesso e poco dopo decidono di sposarsi. Il padre di Umberto lavora all'epoca come ragioniere. Durante la guerra, la famiglia lascia Milano per sfuggire ai bombardamenti. I bambini non vanno a scuola, è la madre che si occupa di istruirli.

Nel 1944, al ritorno a Milano, il giovane Umberto non può riprendere la scuola. Già da diversi anni soffre di vari problemi di salute e deve spesso rimanere allettato. È in questo periodo che inizia a dipingere e a disegnare, realizzando paesaggi ad acquarello a partire da cartoline postali. Ma è ben lontano dall'idea di essere o di voler diventare artista. Per lui la pittura è soltanto un modo per vincere la noia e trascorrere le giornate troppo lunghe rinchiuso in camera. Finalmente, recupera la salute e può tornare a scuola. Il suo professore di educazione artistica non tarda a notare le doti di questo pittore in erba che ha imparato da autodidatta le basi del disegno. Umberto vince peraltro regolarmente i concorsi organizzati dall'insegnante. È quest'ultimo a consigliare ai genitori di iscrivere il figlio al liceo artistico di Brera.

Al termine del liceo, il padre gli offre la possibilità di scegliere tra l'Accademia di Belle Arti e il Politecnico, un corso di studi che gli permetterebbe di diventare architetto. Umberto opta per la seconda soluzione, compila la pratica di iscrizione ma, sulla strada per l'università, cambia idea. Butta i moduli in un cestino, confessandosi alla fine che ciò che desidera più di tutto è fare il pittore. E si iscrive all'Accademia di Brera. All'epoca si soleva scegliere una specialità: pittura, scultura o decorazione. Decide per la decorazione e si iscrive allo studio di Achille Funi. Funi era un artista stimato che si era fatto conoscere durante il periodo fascista. Amico di Costanzo Ciano, viceré di Libia, aveva realizzato numerosi progetti di decorazione e affreschi in Italia e in Libia. Benché fosse stato vicino ai cubo-futuristi nel periodo precedente alla prima guerra mondiale, Funi si era fatto conoscere soprattutto come uno dei fautori del "ritorno all'ordine" e del neoclassicismo italiano. Durante i suoi anni di formazione Umberto realizza numerosi affreschi con il suo professore, introducendo a volte surrettiziamente il proprio autoritratto, come nel caso di una scena raffigurante un gruppo di monaci in udienza presso il cardinale Borromeo. Mariani ha ventidue anni, impara il mestiere, certo, ma cerca un linguaggio pittorico che sia più in sintonia con i suoi interessi di allora.

Durante gli anni del dopoguerra, negli ambienti di sinistra in Italia si parlava molto di realismo socialista, un tema che l'artista evocava talvolta anche con il padre, che era iscritto al partito comunista italiano dall'inizio degli anni trenta. Guttuso era uno dei rappresentanti emblematici di questa pittura impegnata, come Pignon e Picasso in Francia.

E poi c'erano i pittori astratti, come Emilio Vedova, Piero Dorazio o Afro… Ma lui non si sente vicino né agli uni né agli altri. Sarà invece l'opera di Goya, scoperta in occasione di una mostra dedicata ai *Capricci* e ai *Disastri della guerra*, a nutrire la sua immaginazione e permeare il suo lavoro dell'epoca. Paradossalmente, Goya è per lui un modello più vivo e più ispiratore di numerosi suoi contemporanei. A suo avviso, solleva "questioni umane e sociali molto profonde".

Nel 1958, al termine degli studi, Umberto vince un premio dell'accademia e si vede offrire un soggiorno a Bruxelles per visitare l'esposizione universale.

Qui vede per la prima volta una serie di dipinti di Permeke, pittore belga naturalista dagli accenti impressionisti. È un colpo di fulmine e una nuova fonte di ispirazione per il pittore, che dipingerà tele in questa vena fin verso il 1962 o 1963. Nel frattempo deve compiere il servizio militare, terminato il quale torna a lavorare nello studio di Funi. Partecipa a importanti progetti di decorazione, tra cui quello della basilica di San Pietro in Vaticano e i grandi affreschi della cupola e dell'abside del santuario di Sant'Antonio a Rimini.

Nel 1963 Umberto conosce Ritva Raitsalo, giovane designer di origine finlandese. Se ne innamora e qualche mese dopo parte in macchina da Milano per raggiungerla a Helsinki. I due decidono di girare il paese alla scoperta delle architetture di Alvar Aalto. I loro vagabondaggi li fanno approdare a Rovaniemi, città situata a qualche chilometro dal circolo polare dove il celebre architetto aveva

disegnato numerosissimi edifici. Durante questo viaggio Umberto dipinge paesaggi in riva al mare, alternando composizioni a tempera e a pastello su carta con altre ad acrilico su tela. I due innamorati si sposano nel 1965.
Al ritorno in Italia Umberto si stabilisce a Milano in uno studio situato in via Andrea del Sarto. C'è un giardino in un cortile interno che diventerà il tema dominante della sua pittura. Sempre nel 1965 si verifica un grande sconvolgimento nel suo lavoro. Durante un viaggio a Torino scopre l'opera del pittore inglese Sutherland ed è uno shock estetico di quelli che raramente ha provato fino ad allora. "Le piante somigliavano a uccelli, gli uccelli si trasformavano in fiori..." Era, dice, "l'emozione dell'ambiguità": un universo strano, insieme onirico e familiare, che lo ispirerà per un anno intero finché non riuscirà a poco a poco a staccarsi dal suo modello.
L'artista è in piena trasformazione, così come la città in cui vive e lavora. Da città industriale, Milano sta avviandosi a diventare una capitale internazionale della moda e del design. Questa è anche la grande epoca della rivista "Domus", di Jacobsen, Panton, Saarinen, Rietveld, Sottsass, Aulenti e Colombo... Una delle grandi sfide artistiche e intellettuali dell'epoca consisteva, secondo l'artista, "nel confronto tra natura e artificio". Ed è ciò che appare peraltro chiaramente nelle sue tele di quel periodo. Da uno stretto punto di vista formale, i suoi lavori dal 1967 al 1974 sono perfettamente allineati ai tempi. Si avverte con chiarezza l'influenza congiunta di varie correnti: la pop art inglese e americana (ricordiamo che, nel 1964, Umberto si trovava a Venezia e aveva visitato la famosa Biennale durante la quale Rauschenberg aveva ricevuto il Gran Premio), la psichedelia e il lavoro di Konrad Klapheck, Allen Jones e Domenico Gnoli. Mariani s'interessa anche alle opere della Figurazione narrativa, un gruppo di artisti sostenuti dal critico francese Gérald Gassiot-Talabot di cui incontra i principali esponenti in occasione di un viaggio a Parigi nel 1967.
Ma c'è anche, e soprattutto, senza che sia altrettanto evidente, una filiazione con gli artisti della Nuova oggettività tedesca. Mariani era un assiduo visitatore della Galleria del Levante, che esponeva all'epoca Christian Schad, Otto Dix, George Grosz, Max Beckmann e Franz Radziwill: artisti che, con le loro tele meticolosamente rifinite e caratterizzate dalla resa quasi tattile della materia, lasciarono una forte impressione sul pittore, secondo quanto affermato da lui stesso.
Guanti di raso o di gomma, stivali di pelle, frammenti di corpo femminile, strane forme vegetali, oggetti emblematici del design dell'epoca... Ci sono tutti gli ingredienti di un erotismo feticista collegato alla sensualità dei materiali, l'opulenza dolce delle forme del design combinate il più delle volte con due parti dell'anatomia femminile che sembrano affascinare particolarmente il pittore: la gamba e l'avambraccio. Mariani compone così una singolare galleria di ritratti, assemblando una sorta di marionette "antropomorfe". Una pila di oggetti finisce per evocare una testa con un sorriso caricaturale o un corpo grottesco, come in certi quadri di Enrico Baj. Un cuscino trapuntato serve a disegnare i contorni della testa del *Presidente dell'Associazione cliniche neuropsichiatriche*, mentre il ricevitore di un telefono diventa un paio di occhi azzurri e fissi per il *Conservatore della Biblioteca nazionale* e un filo elettrico ritorto evoca le labbra della *Vergine incognita*.
Composte alla maniera di una trama o di una griglia che alterna linee verticali e orizzontali, le tele "vegetali" di Umberto possedevano già quel carattere frontale che si ritrova qui, ma accentuato questa volta da una luce bianca e fissa, quasi clinica, come quella che si potrebbe trovare in una sala operatoria o nello studio di un fotografo. Siamo di fronte a una sorta di *cadavre exquis*, un rebus in cui i vari elementi sono impilati gli uni sugli altri o incastrati gli uni negli altri. È al tempo stesso qualcosa di meccanico e organico, naturale e artificiale, monumentale e copulatorio. E c'è una piacevolezza nello scoprire oggi queste opere dai colori smaglianti che sembrano comporre un inventario testamentario, un museo immaginario degli oggetti e dei fantasmi dell'epoca.
Questo periodo della vita dell'artista è anche contrassegnato da intensi scambi artistici e numerose discussioni con i colleghi milanesi Paolo Baratella, Fernando De Filippi e Giangiacomo Spadari, pittori con cui Mariani considera in retrospettiva di avere avuto "affinità più ideologiche che puramente artistiche". Nel 1968 i quattro artisti vengono invitati con Vittorio Gobbi a partecipare a Parigi al Salon de la Jeune Peinture, durante il quale realizzano un'"installazione-ambiente" intorno alla figura emblematica di un agente di polizia. All'unisono con quanto avviene allora a Parigi, Milano diventa un focolaio di contestazione politica e gli artisti, tra cui Mariani, manifestano contro la gestione delle istituzioni culturali; manifestazioni che culmineranno con l'occupazione simbolica della Triennale di Milano e della Biennale di Venezia. È anche un momento importante dal punto di vista del riconoscimento dell'opera di Mariani. Il critico francese Edouard Jaguer, che ha scoperto il suo lavoro grazie all'intervento amichevole di Enrico Baj, organizza la prima mostra personale dell'artista in Belgio alla Galerie Arcanes e ne pubblica le opere sulla sua rivista "Phases". L'artista espone anche in Finlandia, al Nykytaiteen Museo di Tampere, e le sue opere

ottengono una collocazione di rilievo durante la VIe Exposition internationale de Knokke-Heist. Mariani si dedica in seguito a un ciclo di opere emblematiche dell'ideologia post '68 ispirato all'arte di Daumier, artista di cui si ritrovavano già accennati lo spirito satirico e il senso innato della caricatura politica irriverente delle sue tele precedenti.
È durante questo periodo di intensa attività creativa, ma anche politica, che il suo percorso artistico comincia ad assumere un carattere più coerente e strutturato. La sua tecnica evolve con l'uso dell'aerografo, traducendosi nella realizzazione di una serie di quadri intitolata *La citazione differente* e comprendente, tra gli altri, un omaggio a Piero Manzoni. È qui che il motivo del drappeggio fa la sua prima vera comparsa nella sua opera. A questo proposito, Mariani riconosce con piacere che l'uso che fa allora di questo tema o motivo è direttamente influenzato dalla famosa serie degli *Achromes* di Manzoni, artista per cui nutre una vera e propria ammirazione.
Nel 1974 Mariani realizza i primi dipinti della serie *Alfabeto afono*, iniziata con la commissione da parte di un celebre ristorante milanese, il Saint Andrews, per il quale realizza un dipinto che raffigura le lettere "S" e "A". Secondo Mariani, questo lavoro rispecchia le preoccupazioni intellettuali dell'epoca collegate al tema della comunicazione o dell'incomunicabilità, una corrente di pensiero di cui Lacan, secondo l'artista, era uno dei più importanti esponenti. Mariani si domanda allora: "Come dare una forma plastica a un concetto così letterario e così astratto?". È così, afferma, che ha pensato di camuffare o coprire con un velo l'alfabeto che è "la fonte e il fondamento della nostra comunicazione verbale". Al duplice aspetto, visivo e fonico, della lettera corrisponde il duplice aspetto del drappeggio, velo e bavaglio.
Visivamente, questo lavoro è singolare per l'estrema sobrietà delle composizioni che si riducono d'ora in poi all'inclusione di una forma stilizzata (questa o quella lettera ridotta a oggetto geometrico) nell'ambito della tela. Si ritrovano il gusto e l'interesse di Mariani per la resa dei materiali e delle texture, ma pervasa questa volta da una forma di solennità e monumentalità. C'è anche qualcosa di più radicale, la ricerca di una presenza non più soltanto visiva ma anche fisica del quadro, considerato come oggetto o struttura materiale nello spazio espositivo.
È da queste ricerche e da queste considerazioni che nasce la serie *Teorema*, a cui l'artista si dedica dal 1977 al 1980. Mariani lavora allora sulla forma del rettangolo allungato, direttamente mutuata dall'architettura molto particolare delle sale del museo di Ferrara dove aveva esposto. L'approccio dell'artista si radicalizza un po' di più: siamo ora molto lontani dagli arabeschi pop e psichedelici, come se il pendolo dell'arte, dopo essere arrivato a fine corsa, ripartisse in direzione opposta. Da questo momento l'artista lavora tra la messinscena diretta dei materiali e la loro rappresentazione. Pennarello, olio o acrilico su tela: Mariani realizza composizioni monocrome bianche o nere che raffigurano ora superfici quasi lisce, ora drappeggi. "Passavo", dichiara l'arista, "dalla rappresentazione dell'oggetto all'oggetto pittorico stesso e alla sua materialità. Utilizzavo pellicola di plastica, tessuto… combinavo illusione e realtà, visione e materia."
Paradossalmente, questa serie di opere molto specifica non conduce l'artista allo stile spoglio e all'accentuazione progressiva del carattere astratto e minimalista del suo lavoro dell'epoca. Infatti, il lavoro di Mariani si suddivide in due filoni distinti: il primo, intitolato *Relitti di scena*, porta alla famosa serie *Forma celata* – un ciclo di opere a cui l'artista ha lavorato dal 1991 fino a oggi – mentre il secondo consiste in una sorta di taccuino di viaggio intitolato *Autobiografico*.
Così come l'*Alfabeto afono* deve essere visto nel contesto più ampio delle preoccupazioni intellettuali del post '68 connesse all'importanza crescente delle scienze umane (psicanalisi e linguistica, specialmente) e delle questioni inerenti al linguaggio e alla comunicazione, i *Relitti di scena* non sono dissociabili dalla situazione molto particolare dell'arte in Italia all'inizio degli anni ottanta. In Europa come negli Stati Uniti è il momento del ritorno della figurazione – o in ogni caso di uno spiccato interesse per le pratiche pittoriche figurative – che si traduce fra l'altro nella comparsa della Figurazione libera in Francia, del neoespressionismo in Germania e della Transavanguardia in Italia. Achille Bonito Oliva, l'ideatore della denominazione di quest'ultima, insisteva sul carattere "teatrale" dell'opera pittorica, mentre da parte loro i pittori vicini a questo movimento invocavano un "ritorno alle forme tradizionali della pittura", esaltando il carattere soggettivo dell'arte, propugnando il ricorso al mito e all'immaginazione e la mescolanza dei generi e delle citazioni.
Pur senza appartenere al movimento, Mariani era particolarmente ricettivo a queste idee e, come testimoniano già alcune opere del 1979 (per esempio, *Il luogo dell'illusione* o *Teorema: tela + oggetto*), aveva imboccato quella che lui stesso chiama "la via della teatralità". Gioco di luce, drappeggio o tenda, combinazione di oggetti e di immagini… Alcuni sottolineavano allora il carattere pirandelliano del suo lavoro, a cavallo tra vita reale e teatro. Mariani guarda con rinnovato interesse le tele di Giorgio de Chirico e René Magritte, che

considera messinscene a pieno titolo, e osserva in particolare gli effetti prospettici, le suddivisioni degli spazi, la disposizione degli oggetti e degli accessori, che traspone in maniera tridimensionale, utilizzando strutture in rilievo. Lavora meticolosamente, realizzando ogni anno una decina di opere in uno spirito barocco, dove si combinano elementi ricorrenti: la penna, la squadra, la tenda, a volte una lettera in rilievo… Ogni opera è concepita come una vera e propria installazione che si inserisce nell'architettura circostante ed è illuminata con una luce radente che sottolinea ombre e anfrattuosità, accentuando la drammaturgia dell'opera. Qui si ritrova il carattere frammentario delle composizioni degli anni sessanta e settanta, ma questa volta in modo concreto e tangibile, come se la cornice dell'immagine si fosse frantumata e i pezzi del quadro si sparpagliassero sulla parete.

A poco a poco, seguendo la logica interna dello sviluppo della sua opera, il movimento del pendolo porta di nuovo Mariani a limitare progressivamente il numero di elementi che intervengono nella composizione. Con le due serie *Ferri* e *Specchi*, gli elementi che fino ad allora si erano moltiplicati e proiettati fuori dalla cornice si fanno meno numerosi e tornano via via all'interno. L'artista lavora principalmente con cornici di forma ovale su cui dipinge drappeggi con l'aerografo. A questo si aggiungono pezzi in acciaio Cor-ten, forme di legno scolpito e dorato, oppure lamine di piombo. È in atto una sorta di gioco costante tra positivo e negativo: ora la forma di un oggetto appare in rilievo (una lettera, per esempio), ora ci sono semplicemente i contorni della sua silhouette cava. A volte un punto interrogativo è abbinato a una cifra o a un altro segno di punteggiatura. L'aspetto teatrale e metafisico del lavoro permane, ma in modo più frugale e più sobrio. Sono, a detta dell'artista, strani specchi in cui si riflette non la nostra immagine ma quella dei nostri interrogativi.

Nel 1990, lavorando a un nuovo omaggio a de Chirico raffigurante una spiaggia, Mariani utilizza una lamina di piombo che plasma in modo da suggerire il moto ondeggiante della bandiera al vento. Senza che ne abbia veramente coscienza in quel momento, questi piccoli pezzi di drappeggio avranno il ruolo di un detonatore. In effetti, è tutto lì sotto i suoi occhi da molto tempo. Il drappeggio non si accontenta di pervadere discretamente tutta la storia dell'arte che lo appassiona, dall'Antica Grecia e da Roma fino al Rinascimento e poi al XVIII secolo. Dipinto o scolpito, il drappeggio è ovunque e occupa un posto preminente nella rappresentazione dell'essere umano. E più gli presta attenzione, più scopre con quale sottigliezza, con quale ingegnosità ed eleganza ogni artista abbia trattato questo tema che era tutto meno che accessorio. Ci si è molto dilungati su ciò che il drappeggio nasconde e al tempo stesso rivela, sulla simbologia dei colori scelti e su tante altre cose ancora. Lo stesso Mariani, sin dai suoi esordi di pittore, ha amato i drappeggi di raso, i cuscini profondi e morbidi del design degli anni sessanta, poi quelli dei veli che ricoprivano il suo alfabeto e infine i grandi sipari teatrali che si dispiegavano nelle sue composizioni barocche. Forse non esiste una risposta univoca che permetta di spiegare questa fascinazione per le pieghe, ma al di là delle congetture sull'origine o sul perché di una tale passione, ciò che importa è vedere semplicemente ciò che l'artista ne ha fatto, quale forma le ha dato.

In fondo c'è sempre stata in Mariani questa "questione pratica" – pittorica e/o scultorea – che consisteva nel chiedersi come animare la superficie della tela, che presenza, che rilievo darle. La questione stessa rimanda a un intero capitolo della storia dell'arte italiana del dopoguerra, a uno spazio di ricerca artistica che era stato aperto ed esplorato innanzitutto da Fontana con lo spazialismo e i suoi famosi "buchi" e i suoi "tagli", e in seguito con le ricerche di artisti come Paolo Scheggi, Enrico Castellani, Agostino Bonalumi o anche Dadamaino e i suoi *Volumi*. La forza di Mariani sta nell'aver trovato la sua strada tra i suoi pari, di aver saputo capirli e apprezzarli pur riuscendo a distinguersene, per proporre infine qualcosa di unico e di singolare che appartiene soltanto a lui. Così, secondo me, al di là delle innegabili qualità plastiche delle sue opere, della sontuosità della sua tavolozza, della precisione e della maestosità delle sue composizioni, Mariani possiede un linguaggio plastico che è soltanto suo. Ed è questo che lo rende al tempo stesso unico e insostituibile, e che contribuisce allo sviluppo dell'arte italiana oggi.

Mariani è sempre stato all'ascolto delle cose, del mondo che lo circonda e dei materiali che usa. Quando ha cominciato a lavorare con lamine di piombo, ha sentito, dice, di tenere tra le mani un tessuto denso e pesante, un materiale "muto" con il quale avrebbe potuto passare dall'illusione di rilievo al rilievo stesso. È qui che le tessere del puzzle si sono incastrate e ha potuto fondere le sue ricerche sul drappeggio per "dare corpo al suo desidero di andare oltre la rappresentazione, di riuscire ad animare la superficie del quadro, a infondergli una vita e una presenza non soltanto fisica ma anche spirituale". Gli artisti citati in precedenza sfruttavano l'elasticità della tela per creare un effetto di rilievo e di tensione agli occhi dello spettatore, un fenomeno descritto dalla parola "estroflessione". In Mariani il procedimento è inverso: la piega sprofonda nella tela e rimanda non più all'idea di rilievo o di sporgenza

Pages 138–139
Exhibition *Mariani* chez *Capucci*, Villa Bardini, Florence, 2016

ma di profondità (introflessione). Pertanto, se si volesse avvicinare il suo lavoro a quello di altri spiriti affini, sarebbe forse più giusto e pertinente evocare Fortuny e Capucci, due grandissimi stilisti di moda italiani che, ognuno a suo modo, hanno lavorato con e dentro le pieghe.

Questo paragone o avvicinamento non deve però indurci in errore. Qui non c'è posto per il caso o l'accidentale, contrariamente a quanto può avvenire con un pezzo di tessuto. In Mariani, il drappeggio è oggetto di una messinscena, di una costruzione rigorosa. Benché il lavoro del disegno preparatorio sia molto intuitivo, secondo quanto dice lo stesso Mariani, ogni composizione è infatti elaborata con cura prima di essere meticolosamente eseguita. L'ampiezza dei movimenti ondulatori, la dimensione dei vuoti e delle sporgenze, la disposizione delle pieghe... tutto è oggetto di una riflessione sullo spazio che si inscrive, a detta dell'artista, nella tradizione nata dal Rinascimento in cui la prospettiva permetteva di dirigere lo sguardo e disporre il mondo secondo un ordine geometrico intangibile. "Questa è la grande tradizione italiana in cui aspiro inserirmi", dice Mariani, che aggiunge: "Quando lavoro, penso sempre ai grandi maestri del passato".

A volte la composizione del drappeggio, la monocromia e la presenza dell'opera bastano a se stesse, a volte Mariani reintroduce una "forma celata" rifacendosi all'idea di una tenda che ricopre un oggetto fisico di cui intuiamo l'esistenza senza poterlo vedere direttamente. A questo proposito, Gérard-Georges Lemaire commenta in modo calzante: "Umberto Mariani è riuscito a fare della sua arte una strana e affascinante versione della persistenza della pittura come mezzo di espressione del suo tempo e di una visione concettuale di tale pittura. In altri termini, le sue creazioni sono 'quadri' nel senso classico, ma con un soggetto ridotto a manifestazione oggettuale e puramente referenziale che si pone come una visione della mente. Compiuto questo rovesciamento di prospettiva, il 'quadro' risorge sotto un nuovo aspetto e può essere vissuto dallo spettatore come oggetto sia di contemplazione che di meditazione. È in questo che risiedono la forza e la bellezza del suo percorso estetico".

Talvolta l'artista riceve in maniera del tutto inattesa una sorta di conferma delle sue intuizioni, come durante uno dei suoi viaggi in Mali e poi in Niger, dove fa la conoscenza delle tribù Tuareg. "Era uno shock artistico: l'impressione", racconta, "di ritrovarsi davanti alle proprie opere, come se esse avessero preso vita." Da qui deriverà del resto un ciclo di lavori intitolato *Taghelmoust: il velo* (il tradizionale drappeggio che ricopre il capo e il volto dei Tuareg), comprendente tutta una serie di sculture e quadri color indaco: "Il penultimo colore dello spettro, un misto di blu e di viola che mi ipnotizza", afferma Mariani. Come fa ognuna delle tinte e sfumature che usa in modo monocromatico: rosso vivo, oro, argento, giallo solare, malva, verde intenso, grigio scuro o rosa stridente...

Come si è detto in precedenza, quando inizia il ciclo *Relitti di scena*, che gli permette di rivisitare non soltanto la pittura metafisica italiana ma anche certi aspetti del surrealismo, Mariani comincia a tenere un "diario autobiografico" di un genere molto particolare, che assumerà poi la forma di un taccuino di viaggio. È una parte della sua opera appassionante, un po' ai margini, come se fosse clandestina. Ma permette, in retrospettiva, di capire dove si sta dirigendo l'artista e che cosa si prepara a compiere. In Mariani, il punto di partenza è sempre riflessivo; è un punto di ritorno a sé e alle esperienze estetiche, emozionali o intellettuali che sono alla base della pratica a cui si accinge a dedicarsi. Il lavoro gli permette di risolvere questioni o integrare esperienze vissute dando loro una forma sensibile che abbia un senso ai suoi occhi. È un'ermeneutica applicata alle proprie esperienze. In maniera emblematica e radicale, la primissima opera della serie *Autobiografico* rappresenta la data di nascita dell'artista. Seguono, a seconda delle circostanze e degli eventi, tele che recano la data di un incontro importante, di un avvenimento collegato alla sua carriera di artista, alla vita dei suoi cari o di alcuni amici. Vi sono anche forme di annotazione, come rapporti lapidari sui suoi stati d'animo (*OK* oppure *Crisis*). Ogni quadro è come un marcatore della memoria.

Da un punto di vista formale, si pensa ovviamente ai *Date Paintings* di Kawara e agli imballaggi di Christo, ma anche alle pieghe degli *Achromes* di Manzoni. I formati orizzontali sono allungati, come cartelli stradali. Su sfondi monocromi uniti, usando un carattere tipografico senza grazie, l'artista dipinge semplici date o nomi di luoghi: Titicaca, Lakagikar, Ulan Bator, Xinjiang, Rajasthan, Ténéré... Si scopre allora l'altro aspetto della vita dell'artista, quello del viaggiatore appassionato che ha girato tutto il mondo, con una predilezione per le terre inaccessibili o remote, gli altipiani montagnosi e i mari polari. Sorprendentemente, questa passione per il viaggio è arrivata piuttosto tardi nella sua vita. È verso i cinquant'anni che l'artista si è messo a esplorare il pianeta, percorrendo pianure e montagne, pieghe e anfratti dei paesaggi che chiama "le rughe del mondo", così come percorre con la mano e con lo sguardo le pieghe e gli anfratti del drappeggio quando lavora nel suo studio, per fare emergere o estrarre da ogni giorno che passa tutta la profonda bellezza.

Parigi, febbraio 2016

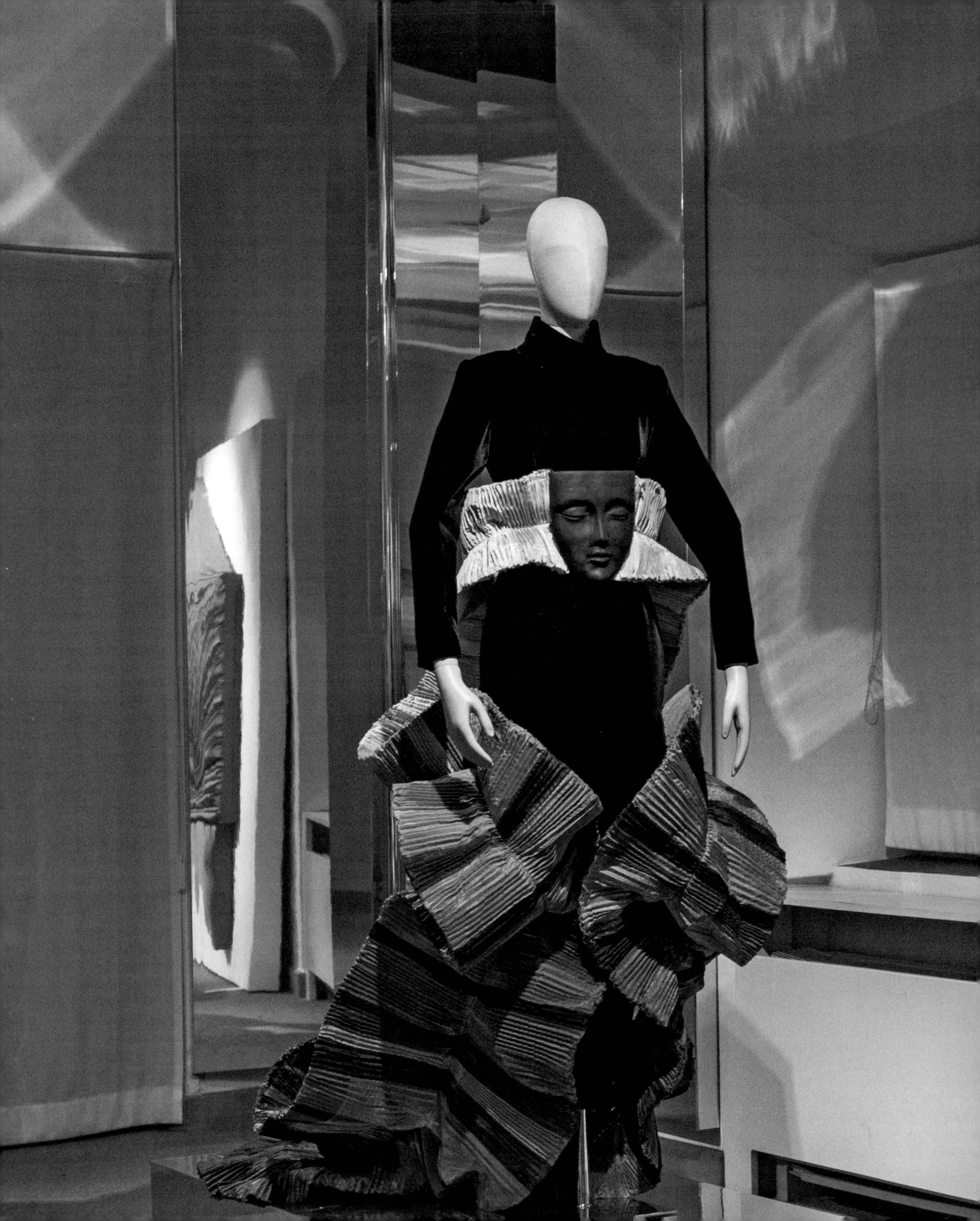

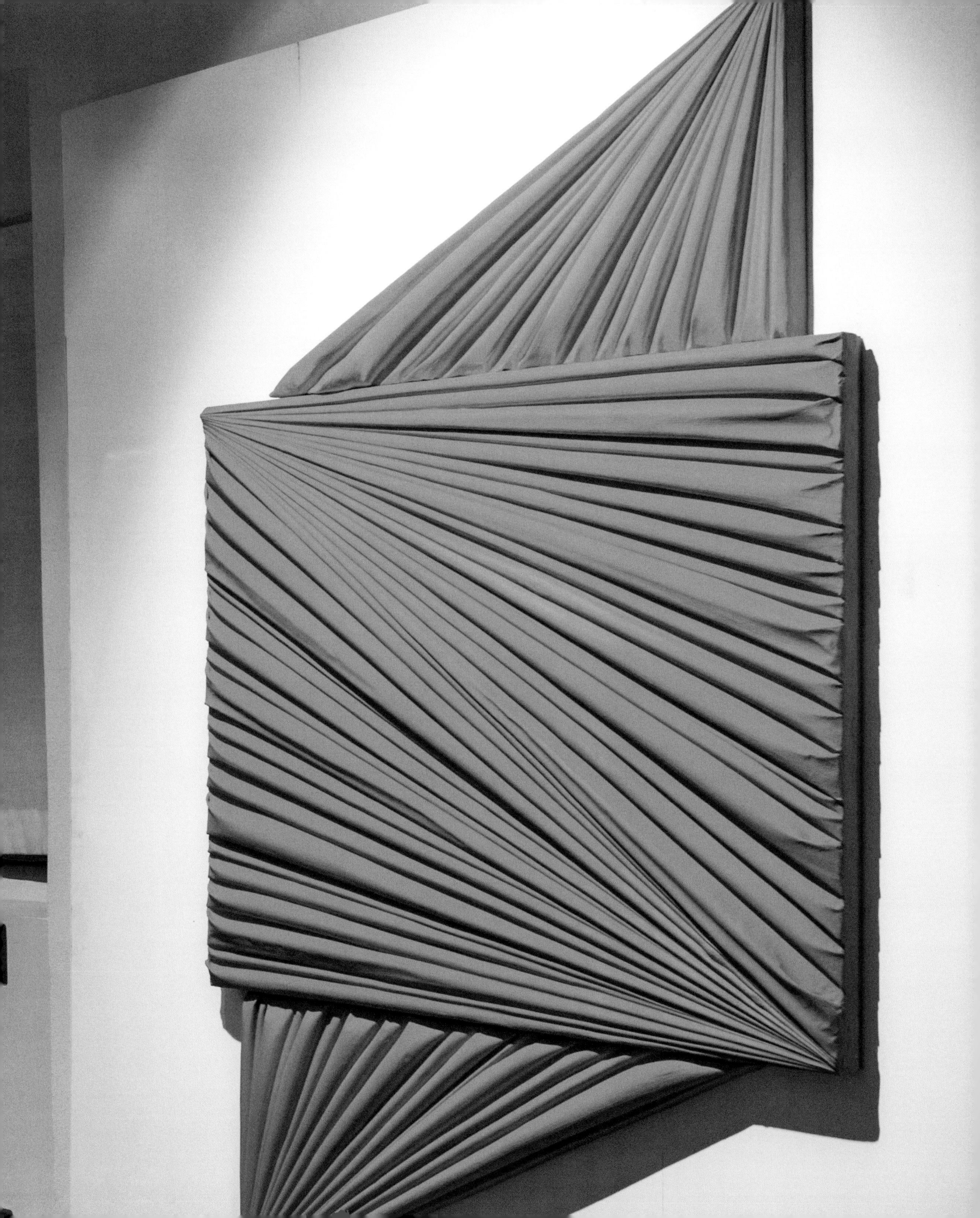

Intorno alla bellezza

Umberto Mariani

Solo la bellezza potrà salvarci
F.M. Dostoevskij

Può sorprendere che uno scrittore come Dostoevskij che, come autore, nella sua letteratura ha trattato soprattutto temi del demoniaco e ha descritto personaggi dannati, sconfitti, disperati, ebbene, sorprende che proprio lui deponga ogni speranza nella *bellezza*.
Ma la bellezza non si manifesta soltanto attraverso forme e contenuti sereni e gratificanti.
La storia dell'arte e della letteratura ci ha fornito prove che la bellezza sta anche nella tragedia greca e nei *terribilia*.
La *Crocifissione* di Grünewald a Colmar rappresenta quanto di più orrido si possa immaginare. Cristo in croce con il corpo ricoperto di pustole infette è un'immagine al limite della disperazione e del disgusto. Ma, a mio avviso, rientra certo nell'ambito dell'arte nobile e sublime.
Allo stesso modo *Le pitture nere* della Quinta del Sordo di Goya al Prado non vogliono certo rasserenarci. Recano in sé un messaggio drammatico e inquietante. La straordinaria qualità della pittura che le compone non vuole in alcun modo elidere il senso di tragedia che le attraversa, e malgrado questo noi non possiamo che definirle belle, anzi bellissime.
"Credo che, oggi più che mai, l'artista abbia questa missione parareligiosa da compiere: tenere accesa la fiamma di una visione interiore."
Questo che ho citato non è il pensiero di un "Nazareno" del XIX secolo, ma un aforisma di Marcel Duchamp datato 1960. Di lì a poco il mondo dell'arte sarebbe stato invaso da immagini appena degne di un supermarket, scatolette del lucido per scarpe, zuppe in barattolo, foto Polaroid, una serie infinita di celebrazioni consumistiche, esaltazioni feticistiche della banalità quotidiana. Le categorie del bello, del sublime, della spiritualità sarebbero state cancellate e considerate con arrogante disprezzo. Le avanguardie storiche, come testimonia il pensiero di Duchamp, aspiravano a rigenerare l'uomo, a conferirgli una dignità moderna, attuale, contemporanea. Basta leggere gli scritti di Boccioni, di Malevič, di Kandinsky.
Kandinsky, Chagall e Klimt facevano esplicito riferimento alla pittura e alle icone bizantine e russe, forse i punti più alti nella storia dell'arte, espressioni di un pensiero e di un sentimento interiore.
Con il mio lavoro faccio riferimento costante a forme e soggetti che appartengono da sempre alla storia dell'arte: al *drappeggio*, al *panneggio* e anche ad altre forme archetipe come l'ellisse, l'uovo e la croce.
Il mio panneggio, le mie pieghe, non hanno nulla di veristico e nemmeno di realistico, semmai fanno ricorso a forme e significati simbolici.
Si sviluppano all'interno di una logica geometrica e si avvalgono di ritmi e spazi lineari. Sono lontani dai volumi di Masaccio, dalle architetture di Piero e dalle enfatiche turbolenze barocche. Senza dubbio sono invece parenti stretti dell'iconografia simbolica (oggi si direbbe astratta, mentale, concettuale) e, per certi versi, labirintica del mondo bizantino.
Gerhard Richter, Umberto Eco e Renzo Piano da tempo riaffermano il profondo valore dell'"idea del bello".
Alla fine del Settecento Goethe scriveva nelle sue *Massime e riflessioni*: "La perfezione esiste già quando viene compiuto il necessario; la bellezza, quando viene eseguito il necessario, purché resti celato".
Oscar Wilde ci dice: "La bellezza è una forma del Genio, anzi, è più alta del Genio perché non necessita di spiegazioni. Essa è uno dei grandi fatti del mondo, come la luce solare, la primavera, il riflesso nell'acqua scura di quella conchiglia d'argento che chiamiamo luna".
Orgogliosamente faccio mie queste parole e intendo utilizzarle come breve introduzione al mio lavoro degli ultimi trent'anni, rivolto appunto alla "forma celata".
Con altrettanto orgoglio mi reputo partecipe del *made in Italy*, macroscopico e recente fenomeno, economico e al tempo stesso culturale, che accomuna bellezza e bontà.

Milano, novembre 2014

Umberto Mariani, l'inflessione infinita

Bruno Corà

Premessa

Se il tempo – nel nostro caso quello relativo all'osservazione del lavoro compiuto – ha qualche valore essenziale, allora varrà la pena di dire che molto di esso è trascorso da quando ho visto per la prima volta l'opera di Umberto Mariani. Da circa mezzo secolo, infatti – si era nel 1966 – quando a Milano, all'inizio del mio tirocinio, mi capitò di fare l'esperienza conoscitiva, insieme a quelle di Mariani, delle opere di Romagnoni, di Baruchello, di Adami, di Pardi e altri segnalatimi dal carissimo amico Giangiacomo Spadari che, in seguito, con alcuni di loro, mi favorì l'incontro.

Ma dovevano trascorrere numerosi anni ancora prima che avessi l'opportunità di misurarmi in senso ermeneutico con la pittura di Mariani, che pur seguivo. Ciò avvenne nel 1975, in occasione dell'esposizione del ciclo di dipinti *Alfabeto afono* per il quale non esitai – dietro suo invito – a formulare un breve testo critico. Di esso, tuttora, alcune affermazioni e alcuni punti mi appaiono resistere nel momento in cui mi accingo a compiere una nuova riflessione sull'opera più recente di Mariani. E per scendere alla testualità, mi riferisco alle denotazioni espresse relativamente alla qualità "ambigua" di quella sua pittura. "Mariani ha coniugato ulteriormente e in modo più serrato", scrivevo allora,

"i termini della sua definizione globale di certa ambiguità della realtà: ambiguità del linguaggio artistico, ambiguità della lingua e dei suoi codici, ambiguità oggettiva di una sua immagine come equivalente dell'ambiguità dei messaggi che la realtà invia"[1].

Nel far osservare che, diversamente dai cicli di pittura precedenti, le *Serre*, 1966, la *Contestazione mondana: Flower Power*, 1967, e gli altri enunciati e temi in cui oggetti e forme vegetali antropometriche, pur nella sintesi delle associazioni, rendevano assolutamente decifrabili i messaggi emblematici fortemente intrisi dell'estetica consumistica anni sessanta, nelle icono-lettere dell'*Alfabeto afono*, invece, la comprensione del loro senso doveva "superare due ordini di lettura: il primo ancora sulle forme dell'immagine, il secondo su ciò che esse potrebbero significare essendo lettere iniziali (o isolate) di una parola ignota, in più private della loro capacità fonetica"[2]. Inoltre denotavo come, sin dagli anni immediatamente precedenti il 1970, Mariani avesse già evidenziato inquietanti forme sotto le guaine, le membrane similpelle e sotto le fogge di attraenti e "agitati panneggi". Infine, proprio del panneggio ponevo in evidenza come questo tema figurativo che Mariani, in seguito, non ha mancato di sottolineare, in quanto appartenente a tutte le civiltà e a tutti i tempi, nel fasciare, raffreddare e nascondere, si caricava anche di un aspetto "drammatico" nel richiamare il sudario.

Mi è stato di grande conforto leggere, alcuni anni dopo, che su quelle mie stesse osservazioni dedicate all'ambiguità delle immagini di Mariani, all'*Alfabeto afono* e non solo, fosse tornato con interesse Guido Ballo[3] approfondendo alcuni aspetti di quella proprietà inalterabile mai perduta da Mariani.

Il più recente e attuale ciclo di opere di Mariani, di cui ho potuto osservare le immagini, al culmine della loro congenita valenza illusoria, mi hanno indotto a compiere un viaggio sino al suo studio di Milano, con l'indubbio vantaggio di aver potuto constatare, una volta di più, quale effettivo ruolo svolga la sua mano-mente nella creazione delle opere. Nonostante perizia, abilità e magistero sembrino virtù obsolete e tramontate per far posto ad altri attributi dell'impulso generativo in arte, quando esse si manifestano generosamente non è però invano. Così, di fronte alle numerose opere ancora in elaborazione e a quelle già terminate, tutte le valenze pittoriche e plastiche di cui avevo percepito dalle immagini la forza obiettiva si sono rivelate con ancor maggiore incisività. La visita nello studio di un pittore come lui continua a rivelarsi come uno dei momenti più fecondi all'osservatore interessato a comprendere sia il linguaggio sia i processi elaborativi che sono all'origine tanto della forma che dell'immagine complessiva dell'opera.

Dall'ambiguo al vero, dalla superficie al rilievo

Delle opere denominate "piombi" che dal 1991prendono forma da quel metallo impiegato nella fornitura in lamina, Mariani è giunto a costruire un variegato paradigma che eguaglia, se non addirittura supera, quello già espresso con l'*Alfabeto afono*. Esse, infatti, nell'elaborazione concepita da Mariani hanno assunto aspetti pittorico-plastici e morfologie difformi, ma come variazioni pressoché inesauribili di un immaginario modello che, lungi dall'esistere come oggetto di riferimento, ha tuttavia sede nella mente dell'artista che si riserva, in tal senso, libertà d'azione e di modificazione rispetto a un'idea pura e come tale non obbligante né rigida, ma nondimeno esigente nel pretendere esiti egualmente ideali.

I primi "piombi" che si manifestano come superfici a rilievo recano la titolazione *La forma celata*, 1991. In essi si evidenziano numerose modalità che, se appaiono riconducibili alla sua pittura degli anni dell'*Alfabeto afono*, 1974-1976, a base di pieghe e di "forme celate", ossia sottostanti la mimetica rappresentazione di un tessuto che nasconde – nel caso evocato, scatolari lettere dell'alfabeto –, in

realtà includono altri "passaggi" di elaborazione successiva a quelle opere. Pertanto, si tratta sia delle declinazioni del ciclo *Teorema*, dal 1977 in poi, sia di quelle del ciclo *Il luogo dell'illusione*, 1979-1980, dei *Relitti di scena*, 1980-1994, dello *Zodiaco*, 1981-1983, degli *Specchi*, 1985-1993, sia infine del ciclo denominato *Autobiografico*, dal 1977.
Le stazioni di questo cammino così particolarmente significativo avevano condotto Mariani, fase dopo fase, nel corso di oltre un decennio, a introdurre nell'opera, accanto alla tela dipinta con acrilici, gli oli su tela e poi materiali diversi: dal jersey allo chiffon di seta, al ferro forgiato, al legno scolpito, alla foglia d'oro, al gesso, al metacrilato, al Kristall e infine alla lamina di piombo. Questo percorso, non certo automatico bensì impegnativo, poneva in risalto l'esigenza di Mariani di liberarsi dall'esercizio metaforico della "rappresentazione" per giungere a un grado progressivo d'inveramento che dall'ambiguità lo conducesse all'illusorietà realistica di esso. Se prima le pieghe del tessuto rappresentato erano esito di pura rappresentazione pittorica, in seguito egli le sostituirà con pieghe di vero tessuto.
Fin qui, il suo salto dalla pittura "rappresentata" a quella "presentante". Ma, successivamente, con la lamina di piombo piegata su tavola, l'interesse di Mariani si è rivolto essenzialmente alla resa fenomenologica di quella materia che, non solo è protagonista reale dell'immagine dell'opera dalla superficie strutturata in pieghe, ma è altresì provvista di un'esponenza di duttilità tale da essere in grado di "celare" o "ostentare", sotto o sopra la sua superficie, forme geometriche di ogni tipo o lettere alfabetiche attraverso impronte recanti diversa quota. In questa "meditazione" morfologica giocano un ruolo essenziale le pieghe della lamina di piombo, la luce, l'ombra, la superficie e la profondità delle pieghe e le impronte delle forme celate di oggetti per lo più assenti.
Questa fase dei "piombi" ha dunque nuovamente un denominatore comune linguistico costituito dalla *piega* non più simulata e illusoria ma reale e fenomenica con una prospettiva di sviluppo morfologico illimitato.

La piega, la forma illimitata

Nell'osservare i primi "piombi" denominati *La forma celata*, vengono alla mente le celebri "pieghe bagnate" poiché l'acqua che comprime e fa aderire il tessuto al corpo ne rivela attraverso le pieghe la forma ancor più della nudità stessa (Gilles Deleuze). Dalle "pieghe bagnate" a quelle del *Cristo velato* di Giuseppe Sanmartino il passo è breve. Poche opere come quella ci parlano del potere di rivelare-celare, del comprimere e aderire delle pieghe al corpo e dunque alla forma.
In quanto "materia ripiegata", la lamina di piombo elaborata con sistematicità da Mariani, a partire dal '91 sino a oggi, sembra idealmente costituire, a causa della morfologia della *piega* di cui sono investiti totalmente i lavori, la destinataria ideale della riflessione di Deleuze a proposito dell'essenza neobarocca moderna e della sua "anima", proprio attraverso la metafora della "piega". Egli esordisce affermando: "Il Barocco [...] non smette mai di fare pieghe. Questo fenomeno non è una sua invenzione: ci sono tutte le pieghe provenienti dall'Oriente, le pieghe greche, romane, romaniche, gotiche, classiche... Ma il Barocco avvolge e riavvolge le pieghe, le spinge all'infinito, piega su piega, piega secondo piega. Il suo tratto distintivo è rappresentato dalla piega che si prolunga all'infinito"[4].
Dopo averne introdotto l'aspetto formale, Deleuze suggerisce la necessità di un'azione crittografica se si vuole arrivare a comprendere le molteplicità e complessità di quel suo tratto distintivo e giungere a "vedere nei ripiegamenti della materia e 'leggere' nelle pieghe dell'anima"[5].
Prima di addentrarci con brevi accenni in questo percorso ermeneutico, non è inutile ricordare, senza alcuna presunzione di voler attribuire a Mariani il merito, peraltro da lui non rivendicato, di essere con il suo lavoro in sintonia con i principi più avanzati della fisica contemporanea, che essa è giunta alla nozione di curvatura dell'universo e curvatura della materia stessa, a causa di forze attive che la comprimono. Quello di Mariani appare dunque come un lavoro che si coniugherebbe con naturalezza allo *Zeigeist* di questi tempi. Provare allora a "vedere" nei ripiegamenti delle lamine di piombo con le "forme celate" significa passare ritmicamente con lo sguardo da zone in piena luce a zone in penombra o piena ombra, per tornare poi a osservare zone di luce e zone in ombra, senza soluzione di continuità se, come sembra, l'opera senza cornice allude all'estensibilità infinita di quella elaborazione a pieghe della lamina plumbea. E si deve pur dire che opere come *Senza titolo*, 2013 (foglio d'oro su lamina di piombo, 120 x 93 cm), in cui i ripiegamenti della lamina rivestita d'oro irradiano dal centro verso i quattro lati, oltretutto con un taglio diagonale del supporto recante un non apparente piano di scorrimento in atto di slittare, suscitano una spazialità che deborda dal perimetro dell'opera verso l'esterno di essa.
Non diversamente si potrebbe dire del *Senza titolo*, 2014 (lamina di piombo modellata, 80 x 60 cm), le cui irradiazioni delle pieghe argentee dal centro verso i quattro lati procedono con la medesima espansività oltre i bordi del

quadro. La continuità di una piega nell'altra è il principio generativo delle opere di Mariani a base di lamine di piombo. Tale continuità, d'altra parte, è attributo e qualità stessa dello spazio. Non si dimentichi che Boccioni ne ha sottolineato la presenza e lo studio nella scultura *Forme uniche nella continuità dello spazio* (1913), e che Castellani, nel suo testo teorico *Continuità e nuovo* pubblicato in "Azimuth" nel 1959, ha fatto a suo modo riferimento alla continuità dando vita a un'opera con la quale, oggi, il lavoro di Mariani può avere perfino molte valenze da condividere. Nelle strutturazioni delle superfici di Castellani, infatti, ombra e luce, nonché quote positive e negative si alternano e, seppure diversamente, costituiscono un'esperienza non trascurabile, certamente ancor più di quella talvolta richiamata a proposito degli *Achromes* di Piero Manzoni, quando, dopo il 1974, ci si addentra in questa fase dell'impiego della lamina di piombo nell'opera di Mariani.
Inoltre, il *continuum* di pieghe delle "forme celate" in lamine di piombo di Mariani, stando alla riflessione già citata e sviluppata da Deleuze sul barocco e Leibniz, induce a tener conto di un'osservazione del grande filosofo tedesco: "La divisione del continuo non deve essere considerata come quella della sabbia in granelli, ma come quella di un foglio di carta o di una tunica in pieghe [...] senza che il corpo si dissolva mai"[6].
Nasce allora spontanea la domanda: ma l'opera di Mariani è "barocca"? Personalmente ritengo che le sue "pieghe" siano consapevolmente elusive della turbolenza barocca e iconograficamente aderenti al modello labirintico concettuale e mentale.
Le diverse opere osservate nello studio di Mariani e ora esposte mostrano una ricchezza di variazioni che chiamano in causa l'atto del modulare consistente nella modellazione ineguale e continuamente variabile. Leggere nelle pieghe dell'anima di queste opere dovrebbe equivalere a decrittare quelle variazioni come sensibilità espresse in forme. Un esercizio arduo quanto opinabile che si può, più propriamente, sostituire con l'identificazione delle attitudini, dei modi e delle intenzioni che sembrano trasparire dall'azione formativa dei lavori. In tal senso, è possibile individuare, accanto all'atto del piegare la lamina di piombo, quello del ricavarvi una traccia di interruzione lineare delle pieghe, come nell'opera *La forma celata*, 2012 (vinilico e sabbia su lamina di piombo, 80,5 x 60,5 cm), in cui è evidente l'impiego della morfologia "impronta", ma anche l'introduzione di vettorialità opposte in raggruppamenti di pieghe come in *La forma celata*, 2010 (vinilico e sabbia su lamina di piombo, 121,5 x 90,5 cm), e in contiguità di linearità orizzontali, verticali e diagonali come in *Senza titolo*, 2013 (vinilico e sabbia su lamina di piombo, 79,5 x 60,5 cm).
Non poche opere recano celate le forme ovali di possibili specchi o di altri oggetti o simboli (la croce, la freccia, la stella) non osservabili perché se ne presenta la forma, spesso geometrica, senza rivelarne l'identità. Questo esercizio, si deve dire, ha molto a che vedere con riflessioni che si potrebbero ugualmente sviluppare di fronte alle variazioni delle "nature morte" di Morandi o davanti a quelle delle *Ninfee* di Monet o alle numerose versioni della *Sainte-Victoire* di Cézanne, poiché in tutti questi casi e in altri ci si trova di fronte alla volontà dell'artista di compiere la propria meditazione sulla inesauribilità del processo formativo, in relazione alla concezione dello spazio e ai fattori determinanti di esso, a partire proprio da quella modularità senza soluzione di continuità delle pieghe e, tutto sommato, anche dalle variazioni cromatiche impiegate.
Tutte le forme celate infine suscitano l'apparizione fantasmatica e con essa le valenze antinomiche dell'assenza-presenza, che induce l'osservatore ad attivare l'immaginario nel tentativo di risolvere un enigma[7].
Mariani, come gli altri maestri che lo hanno preceduto, è entrato nella fase in cui il pensiero generativo della sua opera, mentre non cessa di dischiudere le proprie domande, al contempo mette in scena la drammaturgia del linguaggio stesso nell'atto di manifestarsi.

[1] Bruno Corà, *Alfabeto afono di Umberto Mariani*, in catalogo della mostra, Sala Comunale, Alessandria, dicembre 1976, s.n.p.
[2] *Ibid.*
[3] Guido Ballo, *Umberto Mariani o dell'Ambiguità Fantastica*, in catalogo della mostra *Umberto Mariani. Opere 1975-1984*, Marie-Louise Jeanneret Art Moderne, Genève, ottobre 1984, pp. 2-3.
[4] Gilles Deleuze, *La piega. Leibniz e il Barocco*, Einaudi, Torino 1990, p. 5.
[5] *Ibid.*
[6] Gottfried Wilhelm von Leibniz, *Opuscules et fragments inédits de Leibniz*, a cura di Louis Couturat, Félix Alcan, Paris 1903, pp. 614-615, ripubblicato in Gilles Deleuze, *op. cit.*
[7] Si richiama qui un primo esempio di *objet caché*, nella celebre opera di Man Ray: *L'énigme d'Isidore Ducasse*, 1920.